CAREER EXAMINATION SERIES

THIS IS YOUR **PASSBOOK**® FOR ...

PROMOTION TEST BATTERY

NATIONAL LEARNING CORPORATION®
passbooks.com

Copyright © 2020 by

National Learning Corporation

212 Michael Drive, Syosset, NY 11791
(516) 921-8888 • www.passbooks.com
E-mail: info@passbooks.com

PUBLISHED IN THE UNITED STATES OF AMERICA

PASSBOOK® SERIES

THE *PASSBOOK® SERIES* has been created to prepare applicants and candidates for the ultimate academic battlefield – the examination room.

At some time in our lives, each and every one of us may be required to take an examination – for validation, matriculation, admission, qualification, registration, certification, or licensure.

Based on the assumption that every applicant or candidate has met the basic formal educational standards, has taken the required number of courses, and read the necessary texts, the *PASSBOOK® SERIES* furnishes the one special preparation which may assure passing with confidence, instead of failing with insecurity. Examination questions – together with answers – are furnished as the basic vehicle for study so that the mysteries of the examination and its compounding difficulties may be eliminated or diminished by a sure method.

This book is meant to help you pass your examination provided that you qualify and are serious in your objective.

The entire field is reviewed through the huge store of content information which is succinctly presented through a provocative and challenging approach – the question-and-answer method.

A climate of success is established by furnishing the correct answers at the end of each test.

You soon learn to recognize types of questions, forms of questions, and patterns of questioning. You may even begin to anticipate expected outcomes.

You perceive that many questions are repeated or adapted so that you can gain acute insights, which may enable you to score many sure points.

You learn how to confront new questions, or types of questions, and to attack them confidently and work out the correct answers.

You note objectives and emphases, and recognize pitfalls and dangers, so that you may make positive educational adjustments.

Moreover, you are kept fully informed in relation to new concepts, methods, practices, and directions in the field.

You discover that you arre actually taking the examination all the time: you are preparing for the examination by "taking" an examination, not by reading extraneous and/or supererogatory textbooks.

In short, this PASSBOOK®, used directedly, should be an important factor in helping you to pass your test.

THE PROMOTION TEST BATTERIES

The Promotion Test Batteries are in-depth tests of the common characteristics that employees must possess in order to succeed in most positions at the Grade 23 and above levels. There are two Promotion Test Batteries. The Promotion Test Battery for Supervisors and Specialists is used for promotions to the Grade 23 through 26 and M-1 levels and is open to all permanent State employees at Grade 18 and higher. The Promotion Test Battery for Mid- and High-Level Managers and Administrators is used for promotions to the Grade 27 through Grade 38 and M-2 through M-8 levels and is open to all permanent State employees at Grade 23 and higher. Test battery results will be used in many promotion examinations, but the battery itself is not a civil service examination. No appointments will be made from the results of the Promotion Test Batteries without a specific examination announcement.

When a promotion eligible list is needed for a specific title using the Batteries, an examination announcement will be issued, inviting applications from State employees in qualifying titles. The announcement will specify how to apply, the minimum qualifications and any additional tests candidates must pass in order to be placed on the resulting eligible list. The examination announcement will specify whether results from the Supervisors, Specialists, Mid-Level Managers and Administrators or High-Level Managers and Administrators Promotion Test Battery will be used in establishing the eligible list. For many titles in the target salary grades, the Promotion Test Battery will be the only written test. For some promotion titles, other tests such as oral tests, training and experience evaluations, performance assessments or additional written tests may also be held prior to creating the eligible list; if so they will be specified on the examination announcement for the promotion title.

If you qualify for the announced examination, you must file an application, and your best score from the annual holding of the appropriate Promotion Test Battery will be combined with your passing scores from any additional tests, as specified in the announcement. Your seniority and veterans' credits, if any, will be included at that time to compute a final examination score and to establish the eligible list.

WHAT THE TEST WILL BE LIKE

There will be separate announcements issued for the Promotion Test Battery for Supervisors and Specialists and for the Promotion Test Battery for Mid- and High-Level Managers and Administrators. The Promotion Test Battery for Supervisors and Specialists will consist of questions in the areas of *Managing and Supervising Subordinate Staff, Written Communication* and *Analysis of Information*. The following is a description of the type of test material in these areas.

Managing and Supervising Subordinate Staff - This portion of the Promotion Test Battery will consist of a written simulation test. Much of the information in this Guide is designed to familiarize you with written simulation tests and to give you an understanding of how to take a written simulation test and of how it will be scored.

Written Communication and *Analysis of Information* - The test questions in both of these areas will be multiple-choice questions. There will be several different formats of multiple-choice questions presented and there will be a separate set of instructions preceding each different format of test questions. Each of the instructions will be somewhat different, so it is important that you read each set of directions carefully and follow them exactly.

The Promotion Test Batteries for Mid- and High-Level Managers and Administrators will consist of questions in the areas of *Management and Supervision* and *Written Communication*. The following is a description of the type of test material in these areas.

Management and Supervision - This portion of the Promotion Test Batteries will consist of a written simulation test. Much of the information in this Guide is designed to familiarize you with written simulation tests and to give you an understanding of how to take a written simulation test and of how it will be scored.

Written Communication - This portion of the Promotion Test Batteries will consist of multiple-choice questions. There will be several different formats of multiple-choice questions presented and there will be a separate set of instructions preceding each different format of test questions. Each of the instructions will be somewhat different, so it is important that you read each set of instructions carefully and follow them exactly.

WHAT THE TEST WILL COVER

Below are detailed descriptions of the areas covered by the Promotion Test Battery for Supervisors and Specialists and the Promotion Test Batteries for Mid- and High-Level Managers and Administrators. The descriptions are similar in many areas but there are some significant differences, so be sure to read the announcement for a description for the Battery you intend to take.

The **Promotion Test Battery for Supervisors** assesses knowledge, skills and abilities in areas of managing and supervising subordinate staff, written communication and analysis of information. The **Promotion Test Battery for Specialists** covers only the areas of written communication and analysis of information. The dimensions covered in these areas are listed on the examination announcement. The following expands on the description by providing illustrative tasks and competencies that may be assessed under the different dimensions. Although the test will cover each of the dimensions, it will not cover every possible task and competency listed under every dimension. Choices and actions within a problem often have impact across several of the dimensions. For instance, a particular problem choice may involve aspects of analyzing information, communicating information and interacting with others. The appropriateness of an action depends on its impact and effectiveness across the dimensions, in the context of the situation presented in the test problem.

Section I – Management and Supervisory Dimensions

A. Analyzing information for problem solution

- Absorb and respond appropriately to new information.
- Analyze potential organizational problems or changing situations.
- Anticipate potential threats or opportunities.
- Assess the various aspects of a problem.
- Determine objectives and strategies.
- Keep abreast of key agency policies and priorities likely to affect the program area.
- Obtain relevant information before making a decision.
- Perceive impact and implications of decisions.

B. Communicating information within an organization and across organizations

- Encourage open communication and input from staff.
- Explain significant goals, activities, policies, and procedures to staff.
- Ask questions to clarify issues.
- Provide a means for regular contact and feedback from clients.
- Train staff how to do their work.
- Anticipate the needs of clients.
- Communicate the organization's vision and mission to staff.
- Encourage regular communication with clients to ensure their needs are met.
- Inform higher level management of program developments.
- Inform staff of developments and their impact on organizational activities.
- Present information to bosses (when, what, how).
- Provide feedback to management.

C. Interacting with others for the purposes of accomplishing work

- Motivate staff to do good work.
- Assist staff with job related problems.
- Coach staff.
- Establish networks with key individuals or groups.
- Manage conflict among staff.
- Coordinate with other parts of the organization to accomplish goals.
- Create a work environment where individuals are treated fairly.
- Encourage trust.
- Gain cooperation from others to obtain information and accomplish goals.
- Involve relevant people in decision making.
- Model high standards of honesty and integrity.
- Obtain support from superiors before taking critical action.
- Resolve problems and reach a workable solution among the parties.
- Respond appropriately to the needs, feelings, and capabilities of staff.
- Show respect for others.
- Work with others to achieve goals.

D. Monitoring quality, quantity and timeliness of work

- Review program for conformance with existing policies.
- Use client feedback system to evaluate delivery of service.
- Advise staff of performance standards.
- Conduct formal performance appraisals.
- Evaluate program performance and project accomplishments.
- Identify potential problems in staff's behavior and take appropriate action.
- Insure that effective internal controls are developed and maintained.
- Keep staff informed of the quality of their own performance.
- Maintain a high level of professional expertise.
- Monitor and evaluate staff work products.
- Monitor programs to identify problems.
- Monitor progress on programs.
- Monitor progress on work assignments.
- Review the quality of work.
- Set standards for work and for handling cases where standards are not met.

E. Designing and implementing action plans

- Establish organizational objectives to provide direction for assignment of resources.
- Initiate self-directed action.
- Negotiate solutions acceptable to the people involved.
- Seek opportunities to move the organization toward its goals.
- Work effectively under pressure.
- Adjust work procedures to avoid future problems.
- Adjust work/action plans as a result of budget changes.
- Determine specific projects or actions to accomplish the goals of the organization.
- Develop strategies with contingency plans to implement goals.
- Establish a balance among competing objectives to accomplish overall organizational goals.
- Make decisions.
- Manage financial aspects of a program or programs.
- Recommend solutions to critical or sensitive problems.
- Show flexibility when conditions change.

F. Assigning and scheduling work

- Match staff's interests, abilities, strengths and weaknesses to the job.
- Adjust work schedules to meet changing priorities.
- Explain the parameters of work assignments.
- Schedule work assignments.
- Set and adjust priorities.
- Set deadlines for project completion.

G. Empowering others to act on their own initiative

- Challenge staff to do good work.
- Encourage innovation.
- Encourage staff to take innovative approaches to problem solving.
- Promote teamwork within the organization.
- Provide recognition and reward for effective performance.
- Share rewards for good work.

Section II - Written Communication and Analysis Dimensions

H. **Developing written communications which are sound in mechanics and content, or reviewing mechanics and content of written communications. Written communications may include memos, letters, reports, RFPs/contracts, meeting minutes, agendas, performance evaluations, press releases, hearing notes, speeches, policy manuals, newsletters, etc. Criteria include:**

- Accuracy, clarity, organization, structure and correct grammar
- Relevance and responsiveness
- Conformity with agency policy
- Soundness of conclusions

I. **Developing appropriate written communications or reviewing appropriateness of written communications. Criteria include:**

- Tone--whether message is conveyed in appropriate manner
- Impression conveyed about the author's agency
- Compliance with outlook of higher management
- Appropriateness for intended audience
- Appropriateness for purpose

J. **Analyzing information**

- Understand and apply material provided in written form.
- Apply logical reasoning to reach sound conclusions.
- Apply logical reasoning to recognize and avoid unsound conclusions.
- Recognize the relevance and relative importance of information.
- Recognize the relative significance of changes in conditions.
- Read, understand and apply information from simple numerical tables.
- Read, understand and apply numerical information embedded in text.
- Understand and apply basic concepts of appropriateness and adequacy of samples.
- Understand and apply basic concepts of means and weighted average.
- Understand and apply basic concepts of cost-effectiveness.
- Recognize simple trends in data.
- Read and interpret simple flow charts representing processes.
- Analyze and understand significance of changes in processes.

The **Promotion Test Batteries for Mid-Level and High-Level Managers and Administrators** assess knowledge, skills and abilities in areas of management and supervision and written communication. The dimensions covered in these two areas are listed on the examination announcement. The following expands on the description by providing illustrative tasks and competencies that may be assessed under the different dimensions. Although the test will cover each of the dimensions, it will not cover every possible task and competency listed under every dimension. Choices and actions within a problem often have impact across several of the dimensions. For instance, a particular problem choice may involve aspects of analyzing information, communicating information and interacting with others. The appropriateness of an action depends on its impact and effectiveness across the dimensions, in the context of the situation presented in the test problem.

Section I – Management and Supervisory Dimensions

A. **Analyzing information for problem solution**

- Absorb and respond appropriately to new information.
- Analyze potential organizational problems or changing situations.
- Anticipate potential threats or opportunities.
- Assess the various aspects of a problem.
- Determine objectives and strategies.
- Explore new work methods and systems using new technology.
- Keep abreast of key agency policies and priorities likely to affect the program area.
- Obtain relevant information before making a decision.
- Perceive impact and implications of decisions.

B. **Communicating information within an organization and across organizations**

- Encourage open communication and input from staff.
- Explain significant goals, activities, policies, and procedures to staff.
- Ask questions to clarify issues.
- Anticipate the needs of clients.
- Communicate the organization's vision and mission to staff.
- Encourage regular communication with clients to ensure their needs are met.
- Inform higher level management of program developments.
- Inform staff of developments and their impact on organizational activities.
- Present information to bosses (when, what, how).
- Provide feedback to management.

C. Interacting with others for the purposes of accomplishing work

- Motivate staff to do good work.
- Assist staff with job related problems.
- Coach staff.
- Establish networks with key individuals or groups.
- Manage conflict among staff.
- Negotiate with internal and external groups to facilitate program implementation
- Coordinate with other parts of the organization to accomplish goals.
- Create a work environment where individuals are treated fairly.
- Encourage trust.
- Establish an environment that encourages innovation.
- Gain cooperation from others to obtain information and accomplish goals.
- Involve relevant people in decision making.
- Model high standards of honesty and integrity.
- Obtain support from superiors before taking critical action.
- Resolve problems and reach a workable solution among the parties.
- Respond appropriately to the needs, feelings, and capabilities of staff.
- Show respect for others.
- Work with others to achieve goals.

D. Monitoring quality, quantity and timeliness of work

- Review program for conformance with existing policies.
- Use client feedback system to evaluate delivery of service.
- Advise staff of performance standards.
- Conduct formal performance appraisals.
- Evaluate program performance and project accomplishments.
- Identify potential problems in staff's behavior and take appropriate action.
- Insure that effective internal controls are developed and maintained.
- Keep staff informed of the quality of their own performance.
- Maintain a high level of professional expertise.
- Make decisions on significant personnel actions.
- Monitor and evaluate staff work products.
- Monitor programs to identify problems.
- Monitor progress on programs.
- Monitor progress on work assignments.
- Review the quality of work.
- Set standards for work and for handling cases where standards are not met.

E. Designing and implementing action plans

- Establish organizational objectives to provide direction for assignment of resources.
- Initiate self-directed action.
- Integrate client expectations into the delivery process or products.
- Negotiate solutions acceptable to the people involved.
- Seek opportunities to move the organization toward its goals.
- Work effectively under pressure.
- Adjust work procedures to avoid future problems.
- Adjust work/action plans as a result of budget changes.
- Determine specific projects or actions to accomplish the goals of the organization.
- Develop strategies with contingency plans to implement goals.
- Establish a balance among competing objectives to accomplish overall organizational goals.
- Get for staff the resources (equipment, knowledge, people) they need to get their work done.
- Make decisions.
- Manage financial aspects of a program or programs.
- Recommend solutions to critical or sensitive problems.
- Show flexibility when conditions change.

F. Assigning and scheduling work

- Match staff's interests, abilities, strengths and weaknesses to the job.
- Provide career growth opportunities for staff.
- Adjust work schedules to meet changing priorities.
- Explain the parameters of work assignments.
- Schedule work assignments.
- Set and adjust priorities.
- Set deadlines for project completion.

G. Empowering others to act on their own initiative

- Challenge staff to do good work.
- Reward good work.
- Share power and authority.
- Establish organizational procedures and policies to empower staff.
- Push authority downward.
- Encourage innovation.
- Encourage staff to take innovative approaches to problem solving.
- Give staff substantial authority and discretion to do work and make decisions.
- Promote teamwork within the organization.
- Provide recognition and reward for effective performance.
- Share rewards for good work.

Section II - Written Communication Dimensions

H. Developing written communications which are sound in mechanics and content, and reviewing mechanics and content of written communications. Written communications may include memos, letters, reports, RFPs/contracts, meeting minutes, agendas, performance evaluations, press releases, hearing notes, speeches, policy manuals, newsletters, etc. Criteria include:

- Accuracy, clarity, organization, structure and correct grammar
- Relevance and responsiveness
- Conformity with agency policy
- Soundness of conclusions

I. Developing appropriate written communications or reviewing appropriateness of written communications. Criteria include:

- Tone--whether message is conveyed in appropriate manner
- Impression conveyed about the author's agency
- Compliance with outlook of higher management
- Appropriateness for intended audience
- Appropriateness for purpose

J. Managing written communication related activities

- Organize and/or coordinate writing efforts of subordinates or peers.
- Oversee revision/disposition of written communications.
- As appropriate, train subordinates on how to approach similar future communications.
- Make sound judgments on trade-offs between completeness and timeliness.
- Correctly distinguish crucial information.
- Recognize the value of positive public relations.
- Utilize means which are effective, efficient, and appropriate to convey information.

HOW TO TAKE A TEST

I. YOU MUST PASS AN EXAMINATION

A. *WHAT EVERY CANDIDATE SHOULD KNOW*

Examination applicants often ask us for help in preparing for the written test. What can I study in advance? What kinds of questions will be asked? How will the test be given? How will the papers be graded?

As an applicant for a civil service examination, you may be wondering about some of these things. Our purpose here is to suggest effective methods of advance study and to describe civil service examinations.

Your chances for success on this examination can be increased if you know how to prepare. Those "pre-examination jitters" can be reduced if you know what to expect. You can even experience an adventure in good citizenship if you know why civil service exams are given.

B. *WHY ARE CIVIL SERVICE EXAMINATIONS GIVEN?*

Civil service examinations are important to you in two ways. As a citizen, you want public jobs filled by employees who know how to do their work. As a job seeker, you want a fair chance to compete for that job on an equal footing with other candidates. The best-known means of accomplishing this two-fold goal is the competitive examination.

Exams are widely publicized throughout the nation. They may be administered for jobs in federal, state, city, municipal, town or village governments or agencies.

Any citizen may apply, with some limitations, such as the age or residence of applicants. Your experience and education may be reviewed to see whether you meet the requirements for the particular examination. When these requirements exist, they are reasonable and applied consistently to all applicants. Thus, a competitive examination may cause you some uneasiness now, but it is your privilege and safeguard.

C. *HOW ARE CIVIL SERVICE EXAMS DEVELOPED?*

Examinations are carefully written by trained technicians who are specialists in the field known as "psychological measurement," in consultation with recognized authorities in the field of work that the test will cover. These experts recommend the subject matter areas or skills to be tested; only those knowledges or skills important to your success on the job are included. The most reliable books and source materials available are used as references. Together, the experts and technicians judge the difficulty level of the questions.

Test technicians know how to phrase questions so that the problem is clearly stated. Their ethics do not permit "trick" or "catch" questions. Questions may have been tried out on sample groups, or subjected to statistical analysis, to determine their usefulness.

Written tests are often used in combination with performance tests, ratings of training and experience, and oral interviews. All of these measures combine to form the best-known means of finding the right person for the right job.

II. HOW TO PASS THE WRITTEN TEST

A. NATURE OF THE EXAMINATION

To prepare intelligently for civil service examinations, you should know how they differ from school examinations you have taken. In school you were assigned certain definite pages to read or subjects to cover. The examination questions were quite detailed and usually emphasized memory. Civil service exams, on the other hand, try to discover your present ability to perform the duties of a position, plus your potentiality to learn these duties. In other words, a civil service exam attempts to predict how successful you will be. Questions cover such a broad area that they cannot be as minute and detailed as school exam questions.

In the public service similar kinds of work, or positions, are grouped together in one "class." This process is known as *position-classification*. All the positions in a class are paid according to the salary range for that class. One class title covers all of these positions, and they are all tested by the same examination.

B. FOUR BASIC STEPS

1) Study the announcement

How, then, can you know what subjects to study? Our best answer is: "Learn as much as possible about the class of positions for which you've applied." The exam will test the knowledge, skills and abilities needed to do the work.

Your most valuable source of information about the position you want is the official exam announcement. This announcement lists the training and experience qualifications. Check these standards and apply only if you come reasonably close to meeting them.

The brief description of the position in the examination announcement offers some clues to the subjects which will be tested. Think about the job itself. Review the duties in your mind. Can you perform them, or are there some in which you are rusty? Fill in the blank spots in your preparation.

Many jurisdictions preview the written test in the exam announcement by including a section called "Knowledge and Abilities Required," "Scope of the Examination," or some similar heading. Here you will find out specifically what fields will be tested.

2) Review your own background

Once you learn in general what the position is all about, and what you need to know to do the work, ask yourself which subjects you already know fairly well and which need improvement. You may wonder whether to concentrate on improving your strong areas or on building some background in your fields of weakness. When the announcement has specified "some knowledge" or "considerable knowledge," or has used adjectives like "beginning principles of..." or "advanced ... methods," you can get a clue as to the number and difficulty of questions to be asked in any given field. More questions, and hence broader coverage, would be included for those subjects which are more important in the work. Now weigh your strengths and weaknesses against the job requirements and prepare accordingly.

3) Determine the level of the position

Another way to tell how intensively you should prepare is to understand the level of the job for which you are applying. Is it the entering level? In other words, is this the position in which beginners in a field of work are hired? Or is it an intermediate or advanced level? Sometimes this is indicated by such words as "Junior" or "Senior" in the class title. Other jurisdictions use Roman numerals to designate the level – Clerk I, Clerk II, for example. The word "Supervisor" sometimes appears in the title. If the level is not indicated by the title, check the description of duties. Will you be working under very close supervision, or will you have responsibility for independent decisions in this work?

4) Choose appropriate study materials

Now that you know the subjects to be examined and the relative amount of each subject to be covered, you can choose suitable study materials. For beginning level jobs, or even advanced ones, if you have a pronounced weakness in some aspect of your training, read a modern, standard textbook in that field. Be sure it is up to date and has general coverage. Such books are normally available at your library, and the librarian will be glad to help you locate one. For entry-level positions, questions of appropriate difficulty are chosen – neither highly advanced questions, nor those too simple. Such questions require careful thought but not advanced training.

If the position for which you are applying is technical or advanced, you will read more advanced, specialized material. If you are already familiar with the basic principles of your field, elementary textbooks would waste your time. Concentrate on advanced textbooks and technical periodicals. Think through the concepts and review difficult problems in your field.

These are all general sources. You can get more ideas on your own initiative, following these leads. For example, training manuals and publications of the government agency which employs workers in your field can be useful, particularly for technical and professional positions. A letter or visit to the government department involved may result in more specific study suggestions, and certainly will provide you with a more definite idea of the exact nature of the position you are seeking.

III. KINDS OF TESTS

Tests are used for purposes other than measuring knowledge and ability to perform specified duties. For some positions, it is equally important to test ability to make adjustments to new situations or to profit from training. In others, basic mental abilities not dependent on information are essential. Questions which test these things may not appear as pertinent to the duties of the position as those which test for knowledge and information. Yet they are often highly important parts of a fair examination. For very general questions, it is almost impossible to help you direct your study efforts. What we can do is to point out some of the more common of these general abilities needed in public service positions and describe some typical questions.

1) General information

Broad, general information has been found useful for predicting job success in some kinds of work. This is tested in a variety of ways, from vocabulary lists to questions about current events. Basic background in some field of work, such as sociology or economics, may be sampled in a group of questions. Often these are principles which have become familiar to most persons through exposure rather than through formal training. It is difficult to advise you how to study for these questions; being alert to the world around you is our best suggestion.

2) Verbal ability

An example of an ability needed in many positions is verbal or language ability. Verbal ability is, in brief, the ability to use and understand words. Vocabulary and grammar tests are typical measures of this ability. Reading comprehension or paragraph interpretation questions are common in many kinds of civil service tests. You are given a paragraph of written material and asked to find its central meaning.

3) Numerical ability

Number skills can be tested by the familiar arithmetic problem, by checking paired lists of numbers to see which are alike and which are different, or by interpreting charts and graphs. In the latter test, a graph may be printed in the test booklet which you are asked to use as the basis for answering questions.

4) Observation

A popular test for law-enforcement positions is the observation test. A picture is shown to you for several minutes, then taken away. Questions about the picture test your ability to observe both details and larger elements.

5) Following directions

In many positions in the public service, the employee must be able to carry out written instructions dependably and accurately. You may be given a chart with several columns, each column listing a variety of information. The questions require you to carry out directions involving the information given in the chart.

6) Skills and aptitudes

Performance tests effectively measure some manual skills and aptitudes. When the skill is one in which you are trained, such as typing or shorthand, you can practice. These tests are often very much like those given in business school or high school courses. For many of the other skills and aptitudes, however, no short-time preparation can be made. Skills and abilities natural to you or that you have developed throughout your lifetime are being tested.

Many of the general questions just described provide all the data needed to answer the questions and ask you to use your reasoning ability to find the answers. Your best preparation for these tests, as well as for tests of facts and ideas, is to be at your physical and mental best. You, no doubt, have your own methods of getting into an exam-taking mood and keeping "in shape." The next section lists some ideas on this subject.

IV. KINDS OF QUESTIONS

Only rarely is the "essay" question, which you answer in narrative form, used in civil service tests. Civil service tests are usually of the short-answer type. Full instructions for answering these questions will be given to you at the examination. But in case this is your first experience with short-answer questions and separate answer sheets, here is what you need to know:

1) Multiple-choice Questions

Most popular of the short-answer questions is the "multiple choice" or "best answer" question. It can be used, for example, to test for factual knowledge, ability to solve problems or judgment in meeting situations found at work.

A multiple-choice question is normally one of three types—

- It can begin with an incomplete statement followed by several possible endings. You are to find the one ending which *best* completes the statement, although some of the others may not be entirely wrong.
- It can also be a complete statement in the form of a question which is answered by choosing one of the statements listed.
- It can be in the form of a problem – again you select the best answer.

Here is an example of a multiple-choice question with a discussion which should give you some clues as to the method for choosing the right answer:

When an employee has a complaint about his assignment, the action which will *best* help him overcome his difficulty is to
   A. discuss his difficulty with his coworkers
   B. take the problem to the head of the organization
   C. take the problem to the person who gave him the assignment
   D. say nothing to anyone about his complaint

In answering this question, you should study each of the choices to find which is best. Consider choice "A" – Certainly an employee may discuss his complaint with fellow employees, but no change or improvement can result, and the complaint remains unresolved. Choice "B" is a poor choice since the head of the organization probably does not know what assignment you have been given, and taking your problem to him is known as "going over the head" of the supervisor. The supervisor, or person who made the assignment, is the person who can clarify it or correct any injustice. Choice "C" is, therefore, correct. To say nothing, as in choice "D," is unwise. Supervisors have and interest in knowing the problems employees are facing, and the employee is seeking a solution to his problem.

2) True/False Questions

The "true/false" or "right/wrong" form of question is sometimes used. Here a complete statement is given. Your job is to decide whether the statement is right or wrong.

SAMPLE: A roaming cell-phone call to a nearby city costs less than a non-roaming call to a distant city.

This statement is wrong, or false, since roaming calls are more expensive.
This is not a complete list of all possible question forms, although most of the others are variations of these common types. You will always get complete directions for

answering questions. Be sure you understand *how* to mark your answers – ask questions until you do.

V. RECORDING YOUR ANSWERS

Computer terminals are used more and more today for many different kinds of exams.

For an examination with very few applicants, you may be told to record your answers in the test booklet itself. Separate answer sheets are much more common. If this separate answer sheet is to be scored by machine – and this is often the case – it is highly important that you mark your answers correctly in order to get credit.

An electronic scoring machine is often used in civil service offices because of the speed with which papers can be scored. Machine-scored answer sheets must be marked with a pencil, which will be given to you. This pencil has a high graphite content which responds to the electronic scoring machine. As a matter of fact, stray dots may register as answers, so do not let your pencil rest on the answer sheet while you are pondering the correct answer. Also, if your pencil lead breaks or is otherwise defective, ask for another.

Since the answer sheet will be dropped in a slot in the scoring machine, be careful not to bend the corners or get the paper crumpled.

The answer sheet normally has five vertical columns of numbers, with 30 numbers to a column. These numbers correspond to the question numbers in your test booklet. After each number, going across the page are four or five pairs of dotted lines. These short dotted lines have small letters or numbers above them. The first two pairs may also have a "T" or "F" above the letters. This indicates that the first two pairs only are to be used if the questions are of the true-false type. If the questions are multiple choice, disregard the "T" and "F" and pay attention only to the small letters or numbers.

Answer your questions in the manner of the sample that follows:

32. The largest city in the United States is
    A. Washington, D.C.
    B. New York City
    C. Chicago
    D. Detroit
    E. San Francisco

1) Choose the answer you think is best. (New York City is the largest, so "B" is correct.)
2) Find the row of dotted lines numbered the same as the question you are answering. (Find row number 32)
3) Find the pair of dotted lines corresponding to the answer. (Find the pair of lines under the mark "B.")
4) Make a solid black mark between the dotted lines.

VI. BEFORE THE TEST

Common sense will help you find procedures to follow to get ready for an examination. Too many of us, however, overlook these sensible measures. Indeed, nervousness and fatigue have been found to be the most serious reasons why applicants fail to do their best on civil service tests. Here is a list of reminders:

- Begin your preparation early – Don't wait until the last minute to go scurrying around for books and materials or to find out what the position is all about.
- Prepare continuously – An hour a night for a week is better than an all-night cram session. This has been definitely established. What is more, a night a week for a month will return better dividends than crowding your study into a shorter period of time.
- Locate the place of the exam – You have been sent a notice telling you when and where to report for the examination. If the location is in a different town or otherwise unfamiliar to you, it would be well to inquire the best route and learn something about the building.
- Relax the night before the test – Allow your mind to rest. Do not study at all that night. Plan some mild recreation or diversion; then go to bed early and get a good night's sleep.
- Get up early enough to make a leisurely trip to the place for the test – This way unforeseen events, traffic snarls, unfamiliar buildings, etc. will not upset you.
- Dress comfortably – A written test is not a fashion show. You will be known by number and not by name, so wear something comfortable.
- Leave excess paraphernalia at home – Shopping bags and odd bundles will get in your way. You need bring only the items mentioned in the official notice you received; usually everything you need is provided. Do not bring reference books to the exam. They will only confuse those last minutes and be taken away from you when in the test room.
- Arrive somewhat ahead of time – If because of transportation schedules you must get there very early, bring a newspaper or magazine to take your mind off yourself while waiting.
- Locate the examination room – When you have found the proper room, you will be directed to the seat or part of the room where you will sit. Sometimes you are given a sheet of instructions to read while you are waiting. Do not fill out any forms until you are told to do so; just read them and be prepared.
- Relax and prepare to listen to the instructions
- If you have any physical problem that may keep you from doing your best, be sure to tell the test administrator. If you are sick or in poor health, you really cannot do your best on the exam. You can come back and take the test some other time.

VII. AT THE TEST

The day of the test is here and you have the test booklet in your hand. The temptation to get going is very strong. Caution! There is more to success than knowing the right answers. You must know how to identify your papers and understand variations in the type of short-answer question used in this particular examination. Follow these suggestions for maximum results from your efforts:

1) Cooperate with the monitor

The test administrator has a duty to create a situation in which you can be as much at ease as possible. He will give instructions, tell you when to begin, check to see that you are marking your answer sheet correctly, and so on. He is not there to guard you, although he will see that your competitors do not take unfair advantage. He wants to help you do your best.

2) Listen to all instructions

Don't jump the gun! Wait until you understand all directions. In most civil service tests you get more time than you need to answer the questions. So don't be in a hurry. Read each word of instructions until you clearly understand the meaning. Study the examples, listen to all announcements and follow directions. Ask questions if you do not understand what to do.

3) Identify your papers

Civil service exams are usually identified by number only. You will be assigned a number; you must not put your name on your test papers. Be sure to copy your number correctly. Since more than one exam may be given, copy your exact examination title.

4) Plan your time

Unless you are told that a test is a "speed" or "rate of work" test, speed itself is usually not important. Time enough to answer all the questions will be provided, but this does not mean that you have all day. An overall time limit has been set. Divide the total time (in minutes) by the number of questions to determine the approximate time you have for each question.

5) Do not linger over difficult questions

If you come across a difficult question, mark it with a paper clip (useful to have along) and come back to it when you have been through the booklet. One caution if you do this – be sure to skip a number on your answer sheet as well. Check often to be sure that you have not lost your place and that you are marking in the row numbered the same as the question you are answering.

6) Read the questions

Be sure you know what the question asks! Many capable people are unsuccessful because they failed to *read* the questions correctly.

7) Answer all questions

Unless you have been instructed that a penalty will be deducted for incorrect answers, it is better to guess than to omit a question.

8) Speed tests

It is often better NOT to guess on speed tests. It has been found that on timed tests people are tempted to spend the last few seconds before time is called in marking answers at random – without even reading them – in the hope of picking up a few extra points. To discourage this practice, the instructions may warn you that your score will be "corrected" for guessing. That is, a penalty will be applied. The incorrect answers will be deducted from the correct ones, or some other penalty formula will be used.

9) Review your answers

If you finish before time is called, go back to the questions you guessed or omitted to give them further thought. Review other answers if you have time.

10) Return your test materials

If you are ready to leave before others have finished or time is called, take ALL your materials to the monitor and leave quietly. Never take any test material with you. The monitor can discover whose papers are not complete, and taking a test booklet may be grounds for disqualification.

VIII. EXAMINATION TECHNIQUES

1) Read the general instructions carefully. These are usually printed on the first page of the exam booklet. As a rule, these instructions refer to the timing of the examination; the fact that you should not start work until the signal and must stop work at a signal, etc. If there are any *special* instructions, such as a choice of questions to be answered, make sure that you note this instruction carefully.

2) When you are ready to start work on the examination, that is as soon as the signal has been given, read the instructions to each question booklet, underline any key words or phrases, such as *least, best, outline, describe* and the like. In this way you will tend to answer as requested rather than discover on reviewing your paper that you *listed without describing*, that you selected the *worst* choice rather than the *best* choice, etc.

3) If the examination is of the objective or multiple-choice type – that is, each question will also give a series of possible answers: A, B, C or D, and you are called upon to select the best answer and write the letter next to that answer on your answer paper – it is advisable to start answering each question in turn. There may be anywhere from 50 to 100 such questions in the three or four hours allotted and you can see how much time would be taken if you read through all the questions before beginning to answer any. Furthermore, if you come across a question or group of questions which you know would be difficult to answer, it would undoubtedly affect your handling of all the other questions.

4) If the examination is of the essay type and contains but a few questions, it is a moot point as to whether you should read all the questions before starting to answer any one. Of course, if you are given a choice – say five out of seven and the like – then it is essential to read all the questions so you can eliminate the two that are most difficult. If, however, you are asked to answer all the questions, there may be danger in trying to answer the easiest one first because you may find that you will spend too much time on it. The best technique is to answer the first question, then proceed to the second, etc.

5) Time your answers. Before the exam begins, write down the time it started, then add the time allowed for the examination and write down the time it must be completed, then divide the time available somewhat as follows:

- If 3-1/2 hours are allowed, that would be 210 minutes. If you have 80 objective-type questions, that would be an average of 2-1/2 minutes per question. Allow yourself no more than 2 minutes per question, or a total of 160 minutes, which will permit about 50 minutes to review.
- If for the time allotment of 210 minutes there are 7 essay questions to answer, that would average about 30 minutes a question. Give yourself only 25 minutes per question so that you have about 35 minutes to review.

6) The most important instruction is to *read each question* and make sure you know what is wanted. The second most important instruction is to *time yourself properly* so that you answer every question. The third most important instruction is to *answer every question*. Guess if you have to but include something for each question. Remember that you will receive no credit for a blank and will probably receive some credit if you write something in answer to an essay question. If you guess a letter – say "B" for a multiple-choice question – you may have guessed right. If you leave a blank as an answer to a multiple-choice question, the examiners may respect your feelings but it will not add a point to your score. Some exams may penalize you for wrong answers, so in such cases *only*, you may not want to guess unless you have some basis for your answer.

7) Suggestions
   a. Objective-type questions
      1. Examine the question booklet for proper sequence of pages and questions
      2. Read all instructions carefully
      3. Skip any question which seems too difficult; return to it after all other questions have been answered
      4. Apportion your time properly; do not spend too much time on any single question or group of questions
      5. Note and underline key words – *all, most, fewest, least, best, worst, same, opposite,* etc.
      6. Pay particular attention to negatives
      7. Note unusual option, e.g., unduly long, short, complex, different or similar in content to the body of the question
      8. Observe the use of "hedging" words – *probably, may, most likely,* etc.
      9. Make sure that your answer is put next to the same number as the question
      10. Do not second-guess unless you have good reason to believe the second answer is definitely more correct
      11. Cross out original answer if you decide another answer is more accurate; do not erase until you are ready to hand your paper in
      12. Answer all questions; guess unless instructed otherwise
      13. Leave time for review

   b. Essay questions
      1. Read each question carefully
      2. Determine exactly what is wanted. Underline key words or phrases.
      3. Decide on outline or paragraph answer

4. Include many different points and elements unless asked to develop any one or two points or elements
5. Show impartiality by giving pros and cons unless directed to select one side only
6. Make and write down any assumptions you find necessary to answer the questions
7. Watch your English, grammar, punctuation and choice of words
8. Time your answers; don't crowd material

8) Answering the essay question

Most essay questions can be answered by framing the specific response around several key words or ideas. Here are a few such key words or ideas:

M's: manpower, materials, methods, money, management
P's: purpose, program, policy, plan, procedure, practice, problems, pitfalls, personnel, public relations
  a. Six basic steps in handling problems:
      1. Preliminary plan and background development
      2. Collect information, data and facts
      3. Analyze and interpret information, data and facts
      4. Analyze and develop solutions as well as make recommendations
      5. Prepare report and sell recommendations
      6. Install recommendations and follow up effectiveness

  b. Pitfalls to avoid
      1. *Taking things for granted* – A statement of the situation does not necessarily imply that each of the elements is necessarily true; for example, a complaint may be invalid and biased so that all that can be taken for granted is that a complaint has been registered
      2. *Considering only one side of a situation* – Wherever possible, indicate several alternatives and then point out the reasons you selected the best one
      3. *Failing to indicate follow up* – Whenever your answer indicates action on your part, make certain that you will take proper follow-up action to see how successful your recommendations, procedures or actions turn out to be
      4. *Taking too long in answering any single question* – Remember to time your answers properly

IX. AFTER THE TEST

Scoring procedures differ in detail among civil service jurisdictions although the general principles are the same. Whether the papers are hand-scored or graded by machine we have described, they are nearly always graded by number. That is, the person who marks the paper knows only the number – never the name – of the applicant. Not until all the papers have been graded will they be matched with names. If other tests, such as training and experience or oral interview ratings have been given, scores will be combined. Different parts of the examination usually have different weights. For example, the written test might count 60 percent of the final grade, and a rating of training and experience 40 percent. In many jurisdictions, veterans will have a certain number of points added to their grades.

After the final grade has been determined, the names are placed in grade order and an eligible list is established. There are various methods for resolving ties between those who get the same final grade – probably the most common is to place first the name of the person whose application was received first. Job offers are made from the eligible list in the order the names appear on it. You will be notified of your grade and your rank as soon as all these computations have been made. This will be done as rapidly as possible.

People who are found to meet the requirements in the announcement are called "eligibles." Their names are put on a list of eligible candidates. An eligible's chances of getting a job depend on how high he stands on this list and how fast agencies are filling jobs from the list.

When a job is to be filled from a list of eligibles, the agency asks for the names of people on the list of eligibles for that job. When the civil service commission receives this request, it sends to the agency the names of the three people highest on this list. Or, if the job to be filled has specialized requirements, the office sends the agency the names of the top three persons who meet these requirements from the general list.

The appointing officer makes a choice from among the three people whose names were sent to him. If the selected person accepts the appointment, the names of the others are put back on the list to be considered for future openings.

That is the rule in hiring from all kinds of eligible lists, whether they are for typist, carpenter, chemist, or something else. For every vacancy, the appointing officer has his choice of any one of the top three eligibles on the list. This explains why the person whose name is on top of the list sometimes does not get an appointment when some of the persons lower on the list do. If the appointing officer chooses the second or third eligible, the No. 1 eligible does not get a job at once, but stays on the list until he is appointed or the list is terminated.

X. HOW TO PASS THE INTERVIEW TEST

The examination for which you applied requires an oral interview test. You have already taken the written test and you are now being called for the interview test – the final part of the formal examination.

You may think that it is not possible to prepare for an interview test and that there are no procedures to follow during an interview. Our purpose is to point out some things you can do in advance that will help you and some good rules to follow and pitfalls to avoid while you are being interviewed.

What is an interview supposed to test?

The written examination is designed to test the technical knowledge and competence of the candidate; the oral is designed to evaluate intangible qualities, not readily measured otherwise, and to establish a list showing the relative fitness of each candidate – as measured against his competitors – for the position sought. Scoring is not on the basis of "right" and "wrong," but on a sliding scale of values ranging from "not passable" to "outstanding." As a matter of fact, it is possible to achieve a relatively low score without a single "incorrect" answer because of evident weakness in the qualities being measured.

Occasionally, an examination may consist entirely of an oral test – either an individual or a group oral. In such cases, information is sought concerning the technical knowledges and abilities of the candidate, since there has been no written examination for this purpose. More commonly, however, an oral test is used to supplement a written examination.

Who conducts interviews?

The composition of oral boards varies among different jurisdictions. In nearly all, a representative of the personnel department serves as chairman. One of the members of the board may be a representative of the department in which the candidate would work. In some cases, "outside experts" are used, and, frequently, a businessman or some other representative of the general public is asked to serve. Labor and management or other special groups may be represented. The aim is to secure the services of experts in the appropriate field.

However the board is composed, it is a good idea (and not at all improper or unethical) to ascertain in advance of the interview who the members are and what groups they represent. When you are introduced to them, you will have some idea of their backgrounds and interests, and at least you will not stutter and stammer over their names.

What should be done before the interview?

While knowledge about the board members is useful and takes some of the surprise element out of the interview, there is other preparation which is more substantive. It *is* possible to prepare for an oral interview – in several ways:

1) Keep a copy of your application and review it carefully before the interview

This may be the only document before the oral board, and the starting point of the interview. Know what education and experience you have listed there, and the sequence and dates of all of it. Sometimes the board will ask you to review the highlights of your experience for them; you should not have to hem and haw doing it.

2) Study the class specification and the examination announcement

Usually, the oral board has one or both of these to guide them. The qualities, characteristics or knowledges required by the position sought are stated in these documents. They offer valuable clues as to the nature of the oral interview. For example, if the job involves supervisory responsibilities, the announcement will usually indicate that knowledge of modern supervisory methods and the qualifications of the candidate as a supervisor will be tested. If so, you can expect such questions, frequently in the form of a hypothetical situation which you are expected to solve. NEVER go into an oral without knowledge of the duties and responsibilities of the job you seek.

3) Think through each qualification required

Try to visualize the kind of questions you would ask if you were a board member. How well could you answer them? Try especially to appraise your own knowledge and background in each area, *measured against the job sought*, and identify any areas in which you are weak. Be critical and realistic – do not flatter yourself.

4) Do some general reading in areas in which you feel you may be weak

For example, if the job involves supervision and your past experience has NOT, some general reading in supervisory methods and practices, particularly in the field of human relations, might be useful. Do NOT study agency procedures or detailed manuals. The oral board will be testing your understanding and capacity, not your memory.

5) Get a good night's sleep and watch your general health and mental attitude

You will want a clear head at the interview. Take care of a cold or any other minor ailment, and of course, no hangovers.

What should be done on the day of the interview?

Now comes the day of the interview itself. Give yourself plenty of time to get there. Plan to arrive somewhat ahead of the scheduled time, particularly if your appointment is in the fore part of the day. If a previous candidate fails to appear, the board might be ready for you a bit early. By early afternoon an oral board is almost invariably behind schedule if there are many candidates, and you may have to wait. Take along a book or magazine to read, or your application to review, but leave any extraneous material in the waiting room when you go in for your interview. In any event, relax and compose yourself.

The matter of dress is important. The board is forming impressions about you – from your experience, your manners, your attitude, and your appearance. Give your personal appearance careful attention. Dress your best, but not your flashiest. Choose conservative, appropriate clothing, and be sure it is immaculate. This is a business interview, and your appearance should indicate that you regard it as such. Besides, being well groomed and properly dressed will help boost your confidence.

Sooner or later, someone will call your name and escort you into the interview room. *This is it.* From here on you are on your own. It is too late for any more preparation. But remember, you asked for this opportunity to prove your fitness, and you are here because your request was granted.

What happens when you go in?

The usual sequence of events will be as follows: The clerk (who is often the board stenographer) will introduce you to the chairman of the oral board, who will introduce you to the other members of the board. Acknowledge the introductions before you sit down. Do not be surprised if you find a microphone facing you or a stenotypist sitting by. Oral interviews are usually recorded in the event of an appeal or other review.

Usually the chairman of the board will open the interview by reviewing the highlights of your education and work experience from your application – primarily for the benefit of the other members of the board, as well as to get the material into the record. Do not interrupt or comment unless there is an error or significant misinterpretation; if that is the case, do not hesitate. But do not quibble about insignificant matters. Also, he will usually ask you some question about your education, experience or your present job – partly to get you to start talking and to establish the interviewing "rapport." He may start the actual questioning, or turn it over to one of the other members. Frequently, each member undertakes the questioning on a particular area, one in which he is perhaps most competent, so you can expect each member to participate in the examination. Because time is limited, you may also expect some rather abrupt switches in the direction the questioning takes, so do not be upset by it. Normally, a board member will not pursue a single line of questioning unless he discovers a particular strength or weakness.

After each member has participated, the chairman will usually ask whether any member has any further questions, then will ask you if you have anything you wish to add. Unless you are expecting this question, it may floor you. Worse, it may start you off on an extended, extemporaneous speech. The board is not usually seeking more information. The question is principally to offer you a last opportunity to present further qualifications or to indicate that you have nothing to add. So, if you feel that a significant qualification or characteristic has been overlooked, it is proper to point it out in a sentence or so. Do not compliment the board on the thoroughness of their examination – they have been sketchy, and you know it. If you wish, merely say, "No thank you, I have nothing further to add." This is a point where you can "talk yourself out" of a good impression or fail to present an important bit of information. Remember, *you close the interview yourself.*

The chairman will then say, "That is all, Mr. _____, thank you." Do not be startled; the interview is over, and quicker than you think. Thank him, gather your belongings and take your leave. Save your sigh of relief for the other side of the door.

How to put your best foot forward

Throughout this entire process, you may feel that the board individually and collectively is trying to pierce your defenses, seek out your hidden weaknesses and embarrass and confuse you. Actually, this is not true. They are obliged to make an appraisal of your qualifications for the job you are seeking, and they want to see you in your best light. Remember, they must interview all candidates and a non-cooperative candidate may become a failure in spite of their best efforts to bring out his qualifications. Here are 15 suggestions that will help you:

1) Be natural – Keep your attitude confident, not cocky

If you are not confident that you can do the job, do not expect the board to be. Do not apologize for your weaknesses, try to bring out your strong points. The board is interested in a positive, not negative, presentation. Cockiness will antagonize any board member and make him wonder if you are covering up a weakness by a false show of strength.

2) Get comfortable, but don't lounge or sprawl

Sit erectly but not stiffly. A careless posture may lead the board to conclude that you are careless in other things, or at least that you are not impressed by the importance of the occasion. Either conclusion is natural, even if incorrect. Do not fuss with your clothing, a pencil or an ashtray. Your hands may occasionally be useful to emphasize a point; do not let them become a point of distraction.

3) Do not wisecrack or make small talk

This is a serious situation, and your attitude should show that you consider it as such. Further, the time of the board is limited – they do not want to waste it, and neither should you.

4) Do not exaggerate your experience or abilities

In the first place, from information in the application or other interviews and sources, the board may know more about you than you think. Secondly, you probably will not get away with it. An experienced board is rather adept at spotting such a situation, so do not take the chance.

5) If you know a board member, do not make a point of it, yet do not hide it

Certainly you are not fooling him, and probably not the other members of the board. Do not try to take advantage of your acquaintanceship – it will probably do you little good.

6) Do not dominate the interview

Let the board do that. They will give you the clues – do not assume that you have to do all the talking. Realize that the board has a number of questions to ask you, and do not try to take up all the interview time by showing off your extensive knowledge of the answer to the first one.

7) Be attentive

You only have 20 minutes or so, and you should keep your attention at its sharpest throughout. When a member is addressing a problem or question to you, give him your undivided attention. Address your reply principally to him, but do not exclude the other board members.

8) Do not interrupt

A board member may be stating a problem for you to analyze. He will ask you a question when the time comes. Let him state the problem, and wait for the question.

9) Make sure you understand the question

Do not try to answer until you are sure what the question is. If it is not clear, restate it in your own words or ask the board member to clarify it for you. However, do not haggle about minor elements.

10) Reply promptly but not hastily

A common entry on oral board rating sheets is "candidate responded readily," or "candidate hesitated in replies." Respond as promptly and quickly as you can, but do not jump to a hasty, ill-considered answer.

11) Do not be peremptory in your answers

A brief answer is proper – but do not fire your answer back. That is a losing game from your point of view. The board member can probably ask questions much faster than you can answer them.

12) Do not try to create the answer you think the board member wants

He is interested in what kind of mind you have and how it works – not in playing games. Furthermore, he can usually spot this practice and will actually grade you down on it.

13) Do not switch sides in your reply merely to agree with a board member

Frequently, a member will take a contrary position merely to draw you out and to see if you are willing and able to defend your point of view. Do not start a debate, yet do not surrender a good position. If a position is worth taking, it is worth defending.

14) Do not be afraid to admit an error in judgment if you are shown to be wrong

The board knows that you are forced to reply without any opportunity for careful consideration. Your answer may be demonstrably wrong. If so, admit it and get on with the interview.

15) Do not dwell at length on your present job

The opening question may relate to your present assignment. Answer the question but do not go into an extended discussion. You are being examined for a *new* job, not your present one. As a matter of fact, try to phrase ALL your answers in terms of the job for which you are being examined.

Basis of Rating

Probably you will forget most of these "do's" and "don'ts" when you walk into the oral interview room. Even remembering them all will not ensure you a passing grade. Perhaps you did not have the qualifications in the first place. But remembering them will help you to put your best foot forward, without treading on the toes of the board members.

Rumor and popular opinion to the contrary notwithstanding, an oral board wants you to make the best appearance possible. They know you are under pressure – but they also want to see how you respond to it as a guide to what your reaction would be under the pressures of the job you seek. They will be influenced by the degree of poise you display, the personal traits you show and the manner in which you respond.

ABOUT THIS BOOK

This book contains tests divided into Examination Sections. Go through each test, answering every question in the margin. At the end of each test look at the answer key and check your answers. On the ones you got wrong, look at the right answer choice and learn. Do not fill in the answers first. Do not memorize the questions and answers, but understand the answer and principles involved. On your test, the questions will likely be different from the samples. Questions are changed and new ones added. If you understand these past questions you should have success with any changes that arise. Tests may consist of several types of questions. We have additional books on each subject should more study be advisable or necessary for you. Finally, the more you study, the better prepared you will be. This book is intended to be the last thing you study before you walk into the examination room. Prior study of relevant texts is also recommended. NLC publishes some of these in our Fundamental Series. Knowledge and good sense are important factors in passing your exam. Good luck also helps. So now study this Passbook, absorb the material contained within and take that knowledge into the examination. Then do your best to pass that exam.

———

EXAMINATION SECTION

THE "IN-BASKET" EXAMINATION

While the exact format of in-basket exercises will vary, they frequently involve each trainee in a group first individually assuming the role of a manager who is faced with a number of letters, memoirs, and notes to which he must respond in writing within a limited time period. For example, the trainee may be told that he has just returned from vacation and that he must leave on a trip in four hours, during which time he must respond in writing to all the items on his desk.

To further complicate the exercise, you, the trainee, may be told that you have just returned from vacation and must leave on a business trip in five hours. Also, it is a holiday and your secretary is home, and no one else is around the office to help you. There are more inquiries and problems to respond to than is possible in five hours and so you will have to determine the relative priority of the work to be done.

As you can see, the IN-BASKET EXERCISE demands good decision-making skills, rather than learning new facts or acquiring new skills. The time pressure factor may result in your finding out how well you perform under stress.

When these exercises are conducted in an oral format, and after each exercise is finished (time runs out), you may be asked to justify your decisions and actions to the examiner and the other participants when it is held as a group exercise, and then they in turn will evaluate your actions and critique it. The rating, of course, is done differently in competitive examinations.

The fact that this type of exercise can be given to groups of managerial trainees is considered an advantage to management, i.e., it is easier and cheaper to administer than other training methods. This training technique also tests managerial candidates for decision-making abilities, particularly due to the time constraints involved. This is considered a vital skill for most managerial candidates for decision-making abilities, particularly due to the time constraints involved. This is considered a vital skill for most managerial positions and, although other training techniques such as role playing can also provide stress, in-basket exercises do more so and are specifically designed for this purpose.

There are limitations, too. As with in-basket questions pertaining to case study examples, they are in large part hypothetical in nature, or static, in that the managerial candidate does not have to live or "die" with the consequences of a poor decision, except where he/she is rated poorly on an examination.

Some in-basket exercises provide guidelines or suggestions for solution. The candidate may be presented with a problem which requires a series of decisions and actions but is also presented with a number of alternate means of resolving the problem, from which he must choose the best option. Next, the problem may be further developed and you may be provided with a number of new choices to resolve this new, or expanded, problem. It may even be required a third time. Then comes the evaluation and critique.

So with this technique, the trainee receives information evaluating the consequences, good or bad, of his decisions at each decision point in the exercise.

In order to properly critique the trainee's decisions, the examiner must be highly skilled in conducting the exercise and in conducting the critique. At its extremes, the critique, as with performance evaluations, can be so general as to be meaningless or be so specific that the trainee becomes so overwhelmed as to render the whole training exercise pointless.

In-basket exercises are often used in on-the-job management group training programs, together with case studies.

———

Senior Technical Writer/Content Director, Interaxion

You are T. SMITH, the senior technical writer/content director for an eight-year-old business service provider, Interaxion. The primary services provided to its clients are Web hosting, security services, high-capacity Internet access, and information system audits. You and your staff of 4 writers and 2 assistants have recently completed a draft of customer use manuals for a new addition to the service line: a dedicated storage network for clients with large amounts of data. Within the next several months, Interaxion also intends to launch a new download hosting service that will help clients place large files and applications on their own dedicated servers for access.

Interaxion is a medium-sized company that aggressively competes with larger business-to-business service organizations, much of them sprung from existing computer or telecommunications companies. To hold its market share, Interaxion offers a level of service and individual client attention that goes beyond the norm.

The president and CEO of your company, Marlane Liddell, is the engine behind Interaxion's aggressive approach. She is anxious to make Interaxion into a one-stop destination for any and all business-to-business networking services, which explains the rapid schedule of new product/service rollouts—now occurring at a pace of nearly two per year. Many employees privately complain that the grueling pace of development and launch makes work more stressful and error-prone, but the business is growing steadily. While some errors do occur in implementing and documenting services, the departments are managed well enough to correct these mistakes before they cause a significant loss of up-time for clients—if they weren't managed this well, Interaxion would have real problems in customer relations.

As the head of the technical writing department, you are accountable to the Vice President of Customer Relations, Branch Stuckey. He's known as a calm, reasonable man who nevertheless keeps the pressure steady—if his memos or phone calls are not answered within a reasonable amount of time, he is sure to pay a personal visit to ask why. Both he and you share the vision of the technical writing department as the most important medium through which customers receive information about Interaxion's products and services.

You and your staff are responsible for writing the promotional materials and specifications that anchor every service's marketing campaign, and for writing easy-to-follow manuals for their use. You're also accountable for maintaining and updating the Interaxion Web site.

You and Stuckey have jointly decided that the clientele would be well-served by two additional projects. The first, a general technical glossary, is to be available both in print and from Interaxion's Web site, and will help customers to understand the increasingly complex jargon involved in implementing the company's services. You and Stuckey have set a deadline of six months for the launch of this glossary.

Another document you've decided will be helpful is a Frequently Asked Questions (FAQ)/Troubleshooting guide for each of the company's line of services. This will require close collaboration with both the Technical Support and Communications departments. This a project that is of particular interest to the president, who wants a progress report submitted at the end of each month.

As a matter of principle, you try to work no more than a standard 8-to-5 workday. The three-day focus for this exercise is the Monday-Wednesday span of the 23rd through the 25th. The items you find in your in-box are items 1 through 10 and a general information folder compiled by your trusted assistant, Fred. On Tuesday afternoon, a meeting is scheduled from 2 p.m. to 4. p.m. that will include the marketing staff and your department, to discuss reasons why the marketing campaign for Interaxion's security services is not doing well. Tina Niu, Vice President of Marketing, seems to believe it's because the promotional material is too technical and jargony. You met briefly with your staff on Friday to prepare a response to this, but were unsatisfied with the results. You'd like at least another two hours with your writers before meeting with the marketing department.

On the following pages are a list of important departments and personnel at Interaxion, a to-do list, messages, memos, and a planner covering the three-day period. Read the instructions below, then assume you have just arrived Monday morning to find these items in your in-basket.

1. *Look over the list of officers, the planner, the to-do list, and in-basket items quickly, to get an idea of the tasks to be done.*

2. *In the spaces provided in the left margin of the to-do list, indicate the priority of each item, and note how you would dispose of each. Priorities should be labeled in the following manner:*

    AB priorities = those that are both important and urgent
    A priorities = those that are important, but not particularly urgent (can be deferred)
    B priorities = those that are urgent, but not so important
    X priorities = neither urgent nor important

3. *After reading the in-basket items, do the following:*

    a. *First, decide which items can be delegated, and to whom. Use Form B, Delegated Calls and Correspondence, to list and prioritize these items.*
    b. *Next, prioritize the items to which you must respond personally on Form C, Personal Calls and Correspondence.*

4. *Take the planning guide and schedule the tasks you have in front of you. Be sure to allow some "flexible time" to handle any interruptions or crises.*

Interaxion

Important Departments/Personnel:

<u>President/CEO</u>: Marlane Liddell

    <u>VP Marketing</u>: Tina Niu

      Marketing Director: Brian Paulsen

      General Sales Manager: Maxine Patton

    <u>VP Service Delivery</u>: Owen Stark

      Director of Engineering: Anna Karpov

      Chief Information Architect: Juan Machuca

          (Various Project Managers)

    <u>VP Finance</u>: Tom Wilson

      Treasurer: Mary Stravinsky

      Comptroller: Barbara Bernstein

          John Slingsby, Director of Cost Analysis

          Ruth Nielsen, Director of Budgeting and Accounting

    <u>VP Administration and Human Resources</u>: Tariq Nayim

      Director of Human Resources: Amos Otis

      Director of Administration: Nancy Frank

    <u>VP Customer Relations</u>: Branch Stuckey

      Director of Communications: Alvin Gehring

      Director of Technical Support: Hollis Holt

      Chief Technical Writer: T. SMITH

          Terry Appleton, Technical Writer

          Samir Naramayan, Technical Writer/Web Designer

          Jim Mason, Technical Writer

          Tracy Livingston, Associate Writer

            Fred Cummings, Assistant to **T. SMITH**

            Stacia Cocker, Office Assistant

Things to Do:

<u>Priority</u>   <u>Item</u>

_____   •attend meeting on downtime of hosting service. Some clients have fallen below the promised 99.999% uptime, and the company needs to devise ways to improve performance.

Disposition: _____

_____

_____

_____   •meet with technical writing staff for input on the promotion of security services.

Disposition: _____

_____

_____

_____   •meet with staff to outline promotional copy for download hosting service — now looks as if it will be rolled out in about 8 months.

Disposition: _____

_____

_____

_____   •see what's up with Mason's overtime.

Disposition: _____

_____

_____

Things to Do (cont'd):

_____ •contact people who sent in resumes for associate writing job--Sanchez looked best of all, but I'll interview Larkin, too. Reject Yancey and Crespin.

Disposition: _____

_____

_____

_____ •meet with writers to assign updates to manuals for each of the security services. Should take about an hour.

Disposition: _____

_____

_____

_____ •check on the progress of the technical glossary--Mason is falling way, way behind.

Disposition: _____

_____

_____

_____ •check with human resources and budgeting to ask about availability for part-time position, to compile the FAQ/Troubleshooting guide—even with new associate, not enough staff time to devote to this.

Disposition: _____

_____

_____

_____ •proofread/line-edit customer manual (8 hours work at least) for storage network operation, and send it to the printer. Must be done by you personally, and by Thursday morning! Several customers have already purchased network and are waiting.

Disposition: _____

_____

NOTE TO: __T. SMITH__

DATE __20th__ TIME __4:50 p.m.__

WHILE YOU WERE OUT

M __Janet Yancey__

OF _____

PHONE (____) _____
    AREA CODE   NUMBER   EXTENSION

	Telephoned	✓	Please Call
	Called to See You		Will Call Again
	Wants to See You		Returned Your Call

Message __Anxious to speak w/you about associate writer position.__

_____

_____

_____

_____

_____

_____

_____

Item 2

Memorandum

To: T. SMITH
CC: Hollis Holt, Director of Technical Support
From: Alvin Gehring, Director of Communications
Date: 20th
Re: Web site e-mail service

I've been contacted a few times in the past couple of weeks by customers who have visited our Web site and wanted to e-mail us a question. Apparently some of them have clicked on the "e-mail us" hypertext button from a product description page, and nothing has happened.

I know that this is probably a very small-scale problem, and that the more persistent customers will know to simply e-mail us using their own mail programs. But I can't help thinking we might be losing some potential customers without this direct link.

Can you look into this and see what the problem is? I'd like to find out as soon as possible.

Memorandum

To: T. SMITH
CC:
From: Marlane Liddell, CEO and President
Date: 23rd
Re: Updates on troubleshooting guide and arrangement with Sturdevant

---

Just a note to remind you that I'll want to meet with you soon to talk about progress on the FAQ/Troubleshooting Guide.

I've also recently received a letter from Sturdevant Publishing about our arrangement with them. Their $6500 payment is figured into our revenues for the quarter, so we'll need to meet that contract deadline.

Let me know when you're available to meet—and when we do meet, make sure you're ready with the good news.

NOTE TO: _T. SMITH_

DATE _23rd_   TIME _9:00 am_

WHILE YOU WERE OUT

M _Philip Larkin_

OF _____

PHONE (_____) _____ _____
    AREA CODE   NUMBER   EXTENSION

✓	Telephoned		Please Call
	Called to See You		Will Call Again
	Wants to See You		Returned Your Call

Message _Wants to know your decision about associate writer position._

Memorandum

To: T. SMITH
CC: Terry Appleton, Samir Naramayan, Jim Mason, Technical Writers
From: Tracy Livingston, Associate Writer
Date: 23rd
Re: Security services/marketing

I hope this doesn't sound too compulsive, but I know we all worked very hard on the specs and promotional materials for security services, and I can't accept the idea that people aren't buying in because they don't understand our copy.

I conducted a little of my own market research over the weekend—interviewing purchasers from about a dozen clients who've bought other services from us, but went with another company for security. There were a few different reasons, but many clients seem to have placed the blame on some questionable architecture.

When pressed, a few said that they did find some parts of the promotional copy a little hard to follow—but added that it wasn't the factor that affected our buying decision.

We'll need to be careful about how we present this, so it doesn't appear we're shifting blame to Service Delivery. This can be one of the things we decide together when we meet (when are we meeting again? Isn't the meeting with Marketing tomorrow afternoon?).

Before we do meet, I hope you'll all take a look at some of the results of the interviews, enclosed here. It should take about a half-hour to get through them.

Item 6

NOTE TO: __T. SMITH__

DATE __23rd__   TIME __8:24 a.m.__

WHILE YOU WERE OUT

M __Jim Mason__

OF _____

PHONE __(_____)__ _____ _____
          AREA CODE   NUMBER   EXTENSION

✓	Telephoned		Please Call
	Called to See You		Will Call Again
	Wants to See You		Returned Your Call

Message __Will come in at 10:30 a.m. today —
had to take his wife to a rescheduled
hospital appointment. Says he's sorry— the
only time he could do it.__

Memorandum

To: All Department Heads
CC:
From: Marlane Liddell, President and CEO
Date: 23rd
Re: Meeting on hosting service downtime

A reminder: our meeting on resolving the hosting service downtime problem will be this Wednesday, the 25th, from 1 p.m. to 4 p.m.

Enclosed is a short examination of issues, compiled by Alvin Gehring Hollis Holt, and Owen Stark, that will need to be addressed if we are to improve the uptime of our Web hosting service. This is probably the most important problem facing our company today, and we'll all need to work together to resolve it as soon as possible.

Please take a look through the enclosed 30 pages to get an idea of what's holding us back, and try to have some ideas for resolution ready by the time we meet Wednesday.

Item 8

2642 Avenue of the Americas

New York, NY 00000

Sturdevant Publishing

November 10

T. SMITH
Chief Technical Writer
Interaxion
3445 Newton Ave.
Cambridge, MA 00000

Dear T. SMITH:

We at Sturdevant are pleased you've decided to contribute to our forthcoming publication, *The Encyclopedia of Technical Publishing*, to be compiled over the next 9 months and released early next year.

Last month, you agreed to send us a general profile of your company and a specific description of the different forms of writing (manuals, proposals, letters, specifications, etc.) performed by your department, along with a few recent samples of your work.

As you know, payment of $6500 to Interaxion was contingent on the delivery of this information by the end of the current month. We expect that you have every intention of honoring this contract, but we haven't heard from you recently and wanted to extend a reminder to you in any case.

Sincerely,

Bob Francis

Editorial Director

Memorandum

To: T. SMITH
CC: Jim Mason, Technical Writer; Barbara Bernstein, Comptroller
From: Ruth Nielsen, Director of Budgeting and Accounting
Date: 23rd
Re: Overtime

Our records show an unusual amount of overtime charged to the company by your department over the last month. In order to meet our budget targets for the quarter, you'll need to work with your employees to reduce the number of hours they work each week.

If you're unable to reduce these hours, it may be necessary to conduct an internal audit in order to verify their necessity. Of course this is simply adding time and expenditure to the situation, and we'd like to avoid it entirely.

Please let us know how this situation is resolved.

NOTE TO: _T. SMITH_

DATE _23rd_ _____ TIME _7:50 a.m._

WHILE YOU WERE OUT

M _Janet Yancey_

OF _____

PHONE (_____) _____ _____
$\quad$ AREA CODE $\qquad$ NUMBER $\qquad$ EXTENSION

	Telephoned	✓	Please Call
	Called to See You	✓	Will Call Again
	Wants to See You		Returned Your Call

Message _Wants to speak w/ you ASAP about associate writer position - will keep calling._

General Information Folder:

1. Additional interdepartmental memos—about a dozen of them. Don't need a response but should be read for information. Should take about a half hour.

2. Eight news and trade newspapers and magazines—about two hours' worth of reading.

3. About 20 items of junk mail—should be reviewed. Will take about 30 minutes.

4. A detailed report—in addition to Liddell's 30-page report and Livingston's interviews—that need to be studied for possible action. It's a compilation of customer-satisfaction ratings for the company's other services, including their ratings of the documentation for each on a broad range of criteria, including readability, ease of understanding, and thoroughness. This should require about an hour.

DELEGATED CALLS AND CORRESPONDENCE

Priority   _Item_   _Delegated to:_

_____

_____

_____

_____

_____

_____

_____

_____

PERSONAL CALLS AND CORRESPONDENCE

Priority   *Item*   *Response:*

_____

_____

_____

_____

_____

_____

_____

_____

23 Monday	24 Tuesday	25 Wednesday
7 AM		
8		
9		
10		
11		
12 PM		
1		
2		
3		
4		
5		
6 PM		
7		

KEY (CORRECT ANSWERS)

Discussion of Inbox Examination #1:

Senior Technical Writer/Content Director, Interaxion

One of the first things you should realize, when looking over all the information in front of you, is that there won't be enough time within the next three days for you to do the things on your list, as well as the tasks required by your in-box items. This is hardly surprising for a senior worker at a mid-sized company, but you'll have to decide quickly what can be either eliminated from your schedule, or postponed.

To-Do List:

In this case, the prime candidate for elimination is the three-hour meeting on the downtime of the company's hosting service. While the president is anxious about it, and wants input from people from all departments, there's really not much a technical writing staff can do about the problem. You should try to free up these three hours—speaking with the president personally and explaining what needs to be done by you and your staff in the next three days, and offering to send a representative to the meeting who will report back to you.

As chief technical writer, there are two situations that are both important and urgent: your meeting with marketing department to discuss the quality of your staff's promotional materials, and the huge task of editing the manual for Interaxion's storage network users. Since some customers have already purchased the network, they'll need the manual as soon as possible. The meeting with Marketing is on Tuesday, and you have two tasks to complete before then: read through the information supplied by Tracy Livingston, and call the afternoon meeting with the writers on Monday—they'll need to drop everything in the afternoon for this.

Once the most important and urgent items are taken care of, you should turn your attention to tasks that are important, but not as pressing. You'll need to meet with the staff for two further purposes: outlining promotional copy for the company's downloading hosting service (not that urgent, since the rollout isn't for another 8 months), and assigning updates for the manuals for security service users. Since your copy on the promotional materials for these services is being questioned by the marketing department, it's probably best to schedule this meeting after you've met with Marketing and these questions have been resolved. You'll also need to see if you can find a way to hire part-time help for compiling the FAQ/Troubleshooting guide, since this is of extreme importance to the president.

Urgent matters that aren't quite as significant as the others facing you right now are the progress of the technical glossary—not due out for another six months—and the related problem of Jim Mason's excessive overtime. His memo about taking his wife to the hospital hints that he might be going through some personal problems, and if they're affecting his work, this situation needs to be resolved soon.

Discussion (cont'd)

Delegated Calls and Correspondence:

Janet Yancey may insist on speaking with you personally, but it may simply be that she wants a yes or no answer regarding her hiring. For now, it should be enough to have your assistant send her a letter. Assuming Fred is informed about the progress of your arrangements with Sturdevant—and assuming the contract is being honored—he can also send a reply to them. The e-mail problem, presented in the memo from Hollis Holt, is best left to the expertise of your Web designer, Samir Naramayan.

Personal Calls and Correspondence:

It appears that the news on the progress of the FAQ/Troubleshooting guide is not that good, but you'll need to set up a meeting with the president anyway to tell her so. It might be a good time to state your case about needing more help. You should send a memo to set a meeting time, and to reassure her about the arrangement with Sturdevant.

Since you do intend to interview Philip Larkin about the associate writer position, you should probably call him personally to set this up—though some managers might leave this to an assistant. It's acceptable to include this in the "delegated" column as well.

The memo from the president is simply a re-statement of your obligation to attend the hosting service downtime meeting—and you've determined you can't do this. You should make every attempt to speak with the president personally, to explain why, and to see if sending your assistant is acceptable. You should also give the 30-page report to your assistant, Fred, to have him either outline it for you or see if any of it is relevant to the technical writing staff at all.

Jim Mason appears to be in some trouble, and he may need your help to resolve it—especially since his problems are being noticed by the budgeting department. Since it would be best to discuss it privately, out of the office, you might meet him somewhere for lunch and try to work things out. He'll have to find a way to get things done within a regular 40-hour week.

Planner:

Filling in the planner can be done in a number of ways—as long as everything on your to-do list and in your inbox gets taken care of, and in an appropriate sequence. The most difficult thing to schedule will probably be the meeting with the writers about promotional copy for the security services. It's a short-notice meeting, for one thing, and you'll need to look over Livingston's interviews first. The meeting must happen before the Tuesday meeting with marketing—and Since Jim Mason won't be in until 10:30 on Monday, it will have to take place after that. The tight window requires that the meeting happen Monday afternoon or Tuesday morning. Items such as progress on other projects can be discussed briefly, toward the end of scheduled meetings.

In addition, it wouldn't make sense to schedule the other meeting—regarding the updates to existing security service manuals—until after some of the questions raised by both the marketing department and Livingston's interviews have been resolved. This will have to take place some time on Wednesday.

Things to Do: **22**

_____X_____ •attend meeting on downtime of hosting service. Some clients have fallen below the promised 99.999% uptime, and the company needs to devise ways to improve performance.

Disposition: _____Contact Marlane Liddell personally to explain why you can't make the meeting. Ask if you can send an assistant to take notes, promise to review them later and get back to her with ideas._

_____AB_____ •meet with technical writing staff for input on the promotion of security services.

Disposition: _____Schedule meeting for Monday, the 23rd, after Mason gets in._

_____A_____ •meet with staff to outline promotional copy for download hosting service —now looks as if it will be rolled out in about 8 months.

Disposition: _____Schedule after more urgent meetings—maybe combine with manual update meeting._

_____B_____ •see what's up with Mason's overtime.

Disposition: _____Meet with him soon and privately, away from other writers._

_____A_____ •contact people who sent in resumes for associate writing job--Sanchez looked best of all, but I'll interview Larkin, too. Reject Yancey and Crespin.

Disposition: _____Have Fred send letter to Yancey and Crespin; call Larkin and Sanchez personally to set up interviews_

Things to Do (cont'd):

_____A_____ •meet with writers to assign updates to manuals for each of the security services. Should take about an hour.

Disposition: _____*Schedule meeting after all other concerns regarding security*

*services documentation have been cleared up—no sooner than Wednesday.*_____

_____B_____ •check on the progress of the technical glossary--Mason is falling way, way behind.

Disposition: _____*A quick check that can be slipped in at the end of another*

*meeting—try for Monday or Wednesday.*_____

_____A_____ •check with human resources and budgeting to ask about availability for part-time position, to compile the FAQ/Troubleshooting guide—even with new associate, not enough staff time to devote to this.

Disposition: _____*Contact them personally, during flex time, before scheduling*

*meeting with Marlane Liddell.*_____

_____AB_____ •proofread/line-edit customer manual (8 hours work at least) for storage network operation, and send it to the printer. Must be done by you personally, and by Thursday morning! Several customers have already purchased network and are waiting.

Disposition: _____*Try to fit in big time blocks to devote to this—give it your*

*full attention.*_____

DELEGATED CALLS AND CORRESPONDENCE

Priority	_Item_	_Delegated to:_
X	#1 — Yancey call	Fred
A	#2 — Holt memo	Samir
X	#8 — Sturdevant letter	Fred will write response
X	#10 — Yancey call	Fred
_____		
_____		
_____		
_____		

PERSONAL CALLS AND CORRESPONDENCE

Priority	Item	Response:
A	#3—Liddell memo	Brief memo
A	#4—Larkin call	Phone call for interview
AB	#7—Liddell memo	Personal visit
A	#9—Nielsen memo	Meet w/ Mason and write memo
____		
____		
____		
____		

	23 Monday	24 Tuesday	25 Wednesday
7 AM			
8	flex-time: delegate, make calls, set up meeting	flex-time: reading, sorting work on storage network manual	read customer sat. report
9	reading: interdept. memos, trade publications		flex-time: schedule interviews
10			work on storage network manual
11			
12 PM		lunch, meeting w/ Mason	
1	flex-time: examine Livingston interviews	flex-time: sort through junk mail	meeting w. writers:
2	meeting w. writers:	meeting w/ Marketing	•assign updates to manuals, •outline download promo copy
3	•ideas for response to market-ing,		work on storage network manual
4	•progress of tech. glossary,	work on storage network manual	
5	•FAQ/Troubleshooting guide		
6 PM			
7			

EXAMINATION SECTION
TEST 1

DIRECTIONS: Each question or incomplete statement is followed by several suggested answers or completions. Select the one that BEST answers the question or completes the statement. *PRINT THE LETTER OF THE CORRECT ANSWER IN THE SPACE AT THE RIGHT.*

1. In public agencies, communications should be based PRIMARILY on a   1._____

    A. two-way flow from the top down and from the bottom up, most of which should be given in writing to avoid ambiguity
    B. multidirection flow among all levels and with outside persons
    C. rapid, internal one-way flow from the top down
    D. two-way flow of information, most of which should be given orally for purposes of clarity

2. In some organizations, changes in policy or procedures are often communicated by word   2._____
of mouth from supervisors to employees with no prior discussion or exchange of view-points with employees.
This procedure often produces employee dissatisfaction CHIEFLY because

    A. information is mostly unusable since a considerable amount of time is required to transmit information
    B. lower-level supervisors tend to be excessively concerned with minor details
    C. management has failed to seek employees' advice before making changes
    D. valuable staff time is lost between decision-making and the implementation of decisions

3. For good letter writing, you should try to visualize the person to whom you are writing,   3._____
especially if you know him.
Of the following rules, it is LEAST helpful in such visualization to think of

    A. the person's likes and dislikes, his concerns, and his needs
    B. what you would be likely to say if speaking in person
    C. what you would expect to be asked if speaking in person
    D. your official position in order to be certain that your words are proper

4. One approach to good informal letter writing is to make letters sound conversational.   4._____
All of the following practices will usually help to do this EXCEPT:

    A. If possible, use a style which is similar to the style used when speaking
    B. Substitute phrases for single words (e.g., *at the present time* for *now*)
    C. Use contractions of words (e.g., *you're* for *you are*)
    D. Use ordinary vocabulary when possible

5. All of the following rules will aid in producing clarity in report-writing EXCEPT: 5._____

    A. Give specific details or examples, if possible
    B. Keep related words close together in each sentence
    C. Present information in sequential order
    D. Put several thoughts or ideas in each paragraph

6. The one of the following statements about public relations which is MOST accurate is that   6.___

    A. in the long run, appearance gains better results than performance
    B. objectivity is decreased if outside public relations consultants are employed
    C. public relations is the responsibility of every employee
    D. public relations should be based on a formal publicity program

7. The form of communication which is usually considered to be MOST personally directed to the intended recipient is the   7.___

    A. brochure   B. film   C. letter   D. radio

8. In general, a document that presents an organization's views or opinions on a particular topic is MOST accurately known as a   8.___

    A. tear sheet   B. position paper
    C. flyer   D. journal

9. Assume that you have been asked to speak before an organization of persons who oppose a newly announced program in which you are involved. You feel tense about talking to this group.
Which of the following rules generally would be MOST useful in gaining rapport when speaking before the audience?   9.___

    A. Impress them with your experience
    B. Stress all areas of disagreement
    C. Talk to the group as to one person
    D. Use formal grammar and language

10. An organization must have an effective public relations program since, at its best, public relations is a bridge to change.
All of the following statements about communication and human behavior have validity EXCEPT: 10.___

    A. People are more likely to talk about controversial matters with like-minded people than with those holding other views
    B. The earlier an experience, the more powerful its effect since it influences how later experiences will be interpreted
    C. In periods of social tension, official sources gain increased believability
    D. Those who are already interested in a topic are the ones who are most open to receive new communications about it

11. An employee should be encouraged to talk easily and frankly when he is dealing with his supervisor.
In order to encourage such free communication, it would be MOST appropriate for a supervisor to behave in a(n)   11.___

    A. sincere manner; assure the employee that you will deal with him honestly and openly
    B. official manner; you are a supervisor and must always act formally with subordinates

    C.   investigative manner; you must probe and question to get to a basis of trust

    D.   unemotional manner; the employee's emotions and background should play no part in your dealings with him

12.   Research findings show that an increase in free communication within an agency GENERALLY results in which one of the following?   12.____

    A.   Improved morale and productivity

    B.   Increased promotional opportunities

    C.   An increase in authority

    D.   A spirit of honesty

13.   Assume that you are a supervisor and your superiors have given you a new-type procedure to be followed.   13.____
Before passing this information on to your subordinates, the one of the following actions that you should take FIRST is to

    A.   ask your superiors to send out a memorandum to the entire staff

    B.   clarify the procedure in your own mind

    C.   set up a training course to provide instruction on the new procedure

    D.   write a memorandum to your subordinates

14.   Communication is necessary for an organization to be effective.   14.____
The one of the following which is LEAST important for most communication systems is that

    A.   messages are sent quickly and directly to the person who needs them to operate

    B.   information should be conveyed understandably and accurately

    C.   the method used to transmit information should be kept secret so that security can be maintained

    D.   senders of messages must know how their messages are received and acted upon

15.   Which one of the following is the CHIEF advantage of listening willingly to subordinates and encouraging them to talk freely and honestly?   15.____
It

    A.   reveals to supervisors the degree to which ideas that are passed down are accepted by subordinates

    B.   reduces the participation of subordinates in the operation of the department

    C.   encourages subordinates to try for promotion

    D.   enables supervisors to learn more readily what the *grapevine* is saying

16.   A supervisor may be informed through either oral or written reports.   16.____
Which one of the following is an ADVANTAGE of using oral reports?

    A.   There is no need for a formal record of the report.

    B.   An exact duplicate of the report is not easily transmitted to others.

    C.   A good oral report requires little time for preparation.

    D.   An oral report involves two-way communication between a subordinate and his supervisor.

17. Of the following, the MOST important reason why supervisors should communicate effectively with the public is to

    A. improve the public's understanding of information that is important for them to know
    B. establish a friendly relationship
    C. obtain information about the kinds of people who come to the agency
    D. convince the public that services are adequate

    17.___

18. Supervisors should generally NOT use phrases like *too hard, too easy,* and *a lot* PRINCIPALLY because such phrases

    A. may be offensive to some minority groups
    B. are too informal
    C. mean different things to different people
    D. are difficult to remember

    18.___

19. The ability to communicate clearly and concisely is an important element in effective leadership.
Which of the following statements about oral and written communication is GENERALLY true?

    A. Oral communication is more time-consuming.
    B. Written communication is more likely to be misinterpreted.
    C. Oral communication is useful only in emergencies.
    D. Written communication is useful mainly when giving information to fewer than twenty people.

    19.___

20. Rumors can often have harmful and disruptive effects on an organization.
Which one of the following is the BEST way to prevent rumors from becoming a problem?

    A. Refuse to act on rumors, thereby making them less believable.
    B. Increase the amount of information passed along by the *grapevine.*
    C. Distribute as much factual information as possible.
    D. Provide training in report writing.

    20.___

21. Suppose that a subordinate asks you about a rumor he has heard. The rumor deals with a subject which your superiors consider *confidential.*
Which of the following BEST describes how you should answer the subordinate?
Tell

    A. the subordinate that you don't make the rules and that he should speak to higher ranking officials
    B. the subordinate that you will ask your superior for information
    C. him only that you cannot comment on the matter
    D. him the rumor is not true

    21.___

22. Supervisors often find it difficult to *get their message across* when instructing newly appointed employees in their various duties.
The MAIN reason for this is generally that the

    22.___

A. duties of the employees have increased
B. supervisor is often so expert in his area that he fails to see it from the learner's point of view
C. supervisor adapts his instruction to the slowest learner in the group
D. new employees are younger, less concerned with job security and more interested in fringe benefits

23. Assume that you are discussing a job problem with an employee under your supervision. During the discussion, you see that the man's eyes are turning away from you and that he is not paying attention.
In order to get the man's attention, you should FIRST

    A. ask him to look you in the eye
    B. talk to him about sports
    C. tell him he is being very rude
    D. change your tone of voice

23.____

24. As a supervisor, you may find it necessary to conduct meetings with your subordinates. Of the following, which would be MOST helpful in assuring that a meeting accomplishes the purpose for which it was called?

    A. Give notice of the conclusions you would like to reach at the start of the meeting.
    B. Delay the start of the meeting until everyone is present.
    C. Write down points to be discussed in proper sequence.
    D. Make sure everyone is clear on whatever conclusions have been reached and on what must be done after the meeting.

24.____

25. Every supervisor will occasionally be called upon to deliver a reprimand to a subordinate. If done properly, this can greatly help an employee improve his performance.
Which one of the following is NOT a good practice to follow when giving a reprimand?

    A. Maintain your composure and temper.
    B. Reprimand a subordinate in the presence of other employees so they can learn the same lesson.
    C. Try to understand why the employee was not able to perform satisfactorily.
    D. Let your knowledge of the man involved determine the exact nature of the reprimand.

25.____

KEY (CORRECT ANSWERS)

1.	C		11.	A
2.	B		12.	A
3.	D		13.	B
4.	B		14.	C
5.	D		15.	A
6.	C		16.	D
7.	C		17.	A
8.	B		18.	C
9.	C		19.	B
10.	C		20.	C

21.	B
22.	B
23.	D
24.	D
25.	B

———

TEST 2

DIRECTIONS: Each question or incomplete statement is followed by several suggested answers or completions. Select the one that BEST answers the question or completes the statement. *PRINT THE LETTER OF THE CORRECT ANSWER IN THE SPACE AT THE RIGHT.*

1. Usually one thinks of communication as a single step, essentially that of transmitting an idea.
   Actually, however, this is only part of a total process, the FIRST step of which should be

   A. the prompt dissemination of the idea to those who may be affected by it
   B. motivating those affected to take the required action
   C. clarifying the idea in one's own mind
   D. deciding to whom the idea is to be communicated

   1.____

2. Research studies on patterns of informal communication have concluded that most individuals in a group tend to be passive recipients of news, while a few make it their business to spread it around in an organization.
   With this conclusion in mind, it would be MOST correct for the supervisor to attempt to identify these few individuals and

   A. give them the complete facts on important matters in advance of others
   B. inform the other subordinates of the identify of these few individuals so that their influence may be minimized
   C. keep them straight on the facts on important matters
   D. warn them to cease passing along any information to others

   2.____

3. The one of the following which is the PRINCIPAL advantage of making an oral report is that it

   A. affords an immediate opportunity for two-way communication between the subordinate and superior
   B. is an easy method for the superior to use in transmitting information to others of equal rank
   C. saves the time of all concerned
   D. permits more precise pinpointing of praise or blame by means of follow-up questions by the superior

   3.____

4. An agency may sometimes undertake a public relations program of a defensive nature.
   With reference to the use of defensive public relations, it would be MOST correct to state that it

   A. is bound to be ineffective since defensive statements, even though supported by factual data, can never hope to even partly overcome the effects of prior unfavorable attacks
   B. proves that the agency has failed to establish good relationships with newspapers, radio stations, or other means of publicity
   C. shows that the upper echelons of the agency have failed to develop sound public relations procedures and techniques
   D. is sometimes required to aid morale by protecting the agency from unjustified criticism and misunderstanding of policies or procedures

   4.____

5. Of the following factors which contribute to possible undesirable public attitudes towards   5.__
    an agency, the one which is MOST susceptible to being changed by the efforts of the
    individual employee in an organization is that

    A.   enforcement of unpopular regulations has offended many individuals
    B.   the organization itself has an unsatisfactory reputation
    C.   the public is not interested in agency matters
    D.   there are many errors in judgment committed by individual subordinates

6. It is not enough for an agency's services to be of a high quality; attention must also be   6.__
    given to the acceptability of these services to the general public.
    This statement is GENERALLY

    A.   *false;* a superior quality of service automatically wins public support
    B.   *true;* the agency cannot generally progress beyond the understanding and support
         of the public
    C.   *false;* the acceptance by the public of agency services determines their quality
    D.   *true;* the agency is generally unable to engage in any effective enforcement activity
         without public support

7. Sustained agency participation in a program sponsored by a community organization is   7.__
    MOST justified when

    A.   the achievement of agency objectives in some area depends partly on the activity
         of this organization
    B.   the community organization is attempting to widen the base of participation in all
         community affairs
    C.   the agency is uncertain as to what the community wants
    D.   there is an obvious lack of good leadership in a newly formed community organiza-
         tion

8. Of the following, the LEAST likely way in which a records system may serve a supervisor   8.__
    is in

    A.   developing a sympathetic and cooperative public attitude toward the agency
    B.   improving the quality of supervision by permitting a check on the accomplishment
         of subordinates
    C.   permit a precise prediction of the exact incidences in specific categories for the fol-
         lowing year
    D.   helping to take the guesswork out of the distribution of the agency

9. Assuming that the *grapevine* in any organization is virtually indestructible, the one of the   9.__
    following which it is MOST important for management to understand is:

    A.   What is being spread by means of the *grapevine* and the reason for spreading it
    B.   What is being spread by means of the *grapevine* and how it is being spread
    C.   Who is involved in spreading the information that is on the *grapevine*
    D.   Why those who are involved in spreading the information are doing so

10. When the supervisor writes a report concerning an investigation to which he has been assigned, it should be LEAST intended to provide   10.____

    A. a permanent official record of relevant information gathered
    B. a summary of case findings limited to facts which tend to indicate the guilt of a suspect
    C. a statement of the facts on which higher authorities may base a corrective or disciplinary action
    D. other investigators with information so that they may continue with other phases of the investigation

11. In survey work, questionnaires rather than interviews are sometimes used.   11.____
The one of the following which is a DISADVANTAGE of the questionnaire method as compared with the interview is the

    A. difficulty of accurately interpreting the results
    B. problem of maintaining anonymity of the participant
    C. fact that it is relatively uneconomical
    D. requirement of special training for the distribution of questionnaires

12. In his contacts with the public, an employee should attempt to create a good climate of support for his agency. This statement is GENERALLY   12.____

    A. *false;* such attempts are clearly beyond the scope of his responsibility
    B. *true;* employees of an agency who come in contact with the public have the opportunity to affect public relations
    C. *false;* such activity should be restricted to supervisors trained in public relations techniques
    D. *true;* the future expansion of the agency depends to a great extent on continued public support of the agency

13. The repeated use by a supervisor of a call for volunteers to get a job done is objectionable MAINLY because it   13.____

    A. may create a feeling of animosity between the volunteers and the non-volunteers
    B. may indicate that the supervisor is avoiding responsibility for making assignments which will be most productive
    C. is an indication that the supervisor is not familiar with the individual capabilities of his men
    D. is unfair to men who, for valid reasons, do not, or cannot volunteer

14. Of the following statements concerning subordinates' expressions to a supervisor of their opinions and feelings concerning work situations, the one which is MOST correct is that   14.____

    A. by listening and responding to such expressions the supervisor encourages the development of complaints
    B. the lack of such expressions should indicate to the supervisor that there is a high level of job satisfaction
    C. the more the supervisor listens to and responds to such expressions, the more he demonstrates lack of supervisory ability
    D. by listening and responding to such expressions, the supervisor will enable many subordinates to understand and solve their own problems on the job

15. In attempting to motivate employees, rewards are considered preferable to punishment PRIMARILY because

    A. punishment seldom has any effect on human behavior
    B. punishment usually results in decreased production
    C. supervisors find it difficult to punish
    D. rewards are more likely to result in willing cooperation

15.___

16. In an attempt to combat the low morale in his organization, a high-level supervisor publicized an *open-door* policy to allow employees who wished to do so to come to him with their complaints.
Which of the following is LEAST likely to account for the fact that no employee came in with a complaint?

    A. Employees are generally reluctant to go over the heads of their immediate supervisors.
    B. The employees did not feel that management would help them.
    C. The low morale was not due to complaints associated with the job.
    D. The employees felt that they had more to lose than to gain.

16.___

17. It is MOST desirable to use written instructions rather than oral instructions for a particular job when

    A. a mistake on the job will not be serious
    B. the job can be completed in a short time
    C. there is no need to explain the job minutely
    D. the job involves many details

17.___

18. If you receive a telephone call regarding a matter which your office does not handle, you should FIRST

    A. give the caller the telephone number of the proper office so that he can dial again
    B. offer to transfer the caller to the proper office
    C. suggest that the caller re-dial since he probably dialed incorrectly
    D. tell the caller he has reached the wrong office and then hang up

18.___

19. When you answer the telephone, the MOST important reason for identifying yourself and your organization is to

    A. give the caller time to collect his or her thoughts
    B. impress the caller with your courtesy
    C. inform the caller that he or she has reached the right number
    D. set a business-like tone at the beginning of the conversation

19.___

20. As soon as you pick up the phone, a very angry caller begins immediately to complain about city agencies and *red tape*. He says that he has been shifted to two or three different offices. It turns out that he is seeking information which is not immediately available to you. You believe you know, however, where it can be found. Which of the following actions is the BEST one for you to take?

    A. To eliminate all confusion, suggest that the caller write the agency stating explicitly what he wants.
    B. Apologize by telling the caller how busy city agencies now are, but also tell him directly that you do not have the information he needs.

20.___

C. Ask for the caller's telephone number and assure him you will call back after you have checked further.

D. Give the caller the name and telephone number of the person who might be able to help, but explain that you are not positive he will get results.

21. Which of the following approaches usually provides the BEST communication in the objectives and values of a new program which is to be introduced?   21._____

    A. A general written description of the program by the program manager for review by those who share responsibility

    B. An effective verbal presentation by the program manager to those affected

    C. Development of the plan and operational approach in carrying out the program by the program manager assisted by his key subordinates

    D. Development of the plan by the program manager's supervisor

22. What is the BEST approach for introducing change?   22._____
A

    A. combination of written and also verbal communication to all personnel affected by the change

    B. general bulletin to all personnel

    C. meeting pointing out all the values of the new approach

    D. written directive to key personnel

23. Of the following, committees are BEST used for   23._____

    A. advising the head of the organization

    B. improving functional work

    C. making executive decisions

    D. making specific planning decisions

24. An effective discussion leader is one who   24._____

    A. announces the problem and his preconceived solution at the start of the discussion

    B. guides and directs the discussion according to pre-arranged outline

    C. interrupts or corrects confused participants to save time

    D. permits anyone to say anything at anytime

25. The human relations movement in management theory is basically concerned with   25._____

    A. counteracting employee unrest

    B. eliminating the *time and motion* man

    C. interrelationships among individuals in organizations

    D. the psychology of the worker

KEY (CORRECT ANSWERS)

1.	C	11.	A
2.	C	12.	B
3.	A	13.	B
4.	D	14.	D
5.	D	15.	D
6.	B	16.	C
7.	A	17.	D
8.	C	18.	B
9.	A	19.	C
10.	B	20.	C

21.	C
22.	A
23.	A
24.	B
25.	C

———

COMMUNICATION
EXAMINATION SECTION
TEST 1

DIRECTIONS: Each question or incomplete statement is followed by several suggested answers or completions. Select the one that BEST answers the question or completes the statement. *PRINT THE LETTER OF THE CORRECT ANSWER IN THE SPACE AT THE RIGHT.*

1. In some agencies the counsel to the agency head is given the right to bypass the chain   1.____
   of command and issue orders directly to the staff concerning matters that involve certain
   specific processes and practices.
   This situation *most nearly* illustrates the PRINCIPLE of

   A. the acceptance theory of authority   B. multiple - linear authority
   C. splintered authority   D. functional authority

2. It is commonly understood that communication is an important part of the administrative   2.____
   process.
   Which of the following is NOT a valid principle of the communication process in administration?

   A. The channels of communication should be spontaneous
   B. The lines of communication should be as direct and as short as possible
   C. Communications should be authenticated
   D. The persons serving in communications centers should be competent

3. Of the following, the *one* factor which is generally considered LEAST essential to suc-   3.____
   cessful committee operations is

   A. stating a clear definition of the authority and scope of the committee
   B. selecting the committee chairman carefully
   C. limiting the size of the committee to four persons
   D. limiting the subject matter to that which can be handled in group discussion

4. Of the following, the failure by line managers to accept and appreciate the benefits   4.____
   and limitations of a new program or system *very frequently* can be traced to the

   A. budgetary problems involved
   B. resultant need to reduce staff
   C. lack of controls it engenders
   D. failure of top management to support its implementation

5. If a manager were thinking about using a committee of subordinates to solve an operat-   5.____
   ing problem, which of the following would generally NOT be an *advantage* of such use of
   the committee approach?

   A. Improved coordination   B. Low cost
   C. Increased motivation   D. Integrated judgment

6. Every supervisor has many occasions to lead a conference or participate in a conference   6.___
   of some sort.
   Of the following statements that pertain to conferences and conference leadership, which
   is generally considered to be MOST valid?

   A. Since World War II, the trend has been toward fewer shared decisions and more
      conferences.
   B. The most important part of a conference leader's job is to direct discussion.
   C. In providing opportunities for group interaction, management should avoid consid-
      eration of its past management philosophy.
   D. A good administrator cannot lead a good conference if he is a poor public speaker.

7. Of the following, it is usually LEAST desirable for a conference leader to   7.___

   A. call the name of a person after asking a question
   B. summarize proceedings periodically
   C. make a practice of repeating questions
   D. ask a question without indicating who is to reply

8. Assume that, in a certain organization, a situation has developed in which there is little   8.___
   difference in status or authority between individuals.
   Which of the following would be the *most likely* result with regard to communication
   in this organization?

   A. Both the accuracy and flow of communication will be improved.
   B. Both the accuracy and flow of communication will substantially decrease.
   C. Employees will seek more formal lines of communication.
   D. Neither the flow nor the accuracy of communication will be improved over the
      former hierarchical structure.

9. The main function of many agency administrative officers is "information management."   9.___
   Information that is received by an administrative officer may be classified as active or
   passive, depending upon whether or not it requires the recipient to take some action.
   Of the following, the item received which is *clearly* the MOST active information is

   A. an appointment of a new staff member
   B. a payment voucher for a new desk
   C. a press release concerning a past event
   D. the minutes of a staff meeting

10. Of the following, the one LEAST considered to be a communication barrier is   10.___

    A. group feedback   B. charged words
    C. selective perception   D. symbolic meanings

11. Management studies support the hypothesis that, in spite of the tendency of employees   11.___
    to censor the information communicated to their supervisor, subordinates are *more likely*
    to communicate problem-oriented information UPWARD when they have a

    A. long period of service in the organization
    B. high degree of trust in the supervisor
    C. high educational level
    D. low status on the organizational ladder

12. Electronic data processing equipment can produce more information faster than can be generated by any other means. In view of this, the MOST important problem faced by management at present is to

    A. keep computers fully occupied
    B. find enough computer personnel
    C. assimilate and properly evaluate the information
    D. obtain funds to establish appropriate information systems

12._____

13. A well-designed management information system *essentially* provides each executive and manager the information he needs for

    A. determining computer time requirements
    B. planning and measuring results
    C. drawing a new organization chart
    D. developing a new office layout

13._____

14. It is generally agreed that management policies should be periodically reappraised and restated in accordance with current conditions.
Of the following, the approach which would be MOST effective in determining whether a policy should be revised is to

    A. conduct interviews with staff members at all levels in order to ascertain the relationship between the policy and actual practice
    B. make proposed revisions in the policy and apply it to current problems
    C. make up hypothetical situations using both the old policy and a revised version in order to make comparisons
    D. call a meeting of top level staff in order to discuss ways of revising the policy

14._____

15. Your superior has asked you to notify division employees of an important change in one of the operating procedures described in the division manual. Every employee presently has a copy of this manual.
Which of the following is normally the MOST practical way to get the employees to understand such a change?

    A. Notify each employee individually of the change and answer any questions he might have
    B. Send a written notice to key personnel, directing them to inform the people under them
    C. Call a general meeting, distribute a corrected page for the manual, and discuss the change
    D. Send a memo to employees describing the change in general terms and asking them to make the necessary corrections in their copies of the manual

15._____

16. Assume that the work in your department involves the use of many technical terms. In such a situation, when you are answering inquiries from the general public, it would *usually* be BEST to

    A. use simple language and avoid the technical terms
    B. employ the technical terms whenever possible
    C. bandy technical terms freely, but explain each term in parentheses
    D. apologize if you are forced to use a technical term

16._____

17. Suppose that you receive a telephone call from someone identifying himself as an employee in another city department who asks to be given information which your own department regards as confidential.
Which of the following is the BEST way of handling such a request?

    A. Give the information requested, since your caller has official standing
    B. Grant the request, provided the caller gives you a signed receipt
    C. Refuse the request, because you have no way of knowing whether the caller is really who he claims to be
    D. Explain that the information is confidential and inform the caller of the channels he must go through to have the information released to him

17.___

18. Studies show that office employees place high importance on the social and human aspects of the organization. What office employees like best about their jobs is the kind of people with whom they work. So strive hard to group people who are most likely to get along well together.
Based on this information, it is *most reasonable* to assume that office workers are MOST pleased to work in a group which

    A. is congenial   B. has high productivity
    C. allows individual creativity
    D. is unlike other groups

18.___

19. A certain supervisor does not compliment members of his staff when they come up with good ideas. He feels that coming up with good ideas is part of the job and does not merit special attention.
This supervisor's practice is

    A. *poor,* because recognition for good ideas is a good motivator
    B. *poor,* because the staff will suspect that the supervisor has no good ideas of his own
    C. *good,* because it is reasonable to assume that employees will tell their supervisor of ways to improve office practice
    D. *good,* because the other members of the staff are not made to seem inferior by comparison

19.___

20. Some employees of a department have sent an anonymous letter containing many complaints to the department head. Of the following, what is this *most likely* to show about the department?

    A. It is probably a good place to work.
    B. Communications are probably poor.
    C. The complaints are probably unjustified.
    D. These employees are probably untrustworthy.

20.___

21. Which of the following actions would usually be MOST appropriate for a supervisor to take *after* receiving an instruction sheet from his superior explaining a new procedure which is to be followed?

    A. Put the instruction sheet aside temporarily until he determines what is wrong with the old procedure
    B. Call his superior and ask whether the procedure is one he must implement immediately

21.___

C. Write a memorandum to the superior asking for more details
D. Try the new procedure and advise the superior of any problems or possible improvements

22. Of the following, which one is considered the PRIMARY advantage of using a committee to resolve a problem in an organization?   22._____

    A. No one person will be held accountable for the decision since a group of people was involved
    B. People with different backgrounds give attention to the problem
    C. The decision will take considerable time so there is unlikely to be a decision that will later be regretted
    D. One person cannot dominate the decision-making process

23. Employees in a certain office come to their supervisor with all their complaints about the office and the work. Almost every employee has had at least one minor complaint at some time.   23._____
The situation with respect to complaints in this office may BEST be described as *probably*

    A. *good;* employees who complain care about their jobs and work hard
    B. *good;* grievances brought out into the open can be corrected
    C. *bad;* only serious complaints should be discussed
    D. *bad;* it indicates the staff does not have confidence in the administration

24. The administrator who allows his staff to suggest ways to do their work will *usually* find that   24._____

    A. this practice contributes to high productivity
    B. the administrator's ideas produce greater output
    C. clerical employees suggest inefficient work methods
    D. subordinate employees resent performing a management function

25. The MAIN purpose for a supervisor's questioning the employees at a conference he is holding is to   25._____

    A. stress those areas of information covered but not understood by the participants
    B. encourage participants to think through the problem under discussion
    C. catch those subordinates who are not paying attention
    D. permit the more knowledgeable participants to display their grasp of the problems being discussed

KEYS (CORRECT ANSWERS)

1.	D	11.	B
2.	A	12.	C
3.	C	13.	B
4.	D	14.	A
5.	B	15.	C
6.	B	16.	A
7.	C	17.	D
8.	D	18.	A
9.	A	19.	A
10.	A	20.	B

21. D
22. B
23. B
24. A
25. B

———

TEST 2

DIRECTIONS: Each question or incomplete statement is followed by several suggested answers or completions. Select the one that BEST answers the question or completes the statement. *PRINT THE LETTER OF THE CORRECT ANSWER IN THE SPACE AT THE RIGHT.*

1. For a superior to use *consultative supervision* with his subordinates effectively, it is ESSENTIAL that he

    A. accept the fact that his formal authority will be weakened by the procedure
    B. admit that he does not know more than all his men together and that his ideas are not always best
    C. utilize a committee system so that the procedure is orderly
    D. make sure that all subordinates are consulted so that no one feels left out

1.____

2. The "grapevine" is an informal means of communication in an organization. The attitude of a supervisor with respect to the grapevine should be to

    A. ignore it since it deals mainly with rumors and sensational information
    B. regard it as a serious danger which should be eliminated
    C. accept it as a real line of communication which should be listened to
    D. utilize it for most purposes instead of the official line of communication

2.____

3. The supervisor of an office that must deal with the public should realize that planning in this type of work situation

    A. is *useless* because he does not know how many people will request service or what service they will request
    B. *must be done at a higher level* but that he should be ready to implement the results of such planning
    C. is *useful* primarily for those activities that are not concerned with public contact
    D. is *useful* for all the activities of the office, including those that relate to public contact

3.____

4. Assume that it is your job to receive incoming telephone calls. Those calls which you cannot handle yourself have to be transferred to the appropriate office.
If you receive an outside call for an extension line which is busy, the one of the following which you should do FIRST is to

    A. interrupt the person speaking on the extension and tell him a call is waiting
    B. tell the caller the line is busy and let him know every thirty seconds whether or not it is free
    C. leave the caller on "hold" until the extension is free
    D. tell the caller the line is busy and ask him if he wishes to wait

4.____

5. Your superior has subscribed to several publications directly related to your division's work, and he has asked you to see to it that the publications are circulated among the supervisory personnel in the division. There are eight supervisors involved.
The BEST method of insuring that all eight see these publications is to

    A. place the publication in the division's general reference library as soon as it arrives
    B. inform each supervisor whenever a publication arrives and remind all of them that they are responsible for reading it

5.____

C. prepare a standard slip that can be stapled to each publication, listing the eight supervisors and saying, "Please read, initial your name, and pass along"

D. send a memo to the eight supervisors saying that they may wish to purchase individual subscriptions in their own names if they are interested in seeing each issue

6. Your superior has telephoned a number of key officials in your agency to ask whether they can meet at a certain time next month. He has found that they can all make it, and he has asked you to confirm the meeting.
Which of the following is the BEST way to confirm such a meeting?

    6.___

A. Note the meeting on your superior's calendar
B. Post a notice of the meeting on the agency bulletin board
C. Call the officials on the day of the meeting to remind them of the meeting
D. Write a memo to each official involved, repeating the time and place of the meeting

7. Assume that a new city regulation requires that certain kinds of private organizations file information forms with your department. You have been asked to write the short explanatory message that will be printed on the front cover of the pamphlet containing the forms and instructions.
Which of the following would be the MOST appropriate way of beginning this message?

    7.___

A. Get the readers' attention by emphasizing immediately that there are legal penalties for organizations that fail to file before a certain date
B. Briefly state the nature of the enclosed forms and the types of organizations that must file
C. Say that your department is very sorry to have to put organizations to such an inconvenience
D. Quote the entire regulation adopted by the city, even if it is quite long and is expressed in complicated legal language

8. Suppose that you have been told to make up the vacation schedule for the 18 employees in a particular unit. In order for the unit to operate effectively, only a few employees can be on vacation at the same time.
Which of the following is the MOST advisable approach in making up the schedule?

    8.___

A. Draw up a schedule assigning vacations in alphabetical order
B. Find out when the supervisors want to take their vacations, and randomly assign whatever periods are left to the non-supervisory personnel
C. Assign the most desirable times to employees of longest standing and the least desirable times to the newest employees
D. Have all employees state their own preference, and then work out any conflicts in consultation with the people involved

9. Assume that you have been asked to prepare job descriptions for various positions in your department.
Which of the following are the basic points that should be covered in a *job description*?

    9.___

A. General duties and responsibilities of the position, with examples of day-to-day tasks
B. Comments on the performances of present employees

C. Estimates of the number of openings that may be available in each category during the coming year

D. Instructions for carrying out the specific tasks assigned to your department

10. Of the following, the biggest DISADVANTAGE in allowing a free flow of communications in an agency is that such a free flow   10.____

A. *decreases* creativity
B. *increases* the use of the "grapevine"
C. *lengthens* the chain of command
D. *reduces* the executive's power to direct the flow of information

11. A downward flow of authority in an organization is one example of _____ communication.   11.____

    A. horizontal   B. informal   C. circular   D. vertical

12. Of the following, the one that would *most likely* block effective communication is   12.____

    A. concentration only on the issues at hand   B. lack of interest or commitment
    C. use of written reports   D. use of charts and graphs

13. An ADVANTAGE of the *lecture* as a teaching tool is that it   13.____

A. enables a person to present his ideas to a large number of people
B. allows the audience to retain a maximum of the information given
C. holds the attention of the audience for the longest time
D. enables the audience member to easily recall the main points

14. An ADVANTAGE of the *small-group* discussion as a teaching tool is that   14.____

A. it always focuses attention on one person as the leader
B. it places collective responsibility on the group as a whole
C. its members gain experience by summarizing the ideas of others
D. each member of the group acts as a member of a team

15. The one of the following that is an ADVANTAGE of a *large-group* discussion, when compared to a small-group discussion, is that the large-group discussion   15.____

A. moves along more quickly than a small-group discussion
B. allows its participants to feel more at ease, and speak out more freely
C. gives the whole group a chance to exchange ideas on a certain subject at the same occasion
D. allows its members to feel a greater sense of personal responsibility

---

KEYS (CORRECT ANSWERS)

1.	D	6.	D
2.	C	7.	B
3.	D	8.	D
4.	D	9.	A
5.	C	10.	D

11. D
12. B
13. A
14. D
15. C

———

REPORT WRITING
EXAMINATION SECTION
TEST 1

DIRECTIONS: Each question or incomplete statement is followed by several suggested answers or completions. Select the one that BEST answers the question or completes the statement. *PRINT THE LETTER OF THE CORRECT ANSWER IN THE SPACE AT THE RIGHT.*

Questions 1-4.

DIRECTIONS: Answer Questions 1 through 4 on the basis of the following report which was prepared by a supervisor for inclusion in his agency's annual report.

Line
#

1 On Oct. 13, I was assigned to study the salaries paid
2 to clerical employees in various titles by the city and by
3 private industry in the area.
4 In order to get the data I needed, I called Mr. Johnson at
5 the Bureau of the Budget and the payroll officers at X Corp.—
6 a brokerage house, Y Co.—an insurance company, and Z Inc.—
7 a publishing firm. None of them was available and I had to call
8 all of them again the next day.
9 When I finally got the information I needed, I drew up a
10 chart, which is attached. Note that not all of the companies I
11 contacted employed people at all the different levels used in the
12 city service.
13 The conclusions I draw from analyzing this information is
14 as follows: The city's entry-level salary is about average for
15 the region; middle-level salaries are generally higher in the
16 city government than in private industry; but salaries at the
17 highest levels in private industry are better than city em-
18 ployees' pay.

1. Which of the following criticisms about the style in which this report is written is *most valid*?   1.____

   A. It is too informal.   B. It is too concise.
   C. It is too choppy.   D. The syntax is too complex.

2. Judging from the statements made in the report, the method followed by this employee in performing his research was   2.____

   A. *good;* he contacted a representative sample of businesses in the area
   B. *poor;* he should have drawn more definite conclusions
   C. *good;* he was persistent in collecting information
   D. *poor;* he did not make a thorough study

3. One sentence in this report contains a grammatical error. This sentence *begins* on line number

    A. 4   B. 7   C. 10   D. 13

3.___

4. The type of information given in this report which should be presented in footnotes or in an appendix, is the

    A. purpose of the study
    B. specifics about the businesses contacted
    C. reference to the chart
    D. conclusions drawn by the author

4.___

5. The use of a graph to show statistical data in a report is *superior* to a table because it

    A. features approximations
    B. emphasizes facts and relationships more dramatically
    C. C. presents data more accurately
    D. is easily understood by the average reader

5.___

6. Of the following, the degree of formality required of a written report in tone is *most likely* to depend on the

    A. subject matter of the report
    B. frequency of its occurrence
    C. amount of time available for its preparation
    D. audience for whom the report is intended

6.___

7. Of the following, a distinguishing characteristic of a written report intended for the head of your agency as compared to a report prepared for a lower-echelon staff member, is that the report for the agency head should *usually* include

    A. considerably more detail, especially statistical data
    B. the essential details in an abbreviated form
    C. all available source material
    D. an annotated bibliography

7.___

8. Assume that you are asked to write a lengthy report for use by the administrator of your agency, the subject of which is "The Impact of Proposed New Data Processing Operations on Line Personnel" in your agency. You decide that the *most appropriate* type of report for you to prepare is an analytical report, including recommendations. The MAIN reason for your decision is that

    A. the subject of the report is extremely complex
    B. large sums of money are involved
    C. the report is being prepared for the administrator
    D. you intend to include charts and graphs

8.___

9. Assume that you are preparing a report based on a survey dealing with the attitudes of employees in Division X regarding proposed new changes in compensating employees for working overtime. Three per cent of the respondents to the survey voluntarily offer an unfavorable opinion on the method of assigning overtime work, a question not specifically asked of the employees.

9.____

On the basis of this information, the *most appropriate* and *significant* of the following comments for you to make in the report with regard to employees' attitudes on assigning overtime work, is that

 A. an insignificant percentage of employees dislike the method of assigning overtime work
 B. three per cent of the employees in Division X dislike the method of assigning overtime work
 C. three per cent of the sample selected for the survey voiced an unfavorable opinion on the method of assigning overtime work
 D. some employees voluntarily voiced negative feelings about the method of assigning overtime work, making it impossible to determine the extent of this attitude

10. A supervisor should be able to prepare a report that is well-written and unambiguous. Of the following sentences that might appear in a report, select the one which communicates *most clearly* the intent of its author.

10.____

 A. When your subordinates speak to a group of people, they should be well-informed.
 B. When he asked him to leave, SanMan King told him that he would refuse the request.
 C. Because he is a good worker, Foreman Jefferson assigned Assistant Foreman D'Agostino to replace him.
 D. Each of us is responsible for the actions of our subordinates.

11. In some reports, especially longer ones, a list of the resources (books, papers, magazines, etc.) used to prepare it is included. This list is called the

11.____

 A. accreditation   B. bibliography
 C. summary   D. glossary

12. Reports are usually divided into several sections, some of which are more necessary than others.

12.____

Of the following, the section which is ABSOLUTELY necessary to include in a report is

 A. a table of contents   B. the body
 C. an index   D. a bibliography

13. Suppose you are writing a report on an interview you have just completed with a particularly hostile applicant. Which of the following BEST describes what you should include in this report?

13.____

 A. What you think caused the applicant's hostile attitude during the interview
 B. Specific examples of the applicant's hostile remarks and behavior
 C. The relevant information uncovered during the interview
 D. A recommendation that the applicant's request be denied because of his hostility

14. When including recommendations in a report to your supervisor, which of the following is MOST important for you to do? 14.__

    A. Provide several alternative courses of action for each recommendation
    B. First present the supporting evidence, then the recommendations
    C. First present the recommendations, then the supporting evidence
    D. Make sure the recommendations arise logically out of the information in the report

15. It is often necessary that the writer of a report present facts and sufficient arguments to gain acceptance of the points, conclusions, or recommendations set forth in the report. Of the following, the LEAST advisable step to take in organizing a report, when such argumentation is the important factor, is a(n) 15.__

    A. elaborate expression of personal belief
    B. businesslike discussion of the problem as a whole
    C. orderly arrangement of convincing data
    D. reasonable explanation of the primary issues

16. In some types of reports, visual aids add interest, meaning, and support. They also provide an essential means of effectively communicating the message of the report.
Of the following, the selection of the suitable visual aids to use with a report is LEAST dependent on the 16.__

    A. nature and scope of the report
    B. way in which the aid is to be used
    C. aids used in other reports
    D. prospective readers of the report

17. Visual aids used in a report may be placed either in the text material or in the appendix. Deciding where to put a chart, table, or any such aid *should* depend on the 17.__

    A. title of the report   B. purpose of the visual aid
    C. title of the visual aid   D. length of the report

18. A report is often revised several times before final preparation and distribution in an effort to make certain the report meets the needs of the situation for which it is designed. Which of the following is the BEST way for the author to be sure that a report covers the areas he intended? 18.__

    A. Obtain a co-worker's opinion
    B. Compare it with a content checklist
    C. Test it on a subordinate
    D. Check his bibliography

19. In which of the following situations is an oral report preferable to a written report? When a(n) 19.__

    A. recommendation is being made for a future plan of action
    B. department head requests immediate information
    C. long standing policy change is made
    D. analysis of complicated statistical data is involved

20. When an applicant is approved, the supervisor must fill in standard forms with certain information.
The GREATEST advantage of using standard forms in this situation rather than having the supervisor write the report as he sees fit, is that

    A. the report can be acted on quickly
    B. the report can be written without directions from a supervisor
    C. needed information is less likely to be left out of the report
    D. information that is written up this way is more likely to be verified

20.____

21. Assume that it is part of your job to prepare a monthly report for your unit head that eventually goes to the director. The report contains information on the number of applicants you have interviewed that have been approved and the number of applicants you have interviewed that have been turned down.
Errors on such reports are serious because

    A. you are expected to be able to prove how many applicants you have interviewed each month
    B. accurate statistics are needed for effective management of the department
    C. they may not be discovered before the report is transmitted to the director
    D. they may result in loss to the applicants left out of the report

21.____

22. The frequency with which job reports are submitted should depend MAINLY on

    A. how comprehensive the report has to be
    B. the amount of information in the report
    C. the availability of an experienced man to write the report
    D. the importance of changes in the information included in the report

22.____

23. The CHIEF purpose in preparing an outline for a report is *usually* to insure that

    A. the report will be grammatically correct
    B. every point will be given equal emphasis
    C. principal and secondary points will be properly integrated
    D. the language of the report will be of the same level and include the same technical terms

23.____

24. The MAIN reason for requiring written job reports is to

    A. avoid the necessity of oral orders
    B. develop better methods of doing the work
    C. provide a permanent record of what was done
    D. increase the amount of work that can be done

24.____

25. Assume you are recommending in a report to your supervisor that a radical change in a standard maintenance procedure should be adopted.
Of the following, the MOST important information to be included in this report is

    A. a list of the reasons for making this change
    B. the names of others who favor the change
    C. a complete description of the present procedure
    D. amount of training time needed for the new procedure

25.____

KEY (CORRECT ANSWERS)

1.	A	11.	B
2.	D	12.	B
3.	D	13.	C
4.	B	14.	D
5.	B	15.	A
6.	D	16.	C
7.	B	17.	B
8.	A	18.	B
9.	D	19.	B
10.	D	20.	C

21.	B
22.	D
23.	C
24.	C
25.	A

TEST 2

DIRECTIONS: Each question or incomplete statement is followed by several suggested answers or completions. Select the one that BEST answers the question or completes the statement. *PRINT THE LETTER OF THE CORRECT ANSWER IN THE SPACE AT THE RIGHT.*

1. It is often necessary that the writer of a report present facts and sufficient arguments to gain acceptance of the points, conclusions, or recommendations set forth in the report. Of the following, the LEAST advisable step to take in organizing a report, when such argumentation is the important factor, is a(n)

    A. elaborate expression of personal belief
    B. businesslike discussion of the problem as a whole
    C. orderly arrangement of convincing data
    D. reasonable explanation of the primary issues

    1.____

2. Of the following, the factor which is generally considered to be LEAST characteristic of a good control report is that it

    A. stresses performance that adheres to standard rather than emphasizing the exception
    B. supplies information intended to serve as the basis for corrective action
    C. provides feedback for the planning process
    D. includes data that reflect trends as well as current status

    2.____

3. An administrative assistant has been asked by his superior to write a concise, factual report with objective conclusions and recommendations based on facts assembled by other researchers.
   Of the following factors, the administrative assistant should give LEAST consideratio to

    A. the educational level of the person or persons for whom the report is being prepared
    B. the use to be made of the report
    C. the complexity of the problem
    D. his own feelings about the importance of the problem

    3.____

4. When making a written report, it is often recommended that the findings or conclusions be presented near the beginning of the report.
   Of the following, the MOST important reason for doing this is that it

    A. facilitates organizing the material clearly
    B. assures that all the topics will be covered
    C. avoids unnecessary repetition of ideas
    D. prepares the reader for the facts that will follow

    4.____

5. You have been asked to write a report on methods of hiring and training new employees. Your report is going to be about ten pages long.
   For the convenience of your readers, a brief summary of your findings *should*

    A. appear at the beginning of your report
    B. be appended to the report as a postscript
    C. be circulated in a separate memo
    D. be inserted in tabular form in the middle of your report

    5.____

6. In preparing a report, the MAIN reason for writing an outline is *usually* to   6.

    A. help organize thoughts in a logical sequence
    B. provide a guide for the typing of the report
    C. allow the ultimate user to review the report in advance
    D. ensure that the report is being prepared on schedule

7. The one of the following which is *most appropriate* as a reason for including footnotes in   7.
a report is to

    A. correct capitalization   B. delete passages
    C. improve punctuation   D. cite references

8. A completed formal report may contain all of the following EXCEPT   8.

    A. a synopsis   B. a preface
    C. marginal notes   D. bibliographical references

9. Of the following, the MAIN use of proofreaders' marks is to   9.

    A. explain corrections to be made
    B. indicate that a manuscript has been read and approved
    C. let the reader know who proofread the report
    D. indicate the format of the report

10. Informative, readable and concise reports have been found to observe the following   10.
rules:
    Rule I.   Keep the report short and easy to understand.
    Rule II.   Vary the length of sentences.
    Rule III.   Vary the style of sentences so that, for example, they are not all just sub
              ject-verb, subject-verb.
Consider this hospital laboratory report: The experiment was started in January. The
apparatus was put together in six weeks. At that time the synthesizing process was
begun. The synthetic chemicals were separated. Then they were used in tests on
patients.
Which one of the following choices MOST accurately classifies the above rules into
those which are *violated* by this report and those which are *not*?

    A. II is violated, but I and III are not.
    B. III is violated, but I and II are not.
    C. II and III are violated, but I is not.
    D. I, II, and III are violated.

Questions 11-13.

DIRECTIONS: Questions 11 through 13 are based on the following example of a report. The
                 report consists of eight numbered sentences, some of which are not consis-
                 tent with the principles of good report writing.

(1) I interviewed Mrs. Loretta Crawford in Room 424 of County Hospital. (2) She had collapsed on the street and been brought into emergency. (3) She is an attractive woman with many friends judging by the cards she had received. (4) She did not know what her husband's last job had been, or what their present income was. (5) The first thing that Mrs. Crawford said was that she had never worked and that her husband was presently unemployed. (6) She did not know if they had any medical coverage or if they could pay the bill. (7) She said that her husband could not be reached by telephone but that he would be in to see her that afternoon. (8) I left word at the nursing station to be called when he arrived.

11. A good report should be arranged in logical order. Which of the following sentences from   11.____
the report does NOT appear in its proper sequence in the report? Sentence

    A. 1   B. 4   C. 7   D. 8

12. Only material that is relevant to the main thought of a report should be included.   12.____
Which of the following sentences from the report contains material which is LEAST relevant to this report? Sentence

    A. 3   B. 4   C. 6   D. 8

13. Reports should include all essential information.   13.____
Of the following, the MOST important fact that is *missing* from this report is:

    A. Who was involved in the interview
    B. What was discovered at the interview
    C. When the interview took place
    D. Where the interview took place

Questions 14-15.

DIRECTIONS: Each of Questions 14 and 15 consists of four numbered sentences which constitute a paragraph in a report. They are not in the right order. Choose the numbered arrangement appearing after letter A, B, C, or D which is MOST logical and which BEST expresses the thought of the paragraph.

14.   I.   Congress made the commitment explicit in the Housing Act of 1949, establishing   14.____
        as a national goal the realization of a decent home and suitable environment for
        every American family.
   II.   The result has been that the goal of decent home and suitable environment is
        still as far distant as ever for the disadvantaged urban family.
   III. In spite of this action by Congress, federal housing programs have continued to
        be fragmented and grossly under-funded.
   IV. The passage of the National Housing Act signaled a new federal commitment to
        provide housing for the nation's citizens.

    A. I, IV, III, II   B. IV, I, III, II
    C. IV, I, III, II   D. II, IV, I, III

15.   I.   The greater expense does not necessarily involve "exploitation," but it is often per-   15._
      ceived as exploitative and unfair by those who are aware of the price differences
      involved, but unaware of operating costs.
  II.   Ghetto residents believe they are "exploited" by local merchants, and evidence
      substantiates some of these beliefs.
  III.   However, stores in low-income areas were more likely to be small independents,
      which could not achieve the economies available to supermarket chains and
      were, therefore, more likely to charge higher prices, and the customers were
      more likely to buy smaller-sized packages which are more expensive per unit of
      measure.
  IV.   A study conducted in one city showed that distinctly higher prices were charged
      for goods sold in ghetto stores than in other areas.

    A.   IV, II, I, III   B.   IV, I, III, II
    C.   II, IV, III, I   D.   II, III, IV, I

16. In organizing data to be presented in a formal report, the FIRST of the following steps   16._
should be

    A.   determining the conclusions to be drawn
    B.   establishing the time sequence of the data
    C.   sorting and arranging like data into groups
    D.   evaluating how consistently the data support the recommendations

17. All reports should be prepared with *at least* one copy so that   17._

    A.   there is one copy for your file
    B.   there is a copy for your supervisor
    C.   the report can be sent to more than one person
    D.   the person getting the report can forward a copy to someone else

18. Before turning in a report of an investigation he has made, a supervisor discovers some   18._
additional information he did not include in this report.
Whether he rewrites this report to include this additional information should PRIMA-
RILY depend on the

    A.   importance of the report itself
    B.   number of people who will eventually review this report
    C.   established policy covering the subject matter of the report
    D.   bearing this new information has on the conclusions of the report

---

KEY (CORRECT ANSWERS)

1.	A	11.	B
2.	A	12.	A
3.	D	13.	C
4.	D	14.	B
5.	A	15.	C
6.	A	16.	C
7.	D	17.	A
8.	C	18.	D
9.	A		
10.	C		

PREPARING WRITTEN MATERIALS

EXAMINATION SECTION
TEST 1

DIRECTIONS: Each question consists of a sentence which may be classified appropriately under one of the following four categories:
- A. Incorrect because of faulty grammar or sentence structure;
- B. Incorrect because of faulty punctuation;
- C. Incorrect because of faulty capitalization;
- D. Correct.

Examine each sentence carefully. Then, in the space at the right, indicate the letter preceding the category which is the BEST of the four suggested above. Each incorrect sentence contains only one type of error. Consider a sentence correct if it contains no errors, although there may be other correct ways of expressing the same thought.

1. All the employees, in this office, are over twenty-one years old.   1.____

2. Neither the clerk nor the stenographer was able to explain what had happened.   2.____

3. Mr. Johnson did not know who he would assign to type the order.   3.____

4. Mr. Marshall called her to report for work on Saturday.   4.____

5. He might of arrived on time if the train had not been delayed.   5.____

6. Some employees on the other hand, are required to fill out these forms every month.   6.____

7. The supervisor issued special instructions to his subordinates to prevent their making errors.   7.____

8. Our supervisor Mr. Williams, expects to be promoted in about two weeks.   8.____

9. We were informed that prof. Morgan would attend the conference.   9.____

10. The clerks were assigned to the old building; the stenographers, to the new building.   10.____

11. The supervisor asked Mr. Smith and I to complete the work as quickly as possible.   11.____

12. He said, that before an employee can be permitted to leave, the report must be finished.   12.____

13. An adding machine, in addition to the three typewriters, are needed in the new office.   13.____

14. Having made many errors in her work, the supervisor asked the typist to be more careful.   14.____

15. "If you are given an assignment," he said, "you should begin work on it as quickly as possible."   15.____

16. All the clerks, including those who have been appointed recently are required to work on the new assignment.   16.____

17. The office manager asked each employee to work one Saturday a month.

17.____

18. Neither Mr. Smith nor Mr. Jones was able to finish his assignment on time.

18.____

19. The task of filing these cards is to be divided equally between you and he.

19.____

20. He is an employee whom we consider to be efficient.

20.____

21. I believe that the new employees are not as punctual as us.

21.____

22. The employees, working in this office, are to be congratulated for their work.

22.____

23. The delay in preparing the report was caused, in his opinion, by the lack of proper supervision and coordination.

23.____

24. John Jones accidentally pushed the wrong button and then all the lights went out.

24.____

25. The investigator ought to of had the witness sign the statement.

25.____

KEY (CORRECT ANSWERS)

1. B	11. A
2. D	12. B
3. A	13. A
4. C	14. A
5. A	15. D
6. B	16. B
7. D	17. C
8. B	18. D
9. C	19. A
10. D	20. D

21.	A
22.	B
23.	D
24.	D
25.	A

TEST 2

DIRECTIONS: Each of the following sentences may be classified under one of the following
four options:
  A.   Faulty; contains an error in grammar only
  B.   Faulty; contains an error in spelling only
  C.   Faulty; contains an error in grammar and an error in spelling
  D.   Correct; contains no error in grammar or in spelling

Examine each sentence carefully to determine under which of the above four
options it is BEST classified. Then, in the space at the right, write the letter preceding the option which is the best of the four listed above.

1. A recognized principle of good management is that an assignment should be given to   1.____
    whomever is best qualified to carry it out.

2. He considered it a privilege to be allowed to review and summarize the technical reports   2.____
    issued annually by your agency.

3. Because the warehouse was in an inaccessable location, deliveries of electric fixtures   3.____
    from the warehouse were made only in large lots.

4. Having requisitioned the office supplies, Miss Brown returned to her desk and resumed   4.____
    the computation of petty cash disbursements.

5. One of the advantages of this chemical solution is that records treated with it are not   5.____
    inflamable.

6. The complaint of this employee, in addition to the complaints of the other employees,   6.____
    were submitted to the grievance committee.

7. A study of the duties and responsibilities of each of the various categories of employees   7.____
    was conducted by an unprejudiced classification analyst.

8. Ties of friendship with this subordinate compels him to withold the censure that the sub-   8.____
    ordinate deserves.

9. Neither of the agencies are affected by the decision to institute a program for rehabilitat- 9.____
    ing physically handi-caped men and women.

10. The chairman stated that the argument between you and he was creating an intolerable   10.____
    situation.

Questions 11-25.

DIRECTIONS: Each of the following sentences may be classified under one of the following
four options:

A. Correct
B. Sentence contains an error in spelling
C. Sentence contains an error in grammar
D. Sentence contains errors in both grammar and spelling.

11. He reported that he had had a really good time during his vacation although the farm was located in a very inaccessible portion of the country.　　11.___

12. It looks to me like he has been fasinated by that beautiful painting.　　12.___

13. We have permitted these kind of pencils to accumulate on our shelves, knowing we can sell them at a profit of five cents apiece any time we choose.　　13.___

14. Believing that you will want an unexagerated estimate of the amount of business we can expect, I have made every effort to secure accurate figures.　　14.___

15. Each and every man, woman and child in that untrameled wilderness carry guns for protection against the wild animals.　　15.___

16. Although this process is different than the one to which he is accustomed, a good chemist will have no trouble.　　16.___

17. Insensible to the fuming and fretting going on about him, the engineer continued to drive the mammoth dynamo to its utmost capacity.　　17.___

18. Everyone had studied his lesson carefully and was consequently well prepared when the instructor began to discuss the fourth dimention.　　18.___

19. I learned Johnny six new arithmetic problems this afternoon.　　19.___

20. Athletics is urged by our most prominent citizens as the pursuit which will enable the younger generation to achieve that ideal of education, a sound mind in a sound body.　　20.___

21. He did not see whoever was at the door very clearly but thinks it was the city tax appraiser.　　21.___

22. He could not scarsely believe that his theories had been substantiated in this convincing fashion.　　22.___

23. Although you have displayed great ingenuity in carrying out your assignments, the choice for the position still lies among Brown and Smith.　　23.___

24. If they had have pleaded at the time that Smith was an accessory to the crime, it would have lessened the punishment.　　24.___

25. It has proven indispensible in his compilation of the facts in the matter.　　25.___

KEY (CORRECT ANSWERS)

1.	A		11.	A
2.	D		12.	D
3.	B		13.	C
4.	D		14.	B
5.	B		15.	D
6.	A		16.	C
7.	D		17.	A
8.	C		18.	B
9.	C		19.	C
10.	A		20.	A

21.	B
22.	D
23.	C
24.	D
25.	B

TEST 3

DIRECTIONS: Questions 1 through 5 consist of sentences which may or may not contain errors in grammar or spelling or both. Sentences which do not contain errors in grammar or spelling or both are to be considered correct, even though there may be other correct ways of expressing the same thought. Examine each sentence carefully. Then, in the space at the right, write the letter of the answer which is the BEST of those suggested below:
    A. If the sentence is correct;
    B. If the sentence contains an error in spelling;
    C. If the sentence contains an error in grammar;
    D. If the sentence contains errors in both grammar and spelling.

1. Brown is doing fine although the work is irrevelant to his training.   1.____

2. The conference of sales managers voted to set its adjournment at one o'clock in order to give those present an opportunity to get rid of all merchandise.   2.____

3. He decided that in view of what had taken place at the hotel that he ought to stay and thank the benificent stranger who had rescued him from an embarassing situation.   3.____

4. Since you object to me criticizing your letter, I have no alternative but to consider you a mercenary scoundrel.   4.____

5. I rushed home ahead of schedule so that you will leave me go to the picnic with Mary.   5.____

Questions 6-15.

DIRECTIONS: Some of the following sentences contain an error in spelling, word usage, or sentence structure, or punctuation. Some sentences are correct as they stand although there may be other correct ways of expressing the same thought. All incorrect sentences contain only one error. Mark your answer to each question in the space at the right as follows:
    A. If the sentence has an error in spelling;
    B. If the sentence has an error in punctuation or capitalization;
    C. If the sentence has an error in word usage or sentence structure;
    D. If the sentence is correct.

6. Because the chairman failed to keep the participants from wandering off into irrelevant discussions, it was impossible to reach a consensus before the meeting was adjourned.   6.____

7. Certain employers have an unwritten rule that any applicant, who is over 55 years of age, is automatically excluded from consideration for any position whatsoever.   7.____

8. If the proposal to build schools in some new apartment buildings were to be accepted by the builders, one of the advantages that could be expected to result would be better communication between teachers and parents of schoolchildren.   8.____

9. In this instance, the manufacturer's violation of the law against deseptive packaging was discernible only to an experienced inspector.   9.____

10. The tenants' anger stemmed from the president's going to Washington to testify without consulting them first. 10.____

11. Did the president of this eminent banking company say; "We intend to hire and train a number of these disadvan-taged youths?" 11.____

12. In addition, today's confidential secretary must be knowledgable in many different areas: for example, she must know modern techniques for making travel arrangements for the executive. 12.____

13. To avoid further disruption of work in the offices, the protesters were forbidden from entering the building unless they had special passes. 13.____

14. A valuable secondary result of our training conferences is the opportunities afforded for management to observe the reactions of the participants. 14.____

15. Of the two proposals submitted by the committee, the first one is the best. 15.____

Questions 16-25.

DIRECTIONS: Each of the following sentences may be classified MOST appropriately under one of the following three categories:
A. Faulty because of incorrect grammar
B. Faulty because of incorrect punctuation
C. Correct

Examine each sentence. Then, print the capital letter preceding the BEST choice of the three suggested above. All incorrect sentences contain only one type of error. Consider a sentence correct if it contains none of the types of errors mentioned, even though there may be other ways of expressing the same thought.

16. He sent the notice to the clerk who you hired yesterday. 16.____

17. It must be admitted, however that you were not informed of this change. 17.____

18. Only the employees who have served in this grade for at least two years are eligible for promotion. 18.____

19. The work was divided equally between she and Mary. 19.____

20. He thought that you were not available at that time. 20.____

21. When the messenger returns; please give him this package. 21.____

22. The new secretary prepared, typed, addressed, and delivered, the notices. 22.____

23. Walking into the room, his desk can be seen at the rear. 23.____

24. Although John has worked here longer than she, he produces a smaller amount of work. 24.____

25. She said she could of typed this report yesterday. 25.____

KEY (CORRECT ANSWERS)

1.	D		11.	B
2.	A		12.	A
3.	D		13.	C
4.	C		14.	D
5.	C		15.	C
6.	A		16.	A
7.	B		17.	B
8.	D		18.	C
9.	A		19.	A
10.	D		20.	C

21.	B
22.	B
23.	A
24.	C
25.	A

———

TEST 4

Questions 1-5.

DIRECTIONS: Each of the following sentences may be classified MOST appropriately under one of the following three categories:
- A. Faulty because of incorrect grammar
- B. Faulty because of incorrect punctuation
- C. Correct

Examine each sentence. Then, print the capital letter preceding the BEST choice of the three suggested above. All incorrect sentences contain only one type of error. Consider a sentence correct if it contains none of the types of errors mentioned, even though there may be other correct ways of expressing the same thought.

1. Neither one of these procedures are adequate for the efficient performance of this task.   1._____

2. The typewriter is the tool of the typist; the cash register, the tool of the cashier.   2._____

3. "The assignment must be completed as soon as possible" said the supervisor.   3._____

4. As you know, office handbooks are issued to all new employees.   4._____

5. Writing a speech is sometimes easier than to deliver it before an audience.   5._____

Questions 6-15.

DIRECTIONS: Each statement given in Questions 6 through 15 contains one of the faults of English usage listed below. For each, choose from the options listed the MAJOR fault contained.
- A. The statement is not a complete sentence.
- B. The statement contains a word or phrase that is redundant.
- C. The statement contains a long, less commonly used word when a shorter, more direct word would be acceptable.
- D. The statement contains a colloquial expression that normally is avoided in business writing.

6. The fact that this activity will afford an opportunity to meet your group.   6._____

7. Do you think that the two groups can join together for next month's meeting?   7._____

8. This is one of the most exciting new innovations to be introduced into our college.   8._____

9. We expect to consummate the agenda before the meeting ends tomorrow at noon.   9._____

10. While this seminar room is small in size, we think we can use it.   10._____

11. Do you think you can make a modification in the date of the Budget Committee meeting?   11._____

12. We are cognizant of the problem but we think we can ameliorate the situation.   12._____

13. Shall I call you around three on the day I arrive in the City?   13._____

14. Until such time that we know precisely that the students will be present.   14._____

15. The consensus of opinion of all the members present is reported in the minutes.   15._____

Questions 16-25.

DIRECTIONS: For each of Questions 16 through 25, select from the options given below the MOST applicable choice.
    A. The sentence is correct.
    B. The sentence contains a spelling error only.
    C. The sentence contains an English grammar error only.
    D. The sentence contains both a spelling error and an English grammar error.

16. Every person in the group is going to do his share.   16._____

17. The man who we selected is new to this University.   17._____

18. She is the older of the four secretaries on the two staffs that are to be combined.   18._____

19. The decision has to be made between him and I.   19._____

20. One of the volunteers are too young for this complecated task, don't you think?   20._____

21. I think your idea is splindid and it will improve this report considerably.   21._____

22. Do you think this is an exagerated account of the behavior you and me observed this morning?   22._____

23. Our supervisor has a clear idea of excelence.   23._____

24. How many occurences were verified by the observers?   24._____

25. We must complete the typing of the draft of the questionaire by noon tomorrow.   25._____

————

KEY (CORRECT ANSWERS)

1.	A	11.	C
2.	C	12.	C
3.	B	13.	D
4.	C	14.	A
5.	A	15.	B
6.	A	16.	A
7.	B	17.	C
8.	B	18.	C
9.	C	19.	C
10.	B	20.	D

21.	B
22.	D
23.	B
24.	B
25.	B

PREPARING WRITTEN MATERIAL

PARAGRAPH REARRANGEMENT
COMMENTARY

The sentences which follow are in scrambled order. You are to rearrange them in proper order and indicate the letter choice containing the correct answer at the space at the right.

Each group of sentences in this section is actually a paragraph presented in scrambled order. Each sentence in the group has a place in that paragraph; no sentence is to be left out. You are to read each group of sentences and decide upon the best order in which to put the sentences so as to form as well-organized paragraph.

The questions in this section measure the ability to solve a problem when all the facts relevant to its solution are not given.

More specifically, certain positions of responsibility and authority require the employee to discover connections between events sometimes, apparently, unrelated. In order to do this, the employee will find it necessary to correctly infer that unspecified events have probably occurred or are likely to occur. This ability becomes especially important when action must be taken on incomplete information.

Accordingly, these questions require competitors to choose among several suggested alternatives, each of which presents a different sequential arrangement of the events. Competitors must choose the MOST logical of the suggested sequences.

In order to do so, they may be required to draw on general knowledge to infer missing concepts or events that are essential to sequencing the given events. Competitors should be careful to infer only what is essential to the sequence. The plausibility of the wrong alternatives will always require the inclusion of unlikely events or of additional chains of events which are NOT essential to sequencing the given events.

It's very important to remember that you are looking for the best of the four possible choices, and that the best choice of all may not even be one of the answers you're given to choose from.

There is no one right way to solve these problems. Many people have found it helpful to first write out the order of the sentences, as they would have arranged them, on their scrap paper before looking at the possible answers. If their optimum answer is there, this can save them some time. If it isn't, this method can still give insight into solving the problem. Others find it most helpful to just go through each of the possible choices, contrasting each as they go along. You should use whatever method feels comfortable, and works, for you.

While most of these types of questions are not that difficult, we've added a higher percentage of the difficult type, just to give you more practice. Usually there are only one or two questions on this section that contain such subtle distinctions that you're unable to answer confidently, and you then may find yourself stuck deciding between two possible choices, neither of which you're sure about.

EXAMINATION SECTION
TEST 1

DIRECTIONS: The sentences that follow are in scrambled order. You are to rearrange them in proper order and indicate the letter choice containing the correct answer. *PRINT THE LETTER OF THE CORRECT ANSWER IN THE SPACE AT THE RIGHT.*

1. Below are four statements labeled W., X., Y., and Z.   1.____
   W.   He was a strict and fanatic drillmaster.
   X.   The word is always used in a derogatory sense and generally shows resentment and anger on the part of the user.
   Y.   It is from the name of this Frenchman that we derive our English word, martinet.
   Z.   Jean Martinet was the Inspector-General of Infantry during the reign of King Louis XIV.

   The *PROPER* order in which these sentences should be placed in a paragraph is:

   A. X, Z, W, Y   B. X, Z, Y, W   C. Z, W, Y, X   D. Z, Y, W, X

2. In the following paragraph, the sentences which are numbered, have been jumbled.   2.____
   1.   Since then it has undergone changes.
   2.   It was incorporated in 1955 under the laws of the State of New York.
   3.   Its primary purpose, a cleaner city, has, however, remained the same.
   4.   The Citizens Committee works in cooperation with the Mayor's Inter-departmental Committee for a Clean City.

   The order in which these sentences should be arranged to form a well-organized paragraph is:

   A. 2, 4, 1, 3   B. 3, 4, 1, 2   C. 4, 2, 1, 3   D. 4, 3, 2, 1

Questions 3-5.

DIRECTIONS: The sentences listed below are part of a meaningful paragraph but they are not given in their proper order. You are to decide what would be the *best order* in which to put the sentences so as to form a well-organized paragraph. Each sentence has a place in the paragraph; there are no extra sentences. You are then to answer questions 3 to 5 inclusive on the basis of your rearrangements of these scrambled sentences into a properly organized paragraph.

In 1887 some insurance companies organized an Inspection Department to advise their clients on all phases of fire prevention and protection. Probably this has been due to the smaller annual fire losses in Great Britain than in the United States. It tests various fire prevention devices and appliances and determines manufacturing hazards and their safeguards. Fire research began earlier in the United States and is more advanced than in Great Britain. Later they established a laboratory specializing in electrical, mechanical, hydraulic, and chemical fields.

3. When the five sentences are arranged in proper order, the paragraph starts with the sentence which begins

    3.___

    A. "In 1887..."   B. "Probably this ..."   C. "It tests ..."
    D. "Fire research ..."   E. "Later they ..."

4. In the last sentence listed above, "they" refers to

    4.___

    A. insurance companies
    B. the United States and Great Britain
    C. the Inspection Department
    D. clients
    E. technicians

5. When the above paragraph is properly arranged, it ends with the words

    5.___

    A. "... and protection."   B. "... the United States."
    C. "... their safeguards."   D. "... in Great Britain."
    E. "... chemical fields."

KEY (CORRECT ANSWERS)

1. C
2. C
3. D
4. A
5. C

TEST 2

DIRECTIONS: In each of the questions numbered 1 through 5, several sentences are given. For each question, choose as your answer the group of numbers that represents the *most logical* order of these sentences if they were arranged in paragraph form. *PRINT THE LETTER OF THE CORRECT ANSWER IN THE SPACE AT THE RIGHT.*

1.
   1. It is established when one shows that the landlord has prevented the tenant's enjoyment of his interest in the property leased.
   2. Constructive eviction is the result of a breach of the covenant of quiet enjoyment implied in all leases.
   3. In some parts of the United States, it is not complete until the tenant vacates within a reasonable time.
   4. Generally, the acts must be of such serious and permanent character as to deny the tenant the enjoyment of his possessing rights.
   5. In this event, upon abandonment of the premises, the tenant's liability for that ceases.

   The CORRECT answer is:

   A. 2, 1, 4, 3, 5   B. 5, 2, 3, 1, 4   C. 4, 3, 1, 2, 5
   D. 1, 3, 5, 4, 2

1.____

2.
   1. The powerlessness before private and public authorities that is the typical experience of the slum tenant is reminiscent of the situation of blue-collar workers all through the nineteenth century.
   2. Similarly, in recent years, this chapter of history has been reopened by anti-poverty groups which have attempted to organize slum tenants to enable them to bargain collectively with their landlords about the conditions of their tenancies.
   3. It is familiar history that many of the workers remedied their condition by joining together and presenting their demands collectively.
   4. Like the workers, tenants are forced by the conditions of modern life into substantial dependence on these who possess great political arid economic power.
   5. What's more, the very fact of dependence coupled with an absence of education and self-confidence makes them hesitant and unable to stand up for what they need from those in power.

   The CORRECT answer is:

   A. 5, 4, 1, 2, 3   B. 2, 3, 1, 5, 4   C. 3, 1, 5, 4, 2
   D. 1, 4, 5, 3, 2

2.____

3.
   1. A railroad, for example, when not acting as a common carrier may contract away responsibility for its own negligence.
   2. As to a landlord, however, no decision has been found relating to the legal effect of a clause shifting the statutory duty of repair to the tenant.
   3. The courts have not passed on the validity of clauses relieving the landlord of this duty and liability.
   4. They have, however, upheld the validity of exculpatory clauses in other types of contracts.
   5. Housing regulations impose a duty upon the landlord to maintain leased premises in safe condition.

3.____

6. As another example, a bailee may limit his liability except for gross negligence, willful acts, or fraud.

The CORRECT answer is:

A. 2, 1, 6, 4, 3, 5
D. 5, 3, 4, 1, 6, 2
B. 1, 3, 4, 5, 6, 2
C. 3, 5, 1, 4, 2, 6

4.

1. Since there are only samples in the building, retail or consumer sales are generally eschewed by mart occupants, and in some instances, rigid controls are maintained to limit entrance to the mart only to those persons engaged in retailing.
2. Since World War I, in many larger cities, there has developed a new type of property, called the mart building.
3. It can, therefore, be used by wholesalers and jobbers for the display of sample merchandise.
4. This type of building is most frequently a multi-storied, finished interior property which is a cross between a retail arcade and a loft building.
5. This limitation enables the mart occupants to ship the orders from another location after the retailer or dealer makes his selection from the samples.

The CORRECT answer is:

A. 2, 4, 3, 1, 5
D. 1, 4, 2, 3, 5
B. 4, 3, 5, 1, 2
C. 1, 3, 2, 4, 5

4.___

5.

1. In general, staff-line friction reduces the distinctive contribution of staff personnel.
2. The conflicts, however, introduce an uncontrolled element into the managerial system.
3. On the other hand, the natural resistance of the line to staff innovations probably usefully restrains over-eager efforts to apply untested procedures on a large scale.
4. Under such conditions, it is difficult to know when valuable ideas are being sacrificed.
5. The relatively weak position of staff, requiring accommodation to the line, tends to restrict their ability to engage in free, experimental innovation.

The CORRECT answer is:

A. 4, 2, 3, 1, 3
D. 2, 1, 4, 5, 3
B. 1, 5, 3, 2, 4
C. 5, 3, 1, 2, 4

5.___

KEY (CORRECT ANSWERS)

1. A
2. D
3. D
4. A
5. B

TEST 3

DIRECTIONS: Questions 1 through 4 consist of six sentences which can be arranged in a logical sequence. For each question, select the choice which places the numbered sentences in the *most logical* sequence. *PRINT THE LETTER OF THE CORRECT ANSWER IN THE SPACE AT THE RIGHT.*

1. 1. The burden of proof as to each issue is determined before trial and remains upon the same party throughout the trial.
    2. The jury is at liberty to believe one witness' testimony as against a number of contradictory witnesses.
    3. In a civil case, the party bearing the burden of proof is required to prove his contention by a fair preponderance of the evidence.
    4. However, it must be noted that a fair preponderance of evidence does not necessarily mean a greater number of witnesses.
    5. The burden of proof is the burden which rests upon one of the parties to an action to persuade the trier of the facts, generally the jury, that a proposition he asserts is true.
    6. If the evidence is equally balanced, or if it leaves the jury in such doubt as to be unable to decide the controversy either way, judgment must be given against the party upon whom the burden of proof rests.

    The CORRECT answer is:

    A. 3, 2, 5, 4, 1, 6   B. 1, 2, 6, 5, 3, 4   C. 3, 4, 5, 1, 2, 6
    D. 5, 1, 3, 6, 4, 2

1.____

2. 1. If a parent is without assets and is unemployed, he cannot be convicted of the crime of non-support of a child.
    2. The term "sufficient ability" has been held to mean sufficient financial ability.
    3. It does not matter if his unemployment is by choice or unavoidable circumstances.
    4. If he fails to take any steps at all, he may be liable to prosecution for endangering the welfare of a child.
    5. Under the penal law, a parent is responsible for the support of his minor child only if the parent is "of sufficient ability."
    6. An indigent parent may meet his obligation by borrowing money or by seeking aid under the provisions of the Social Welfare Law.

    The CORRECT answer is:

    A. 6, 1, 5, 3, 2, 4   B. 1, 3, 5, 2, 4, 6   C. 5, 2, 1, 3, 6, 4
    D. 1, 6, 4, 5, 2, 3

2.____

3.
1. Consider, for example, the case of a rabble rouser who urges a group of twenty people to go out and break the windows of a nearby factory.
2. Therefore, the law fills the indicated gap with the crime of inciting to riot.
3. A person is considered guilty of inciting to riot when he urges ten or more persons to engage in tumultuous and violent conduct of a kind likely to create public alarm.
4. However, if he has not obtained the cooperation of at least four people, he cannot be charged with unlawful assembly.
5. The charge of inciting to riot was added to the law to cover types of conduct which cannot be classified as either the crime of "riot" or the crime of "unlawful assembly."
6. If he acquires the acquiescence of at least four of them, he is guilty of unlawful assembly even if the project does not materialize.

The CORRECT answer is:

A. 3, 5, 1, 6, 4, 2   B. 5, 1, 4, 6, 2, 3   C. 3, 4, 1, 5, 2, 6
D. 5, 1, 4, 6, 3, 2

3.____

4.
1. If, however, the rebuttal evidence presents an issue of credibility, it is for the jury to determine whether the presumption has, in fact, been destroyed.
2. Once sufficient evidence to the contrary is introduced, the presumption disappears from the trial.
3. The effect of a presumption is to place the burden upon the adversary to come forward with evidence to rebut the presumption.
4. When a presumption is overcome and ceases to exist in the case, the fact or facts which gave rise to the presumption still remain.
5. Whether a presumption has been overcome is ordinarily a question for the court.
6. Such information may furnish a basis for a logical inference.

The CORRECT answer is:

A. 4, 6, 2, 5, 1, 3   B. 3, 2, 5, 1, 4, 6   C. 5, 3, 6, 4, 2, 1
D. 5, 4, 1, 2, 6, 3

4.____

KEY (CORRECT ANSWERS)

1. D
2. C
3. A
4. B

PREPARING WRITTEN MATERIAL
EXAMINATION SECTION
TEST 1

DIRECTIONS: The following groups of sentences need to be arranged in an order that makes sense. Select the letter preceding the sequence that represents the *BEST sentence order. PRINT THE LETTER OF THE CORRECT ANSWER IN THE SPACE AT THE RIGHT.*

1.   1._____

   I.   A large Naval station on Alameda Island, near Oakland, held many warships in port, and the War Department was worried that if the bridge were to be blown ·up by the enemy, passage to and from the bay would be hopelessly blocked.

   II.   Though many skeptics were opposed to the idea of building such an enormous bridge, the most vocal opposition came from a surprising source: the United States War Department.

   III.   The War Department's concerns led to a showdown at San Francisco City Hall between Strauss and the Secretary of War, who demanded to know what would happen if a military enemy blew up the bridge.

   IV.   In 1933, by submitting a construction cost estimate of $17 million, an engineer named Joseph Strauss won the contract to build the Golden Gate Bridge of San Francisco, which would then become one of the world's largest bridges.

   V.   Strauss quickly ended the debate by explaining that the Golden Gate Bridge was to be a suspension bridge, whose roadway would hang in the air from cables strung between two huge towers, and would immediately sink into three hundred feet of water if it were destroyed.

The best order is
A.   II, III, I, IV, V
B.   I, II, III, V, IV
C.   IV, II, I, III, V
D.   IV, I, III, V, II

2.

I.   Plastic surgeons have already begun to use virtual reality to map out the complex nerve and tissue structures of a particular patient's face, in order to prepare for delicate surgery.

II. A virtual reality program responds to these movements by adjusting the Images that a person sees on a screen or through goggles, thereby creating an "interactive" world in which a person can see and touch three-dimensional graphic objects.

III. No more than a computer program that is designed to build and display graphic images, the virtual reality program takes graphic programs a step further by sensing a person's head and body movements.

IV. The computer technology known as virtual reality, now in its very first stages of development, is already revolutionizing some aspects of contemporary life.

V.   Virtual reality computers are also being used by the space program, most recently to simulate conditions for the astronauts who were launched on a repair mission to the Hubble telescope.

The best order is
A. IV, II, I, V, III
B. III, I, V, II, IV
C. IV, III, II, I, V
D. III, I, II, IV, V

3.

I.   Before you plant anything, the soil in your plant bed should be carefully raked level, a small section at a time, and any clods or rocks that can't be broken up should be removed.

II. Your plant should be placed in a hole that will position it at the same level it was at the nursery, and a small indentation should be pressed into the soil around the plant in order to hold water near it roots.

III. Before placing the plant in the soil, lightly separate any roots that may have been matted together in the container, cutting away any thick masses that can't be separated, so that the remaining roots will be able to grow outward.

IV. After the bed is ready, remove your plant from its container by turning it upside down and tapping or pushing on the bottom — never remove it by pulling on the plant.

V.   When you bring home a small plant in an individual container from the nursery, there are several things to remember while preparing to plant it in your own garden.

The best order is
A. V, IV, III, II, I
B. V, I, IV, III, II
C. I, IV, II, III, V
D. I, IV, V, II, III

4.

I.   The motte and its tower were usually built first, so that sentries could use it as a lookout to warn the castle workers of any danger that might approach the castle.

II.   Though the moat and palisade offered the bailey a good deal of protection, it was linked to the motte by a set of stairs that led to a retractable drawbridge at the motte's gate, to enable people to evacuate and retreat onto the motte in case of an attack.

III.   The *motte* of these early castles was a fortified hill, sometimes as high as one hundred feet, on which stood a palisade and tower.

IV.   The *bailey* was a clear, level spot below the motte, also enclosed by a palisade, which in turn was surrounded by a large trench or moat.

V.   The earliest castles built in Europe were not the magnificent stone giants that still tower over much of the European landscape, but simpler wooden constructions called motte-and-bailey castles.

The best order is
A. V, III, I, IV, II
B. V, IV, I, II, III
C. I, IV, IIII, II, V
D. I, III, II, IV, V

5.

I.   If an infant is left alone or abandoned for a short while, its immediate response is to cry loudly, accompanying its screams with aggressive flailing of its legs and limbs.

II.   If a child has been abandoned for a longer period of time, it becomes completely still and quiet, as if realizing that now its only chance for survival is to shut its mouth and remain motionless.

III.   Along with their intense fear of the dark, the crying behavior of human infants offers insights into how prehistoric newborn children might have evolved instincts that would prevent them from becoming victims of predators.

IV.   This behavior often surprises people who enter a hospital's maternity ward for the first time and encounter total silence from a roomful of infants.

V.   This violent screaming response is quite different from an infant's cries of discomfort or hunger, and seems to serve as either the child's first line of defense against an unwanted intruder, or a desperate attempt to communicate its position to the mother.

The best order is
A. III, II, IV, I, V
B. III, I, V, II, IV
C. I, V, IV, II, III
D. II, IV, I, V, III

6.

I.   When two cats meet who are strangers, their first actions and gestures determine who the "dominant" cat will be, at least for the time being.

II.   Unlike dogs, cats are typically a solitary animal species who avoid social interaction, but they do display specific social responses to each other upon meeting.

III.   This is unlikely, however; before such a point of open hostility is reached, one of the cats will usually take the "submissive" position of crouching down while looking away from the other cat.

IV.   If a cat desires dominance or sees the other cat as a threat to its territory, it will stare directly at the intruder with a lowered tail.

V.   If the other cat responds with a similar gesture, or with the strong defensive posture of an arched back, laid-back ears and raised tail, a fight or chase is likely if neither cat gives in.

The best order is
A. IV, II, I, V, III
B. I, II, IV, V, III
C. I, IV, V, III, II
D. II, I, IV, V, III

7.

I.   A star or planet's gravitational force can best be explained in this way: anything passing through this "dent" in space will veer toward the star or planet as if it were rolling into a hole.

II.   Objects that are massive or heavy, such as stars or planets, "sink" into this surface, creating a sort of dent or concavity in the surrounding space.

III.   Black holes, the most massive objects known to exist in space, create dents so large and deep that the space surrounding them actually folds in on itself, preventing anything that falls in — even light — from ever escaping again.

IV.   The sort of dent a star or planet makes depends on how massive it is; planets generally have weak gravitational pulls, but stars, which are larger and heavier, make a bigger "dent" that will attract more matter.

V.   In outer space, the force of gravity works as if the surrounding space is a soft, flat surface.

The best order is
A. III, V, II, I, IV
B. III, IV, I, V, II
C. V, II, I, IV, III
D. I, V, II, IV, III

8.   8._____

   I.   Eventually, the society of Kyoto gave the world one of its first and greatest
        novels when Japan's most prominent writer, Lady Murasaki Shikibu, wrote
        her chronicle of Kyoto's society, *The Tale of Genji*, which preceded the first
        European novels by more than 500 years.

   II.   The society of Kyoto was dedicated to the pleasures of art; the courtiers
        experimented with new and colorful methods of sculpture, painting, writing,
        decorative gardening, and even making clothes.

   III. Japanese culture began under the powerful authority of Chinese Buddhism,
        which influenced every aspect of Japanese life from religion to politics and art.

   IV. This new, vibrant culture was so sophisticated that all the people in Kyoto's
        imperial court considered themselves poets, and the line between life and art
        hardly existed — lovers corresponded entirely through written verses, and even
        government officials communicated by writing poems to each other.

   V.   In the eighth century, when the emperor established the town of Kyoto as the
        capital of the Japanese empire, Japanese society began to develop its own
        distinctive style.

The best order is
A. V, II, IV, I, III
B. II, I, V, IV, III
C. V, III, IV, I, II
D. III, V, II, IV, I

9.   9._____

   I.   Instead of wheels, the HSST uses two sets of magnets, one which sits on the
        track, and another that is carried by the train; these magnets generate an
        identical magnetic field which forces the two sets apart.

   II.   In the last few decades, railway travel has become less popular throughout the
        world, because it is much slower than travel by airplane, and not much less
        expensive.

   III. The HSST's designers say that the train can take passengers from one town
        to another as quickly as a jet plane — while consuming less than half the energy.

   IV. This repellent effect is strong enough to lift the entire train above the trackway,
        and the train, literally traveling on air, rockets along at speeds of up to 300 miles
        per hour.

   V.   The revolutionary technology of magnetic levitation, currently being tested by
        Japan's experimental HSST (High Speed Surface Transport), may yet bring
        passenger trains back from the dead.

The best order is
A. II, V, I, IV, III
B. II, I, IV, III, V
C. V, II, III, I, IV
D. V, I, III, IV, II

10.

I. When European countries first began to colonize the African continent, their impression of the African people was of a vast group of loosely organized tribal societies, without any great centralized source of power or wealth.

II. The legend of Timbuktu persisted until the nineteenth century, when a French adventurer visited Timbuktu and found that raids by neighboring tribesmen had made the city a shadow of its former self.

III. In the fifteenth century, when the stories of travelers who had traveled Africa's Sudan region began circulating around Europe, this impression began to change.

IV. In 1470, an Italian merchant named Benedetto Dei traveled to Timbuktu and confirmed these rumors, describing a thriving metropolis where rich and poor people worshipped together in the city's many ornate mosques — there was even a university in Timbuktu, much like its European counterparts, where African scholars pursued their studies in the arts and sciences.

V. The travelers' legends told of an enormous city in the western Sudan, Timbuktu, where the streets were crowded with goods brought by faraway caravans, and where there was a stone palace as large as any in Europe.

The best order is
A. III, V, I, IV, II
B. I, II, IV, III, V
C. I, III, V, IV, II
D. II, I, III, IV, V

11.

I. Also, our reference points in sighting the moon may make us believe that its size is changing; when the moon is rising through the trees, it seems huge, because our brains unconsciously compare the size of the moon with the size of the trees in the foreground.

II. To most people, the sky itself appears more distant at the horizon than directly overhead, and if the moon's size — which remains constant — is projected from the horizon, the apparent distance of the horizon makes the moon look bigger.

III. Up higher in the sky, the moon is set against tiny stars in the background, which will make the moon seem smaller.

IV. People often wonder why the moon becomes bigger when it approaches the horizon, but most scientists agree that this is a complicated optical illusion, produced by at least three factors.

V. The moon illusion may also be partially explained by a phenomenon that has nothing to do with errors in our perception — light that enters the earth's atmosphere is sometimes refracted, and so the atmosphere may act as a kind of magnifying glass for the moon's image.

The best order is
A. IV, III, V, II, I
B. IV, II, I, III, V
C. V, II, I, III, IV
D. II, I, III, IV, V

12.   12._____

   I.   When the Native Americans were introduced to the horses used by white explorers, they were amazed at their new alternative — here was an animal that was strong and swift, would patiently carry a person or other loads on its back, and, they later discovered, was right at home on the plains.

   II.   Before the arrival of European explorers to North America, the natives of the American plains used large dogs to carry their travois-long lodgepoles loaded with clothing, gear, and food.

   III.   These horses, it is now known, were not really strangers to North America; the very first horses originated here, on this continent, tens of thousands of years ago, and migrated into Asia across the Bering Land Bridge, a strip of land that used to link our continent with the Eastern world.

   IV.   At first, the natives knew so little about horses that at least one tribe tried to feed their new animals pieces of dried meat and animal fat, and were surprised when the horses turned their heads away and began to eat the grass of the prairie.

   V.   The American horse eventually became extinct, but its Asian cousins were reintroduced to the New World when the European explorers brought them to live among the Native Americans.

The best order is
A. II, I, IV, III, V
B. II, IV, I, III, V
C. I, II, IV, III, V
D. I, III, V, II, IV

13.   13._____

   I.   The dress worn by the dancer is believed to have been adorned in the past by shells which would strike each other as the dancer performed, creating a lovely sound.

   II.   Today's jingle-dress is decorated with the tin lids of snuff cans, which are rolled into cones and sewn onto the dress.

   III.   During the jingle-dress dance, the dancer must blend complicated footwork with a series of gentle hops that cause the cones to jingle in rhythm to a drumbeat.

   IV.   When contemporary Native American tribes meet for a pow-wow, one of the most popular ceremonies to take place is the women's jingle-dress dance.

   V.   Besides being more readily available than shells, the lids are thought by many dancers to create a softer, more subtle sound.

The best order is
A. II, IV, V, I, III
B. IV, II, I, III, V
C. II, I, III, V, IV
D. IV, I, II, V, III

14.

   14.____

I.   If a homeowner lives where seasonal climates are extreme, deciduous shade trees — which will drop their leaves in the winter and allow sunlight to pass through the windows — should be planted near the southern exposure in order to keep the house cool during the summer.

II.   This trajectory is shorter and lower in the sky than at any other time of year during the winter, when a house most requires heating; the northern-facing parts of a house do not receive any direct sunlight at all.

III.   In designing an energy-efficient house, especially in colder climates, it is important to remember that most of the house's windows should face south.

IV.   Though the sun always rises in the east and sets in the west, the sun of the northern hemisphere is permanently situated in the southern portion of the sky.

V.   The explanation for why so many architects and builders want this "southern exposure" is related to the path of the sun in the sky.

The best order is
A. III, I, V, IV, II
B. III, V, IV, II, I
C. I, III, IV, II, V
D. I, II, V, IV, III

15.

   15.____

I.   His journeying lasted twenty-four years and took him over an estimated 75,000 miles, a distance that would not be surpassed by anyone other than Magellan — who sailed around the world — for another six hundred years.

II.   Perhaps the most far-flung of these lesser-known travelers was Ibn Batuta, an African Moslem who left his birthplace of Tangier in the summer of 1325.

III.   Ibn Batuta traveled all over Africa and Asia, from Niger to Peking, and to the islands of Maldive and Indonesia.

IV.   However, a few explorers of the Eastern world logged enough miles and adventures to make Marco Polo's voyage look like an evening stroll.

V.   In America, the most well-known of the Old World's explorers are usually Europeans such as Marco Polo, the Italian who brought many elements of Chinese culture to the Western world.

The best order is
A. V, IV, II, III, I
B. V, IV, III, II, I
C. III, II, I, IV, V
D. II, III, I, IV, V

16.

   I.   In the rain forests of South America, a rare species of frog practices a repro-
ductive method that is entirely different from this standard process.

   II.   She will eventually carry each of the tadpoles up into the canopy and drop
each into its own little pool, where it will be easy to locate and safe from most
predators.

   III. After fertilization, the female of the species, who lives almost entirely on the
forest floor, lays between 2 and 16 eggs among the leaf litter at the base of a
tree, and stands watch over these eggs until they hatch.

   IV. Most frogs are pond-dwellers who are able to deposit hundreds of eggs in
the water and then leave them alone, knowing that enough eggs have been
laid to insure the survival of some of their offspring.

   V.   Once the tadpoles emerge, the female backs in among them, and a tadpole
will wriggle onto her back to be carried high into the forest canopy, where the
female will deposit it in a little pool of water cupped in the leaf of a plant.

The best order is
A. I, IV, III, II, V
B. I, III, V, II, IV
C. IV, III, II, V, I
D. IV, I, III, V, II

17.

   I.   Eratosthenes had heard from travelers that at exactly noon on June 21, in the
ancient city of Aswan, Egypt, the sun cast no shadow in a well, which meant
that the sun must be directly overhead.

   II.   He knew the sun always cast a shadow in Alexandria, and so he figured that if
he could measure the length of an Alexandria shadow at the time when there
was no shadow in Aswan, he could calculate the angle of the sun, and therefore
the circumference of the earth.

   III. The evidence for a round earth was not new in 1492; in fact, Eratosthenes, an
Alexandrian geographer who lived nearly sixteen centuries before Columbus's
voyage (275-195 B.C.), actually developed a method for calculating the circumference of the earth that is still in use today.

   IV. Eratosthenes's method was correct, but his result — 28,700 miles — was about
15 percent too high, probably because of the inaccurate ancient methods of
keeping time, and because Aswan was not due south of Alexandria, as
Eratosthenes had believed.

   V.   When Christopher Columbus sailed across the Atlantic Ocean for the first time in
1492, there were still some people in the world who ignored scientific evidence
and believed that the earth was flat, rather than round.

The best order is
A. I, II, V, III, IV
B. V, III, IV, I, II
C. V, III, I, II, IV
D. III, V, I, II, IV

18.

I. The first name for the child is considered a trial naming, often impersonal and neutral, such as the Ngoni name *Chabwera*, meaning "it has arrived."

II. This sort of name is not due to any parental indifference to the child, but is a kind of silent recognition of Africa's sometimes high infant death rate; most parents ease the pain of losing a child with the belief that it is not really a person until it has been given a final name.

III. In many tribal African societies, families often give two different names to their children, at different periods in time.

IV. After the trial naming period has subsided and it is clear that the child will survive, the parents choose a final name for the child, an act that symbolically completes the act of birth.

V. In fact, some African first-given names are explicitly uncomplimentary, translating as "I am dead" or "I am ugly," in order to avoid the jealousy of ancestral spirits who might wish to take a child that is especially healthy or attractive.

The best order is
A. III, I, II, V, IV
B. III, IV, II, I, V
C. IV, III, I, II, V
D. IV, V, III, I, II

19.

I. Though uncertain of the definite reasons for this behavior, scientists believe the birds digest the clay in order to counteract toxins contained in the seeds of certain fruits that are eaten by macaws.

II. For example, all macaws flock to riverbanks at certain times of the year to eat the clay that is found in river mud.

III. The macaws of South America are not only among the largest and most beautifully colored of the world's flying birds, but they are also one of the smartest.

IV. It is believed that macaws are forced to resort to these toxic fruits during the dry season, when foods are more scarce.

V. The macaw's intelligence has led to intense study by scientists, who have discovered some macaw behaviors that have not yet been explained.

The best order is
A. III, IV, I, II, V
B. III, V, II, I, IV
C. V, II, I, IV, III
D. IV, I, II, III, V

20.   20._____

   I.   Although Maggie Kuhn has since passed away, the Gray Panthers are still waging a campaign to reinstate the historical view of the elderly as people whose experience allows them to make their greatest contribution in their later years.

   II.   In 1972, an elderly woman named Maggie Kuhn responded to this sort of treatment by forming a group called the Gray Panthers, an organization of both old and young adults with the common goal of creating change.

   III.   This attitude is reflected strongly in the way elderly people are treated by our society; many are forced into early retirement, or are placed in rest homes in which they are isolated from their communities.

   IV.   Unlike most other cultures around the world, Americans tend to look upon old age with a sense of dread and sadness.

   V.   Kuhn believed that when the elderly are forced to withdraw into lives that lack purpose, society loses one of its greatest resources: people who have a lifetime of experience and wisdom to offer their communities.

The best order is
A. IV, III, II, V, I
B. IV, II, I, III, V
C. II, IV, III, V, I
D. II, I, IV, III, V

21.   21._____

   I.   The current theory among most anthropologists is that humans evolved from apes who lived in trees near the grasslands of Africa.

   II.   Still, some anthropologists insist that such an invention was necessary for the survival of early humans, and point to the Kung Bushmen of central Africa as a society in which the sling is still used in this way.

   III.   Two of these inventions — fire, and weapons such as spears and clubs — were obvious defenses against predators, and there is archaeological evidence to support the theory of their use.

   IV.   Once people had evolved enough to leave the safety of trees and walk upright, they needed the protection of several inventions in order to survive.

   V.   But another invention, a leather or fiber sling that allowed mothers to carry children while leaving their hands free to gather roots or berries, would certainly have decomposed and left behind no trace of itself.

The best order is
A. I, II, III, V, IV
B. IV, I, II, III, V
C. I, IV, III, V, II
D. IV, III, V, II, I

22.

I. The person holding the bird should keep it in hot water up to its neck, and the person cleaning should work a mild solution of dishwashing liquid into the bird's plumage, paying close attention to the head and neck.

II. When rinsing the bird, after all the oil has been removed, the running water should be directed against the lay of its feathers, until water begins to bead off the surface of the feathers — a sign that all the detergent has been rinsed out.

III. If you have rescued a sea bird from an oil spill and want to restore it to clean and normal living, you need a large sink, a constant supply of running hot water (a little over 100° F), and regular dishwashing liquid.

IV. This cleaning with detergent solution should be repeated as many times as it takes to remove all traces of oil from the bird's feathers, sometimes over a period of several days.

V. But before you begin to clean the bird, you must first find a partner, because cleaning an oiled bird is a two-person job.

The best order is
A. III, I, II, IV, V
B. III, V, I, IV, II
C. III, I, IV, V, II
D. III, IV, V, I, II

23.

I. The most difficult time of year for the Tsaatang is the spring calving, when the reindeer leave their wintering ground and rush to their accustomed calving place, without stopping by night or by day.

II. Reindeer travel in herds, and though some animals are tamed by the Tsaatang for riding or milking, the herds are allowed to roam free.

III. This journey is hard for the Tsaatang, who carry all their possessions with them, but once it's over it proves worthwhile; the Tsaatang can immediately begin to gather milk from reindeer cows who have given birth.

IV. The Tsaatang, a small tribe who live in the far northwest corner of Mongolia, practice a lifestyle that is completely dependent on the reindeer, their main resource for food, clothing, and transport.

V. The people must follow their yearly migrations, living in portable shelters that resemble Native American tepees.

The best order is
A. I, III, II, V, IV
B. I, IV, II, V, III
C. IV, I, III, V, II
D. IV, II, V, I, III

24.

I.   The Romans later improved this system by installing these heated pipe networks throughout walls and ceilings, supplying heat to even the uppermost
floors of a building — a system that, to this day, hasn't been much improved.

II.   Air-conditioning, the method by which humans control indoor temperatures,
was practiced much earlier than most people think.

III.   The earliest heating devices other than open fires were used in 350 B.C. by
the ancient Greeks, who directed air that had been heated by underground
fires into baked clay pipes that ran under the floor.

IV.   Ironically, the first successful cooling system, patented in England in 1831,
used fire as its main energy source — fires were lit in the attic of a building,
creating an updraft of air that drew cool air into the building through ducts
that had underground openings near the river Thames.

V.   Cooling buildings was more of a challenge, and wasn't attempted until 1500:
a water-based system, designed by Leonardo da Vinci, does not appear to
have been successful, since it was never used again.

The best order is
A. III, V, IV, I, II
B. III, I, II, V, IV
C. II, III, I, V, IV
D. IV, II, III, I, V

25.

I.   Cold, dry air from Canada passes over the Rocky Mountains and sweeps
down onto the plains, where it collides with warm, moist air from the waters
of the Gulf of Mexico, and when the two air masses meet, the resulting
disturbance sometimes forms a violent funnel cloud that strikes the earth
and destroys virtually everything in its path.

II.   Hurricanes, storms which are generally not this violent and last much longer,
are usually given names by meteorologists, but this tradition cannot be applied
to tornados, which have a life span measured in minutes and disappear in the
same way as they are born — unnamed.

III.   A tornado funnel forms rotating columns of air whose speed reaches three
hundred miles an hour — a speed that can only be estimated, because no
wind-measuring devices in the direct path of a storm have ever survived.

IV.   The natural phenomena known as tornados occur primarily over the mid-
western grasslands of the United States.

V.   It is here, meteorologists tell us, that conditions for the formation of tornados
are sometimes perfect during the spring months.

The best order is
A. II, IV, V, I, III
B. II, III, I, V, IV
C. IV, V, I, III, II
D. IV, III, I, V, II

KEY (CORRECT ANSWERS)

1.	C		11.	B
2.	C		12.	A
3.	B		13.	D
4.	A		14.	B
5.	B		15.	A
6.	D		16.	D
7.	C		17.	C
8.	D		18.	A
9.	A		19.	B
10.	C		20.	A

21.	C
22.	B
23.	D
24.	C
25.	C

———————

ANALYSIS OF SITUATIONS
DATA EVALUATION AND DATA APPLICATION

SAMPLE QUESTIONS

The passages for this question-type are quite long and complex. Consequently, a *complete* passage, with its associated questions, is not presented here. However, the instructions and directions that follow are the same as those given on the test itself.

INSTRUCTIONS: The passages in this section are followed by two sets of questions: *data evaluation* and *data application*.

In the first set, data evaluation, you will be required to classify certain of the facts presented in each passage on the basis of their importance, as illustrated in the following example:

SAMPLE PASSAGE

Fred North, a prospering hardware dealer in Hillidale, Connecticut, felt that he needed more store space to accommodate a new line of farm equipment and repair parts that he intended to carry. A number of New York City commuters had recently purchased tracts of land in the environs of Hillidale and there had taken up farming on a small scale. Mr. North, foreseeing a potential increase in farming in that area, wanted to expand his business to cater to this market. North felt that the most feasible and appealing recourse open to him would be to purchase the adjoining store property owned by Mike Johnson, who used the premises for his small grocery store. Johnson's business had been on the decline for over a year since the advent of a large supermarket in the town. North felt that Johnson would be willing to sell the property at reasonable terms, and this was important since North, after the purchase of the new merchandise, would have little capital available to invest in the expansion of his store.

DATA EVALUATION

DIRECTIONS: The following items relate to the passage above. Consider each item separately in terms of the passage and, in the answer space at the right, write the letter

    A. if the item is a *Major Objective* in making the decision; that is, one of the outcomes or results sought by the decision maker;

    B. if the item is a *Major Factor* in making the decision; that is, a consideration, explicitly mentioned in the passage, that is basic in determining the decision;

    C. if the item is a *Minor Factor* in making the decision; that is, a secondary consideration that affects the criteria tangentially, relating to a Major Factor rather than to an Objective;

    D. if the item is a *Major Assumption* in making the decision; that is, a supposition or projection made by the decision maker before weighing the variables;

    E. if the item is an *Unimportant Issue* in making the decision; that is, a factor that is insignificant or not immediately relevant to the situation.

1. Increase in farming in the Hillidale area   1._____
2. Acquisition of property for expanding the store   2._____
3. Cost of Johnson's property   3._____
4. State of Johnson's grocery business   4._____
5. Quality of the farm equipment North intends to sell   5._____

The correct designation for number 1 is D, a *Major Assumption*, since North bases his whole expansion project on his supposition that the new commuter-farmers in the Hillidale area are indicative of a trend in that direction.

Number 2 is A, a *Major Objective*, inasmuch as North's immediate purpose is to obtain room for expansion.

B, a Major Factor, is the correct answer for number 3 because North's present lack of capital renders cost a vital consideration.

The best classification of number 4 is C, a *Minor Factor*, because the depreciating value of Johnson's business influences his willingness to sell and also the price he will demand for his property; thus, this factor pertains to 3, the cost of Johnson's property, and is an indirect consideration in the case.

Point 5, finally, is E, an *Unimportant Issue*, for the quality of North's goods has no relevance to the situation at hand; i.e., the desire for room to expand his business.

DATA APPLICATION

A second set of questions, data application, requires judgments based on a comparison of the available alternatives in terms of the relevant criteria, in order to attain the objectives stated in each passage.

DIRECTIONS: Each of the following questions relates to the passage above. For each question, choose the BEST answer and print the letter of the correct answer in the space at the right.

SAMPLE QUESTION

1. *Which* of the following reasons is (are) given for North's decision to expand his business?
   - I.   Potential demand for farm equipment in the Hillidale area
   - II.   Desire to undermine Mike Johnson's business
   - III. Higher profit margin on farm equipment than on hardware

The CORRECT answer is:
  A. I only   B. III only   C. I and II   D. II and III   E. I, II, and III

The correct designation here is A, I only, since the passage clearly states that North anticipates a demand for farm equipment in the Hillidale area and wishes to attract that market.

Alternative II is easily eliminated because there is no indication of competition or malice between North and Johnson, and Johnson's business has, in any case, declined already. Option III, while plausible, is not supported by the passage.

EXAMINATION SECTION
TEST 1

DIRECTIONS: Each question or incomplete statement is followed by several suggested answers or completions. Select the one that BEST answers the question or completes the statement. *PRINT THE LETTER OF THE CORRECT ANSWER IN THE SPACE AT THE RIGHT.*

1. Professional staff members in large organizations are sometimes frustrated by a lack of vital work-related information because of the failure of some middle-management supervisors to pass along unrestricted information from top management.
All of the following are considered to be reasons for such failure to pass along information EXCEPT the supervisors'

    A. belief that information affecting procedures will be ignored unless they are present to supervise their subordinates
    B. fear that specific information will require explanation or justification
    C. inclination to regard the possession of information as a symbol of higher status
    D. tendency to treat information as private property

1.____

2. Increasingly in government, employees' records are being handled by automated data processing systems. However, employees frequently doubt a computer's ability to handle their records properly.
Which of the following is the BEST way for management to overcome such doubts?

    A. Conduct a public relations campaign to explain the savings certain to result from the use of computers
    B. Use automated data processing equipment made by the firm which has the best repair facilities in the industry
    C. Maintain a clerical force to spot check on the accuracy of the computer's record-keeping
    D. Establish automated data processing systems that are objective, impartial, and take into account individual factors as far as possible

2.____

3. Some management experts question the usefulness of offering cash to individual employees for their suggestions.
Which of the following reasons for opposing cash awards is MOST valid?

    A. Emphasis on individual gain deters cooperative effort.
    B. Money spent on evaluating suggestions may outweigh the value of the suggestions.
    C. Awards encourage employees to think about unusual methods of doing work.
    D. Suggestions too technical for ordinary evaluation are usually presented.

3.____

4. The use of outside consultants, rather than regular staff, in studying and recommending improvements in the operations of public agencies has been criticized.
Of the following, the BEST argument in favor of using regular staff is that such staff can better perform the work because they

    A. are more knowledgeable about operations and problems
    B. can more easily be organized into teams consisting of technical specialists
    C. may wish to gain additional professional experience
    D. will provide reports which will be more interesting to the public since they are more experienced

4.____

5. One approach to organizational problem-solving is to have all problem-solving authority centralized at the top of the organization.
However, from the viewpoint of providing maximum service to the public, this practice is UNWISE chiefly because it

    A. reduces the responsibility of the decision-makers
    B. produces delays
    C. reduces internal communications
    D. requires specialists

5.___

6. Research has shown that problem-solving efficiency is optimal when the motivation of the problem-solver is at a moderate rather than an extreme level.
Of the following, probably the CHIEF reason for this is that the problem-solver

    A. will cause confusion among his subordinates when his motivation is too high
    B. must avoid alternate solutions that tend to lead him up blind alleys
    C. can devote his attention to both the immediate problem as well as to other relevant problems in the general area
    D. must feel the need to solve the problem but not so urgently as to direct all his attention to the need and none to the means of solution

6.___

7. Don't be afraid to make mistakes. Many organizations are paralyzed from the fear of making mistakes. As a result, they don't do the things they should; they don't try new and different ideas.
For the effective supervisor, the MOST valid implication of this statement is that

    A. mistakes should not be encouraged, but there are some unavoidable risks in decision-making
    B. mistakes which stem from trying new and different ideas are usually not serious
    C. the possibility of doing things wrong is limited by one's organizational position
    D. the fear of making mistakes will prevent future errors

7.___

8. The duties of an employee under your supervision may be either routine, problem-solving, innovative, or creative. Which of the following BEST describes duties which are both innovative and creative?

    A. Checking to make sure that work is done properly
    B. Applying principles in a practical manner
    C. Developing new and better methods of meeting goals
    D. Working at two or more jobs at the same time

8.___

9. According to modern management theory, a supervisor who uses as little authority as possible and as much as is necessary would be considered to be using a mode that is

    A. autocratic   B. inappropriate
    C. participative   D. directive

9.___

10. Delegation involves establishing and maintaining effective working arrangements between a supervisor and the persons who report to him.
Delegation is MOST likely to have taken place when the

    10.____

    A. entire staff openly discusses common problems in order to reach solutions satisfactory to the supervisor
    B. performance of specified work is entrusted to a capable person, and the expected results are mutually understood
    C. persons assigned to properly accomplish work are carefully evaluated and given a chance to explain shortcomings
    D. supervisor provides specific written instructions in order to prevent anxiety on the part of inexperienced persons

11. Supervisors often are not aware of the effect that their behavior has on their subordinates.
The one of the following training methods which would be BEST for changing such supervisory behavior is

    11.____

    A. essential skills training
    B. off-the-job training
    C. sensitivity training
    D. developmental training

12. A supervisor, in his role as a trainer, may have to decide on the length and frequency of training sessions.
When the material to be taught is new, difficult, and lengthy, the trainer should be guided by the principle that for BEST results in such circumstances, sessions should be

    12.____

    A. longer, relatively fewer in number, and held on successive days
    B. shorter, relatively greater in number, and spaced at intervals of several days
    C. of average length, relatively fewer in number, and held at intermittent intervals
    D. of random length and frequency, but spaced at fixed intervals

13. Employee training which is based on realistic simulation, sometimes known as *game play* or *role play*, is sometimes preferable to learning from actual experience on the job. Which of the following is NOT a correct statement concerning the value of simulation to trainees?

    13.____

    A. Simulation allows for practice in decision-making without any need for subsequent discussion.
    B. Simulation is intrinsically motivating because it offers a variety of challenges.
    C. Compared to other, more traditional training techniques, simulation is dynamic.
    D. The simulation environment is nonpunitive as compared to real life.

14. Programmed instruction as a method of training has all of the following advantages EXCEPT:

    14.____

    A. Learning is accomplished in an optimum sequence of distinct steps
    B. Trainees have wide latitude in deciding what is to be learned within each program
    C. The trainee takes an active part in the learning process
    D. The trainee receives immediate knowledge of the results of his response

15. In a work-study program, trainees were required to submit weekly written performance reports in order to insure that work assignments fulfilled the program objectives.
Such reports would also assist the administrator of the work-study program PRIMARILY to

    A. eliminate personal counseling for the trainees
    B. identify problems requiring prompt resolution
    C. reduce the amount of clerical work for all concerned
    D. estimate the rate at which budgeted funds are being expended

15.___

16. Which of the following would be MOST useful in order to avoid misunderstanding when preparing correspondence or reports?

    A. Use vocabulary which is at an elementary level
    B. Present each sentence as an individual paragraph
    C. Have someone other than the writer read the material for clarity
    D. Use general words which are open to interpretation

16.___

17. Which of the following supervisory methods would be MOST likely to train subordinates to give a prompt response to memoranda in an organizational setting where most transactions are informal?

    A. Issue a written directive setting forth a schedule of strict deadlines
    B. Let it be known, informally, that those who respond promptly will be rewarded
    C. Follow up each memorandum by a personal inquiry regarding the receiver's reaction to it
    D. Direct subordinates to furnish a precise explanation for ignoring memos

17.___

18. Conferences may fail for a number of reasons. Still, a conference that is an apparent failure may have some benefit.
Which of the following would LEAST likely be such a benefit? It may

    A. increase for most participants their possessiveness about information they have
    B. produce a climate of good will and trust among many of the participants
    C. provide most participants with an opportunity to learn things about the others
    D. serve as a unifying force to keep most of the individuals functioning as a group

18.___

19. Assume that you have been assigned to study and suggest improvements in an operating unit of a delegate agency whose staff has become overwhelmed with problems, has had inadequate resources, and has become accustomed to things getting worse. The staff is indifferent to cooperating with you because they see no hope of improvement.
Which of the following steps would be LEAST useful in carrying out your assignment?

    A. Encourage the entire staff to make suggestions to you for change
    B. Inform the staff that management is somewhat dissatisfied with their performance
    C. Let staff know that you are fully aware of their problems and stresses
    D. Look for those problem areas where changes can be made quickly

19.___

20. Which of the following statements about employer-employee relations is NOT considered to be correct by leading managerial experts?

    A. An important factor in good employer-employee relations is treating workers respectfully.
    B. Employer-employee relations are profoundly influenced by the fundamentals of human nature.
    C. Good employer-employee relations must stem from top management and reach downward.
    D. Employee unions are usually a major obstacle to establishing good employer-employee relations.

21. In connection with labor relations, the term *management rights* GENERALLY refers to

    A. a managerial review level in a grievance system
    B. statutory prohibitions that bar monetary negotiations
    C. the impact of collective bargaining on government
    D. those subjects which management considers to be non-negotiable

22. Barriers may exist to the utilization of women in higher level positions. Some of these barriers are attitudinal in nature.
    Which of the following is MOST clearly attitudinal in nature?

    A. Advancement opportunities which are vertical in nature and thus require seniority
    B. Experience which is inadequate or irrelevant to the needs of a dynamic and progressive organization
    C. Inadequate means of early identification of employees with talent and potential for advancement
    D. Lack of self-confidence on the part of some women concerning their ability to handle a higher position

23. Because a reader reacts to the meaning he associates with a word, we can never be sure what emotional impact a word may carry or how it may affect our readers.
    The MOST logical implication of this statement for employees who correspond with members of the public is that

    A. a writer should try to select a neutral word that will not bias his writing by its hidden emotional meaning
    B. simple language should be used in writing letters denying requests so that readers are not upset by the denial
    C. every writer should adopt a writing style which he finds natural and easy
    D. whenever there is any doubt as to how a word is defined, the dictionary should be consulted

24. A public information program should be based on clear information about the nature of actual public knowledge and opinion. One way of learning about the views of the public is through the use of questionnaires.
    Which of the following is of LEAST importance in designing a questionnaire?

    A. A respondent should be asked for his name and address.
    B. A respondent should be asked to choose from among several statements the one which expresses his views.
    C. Questions should ask for responses in a form suitable for processing.
    D. Questions should be stated in familiar language.

25. Assume that you have accepted an invitation to speak before an interested group about a problem. You have brought with you for distribution a number of booklets and other informational material.
Of the following, which would be the BEST way to use this material?

    A. Distribute it before you begin talking so that the audience may read it at their leisure.
    B. Distribute it during your talk to increase the likelihood that it will be read.
    C. Hold it until the end of your talk, then announce that those who wish may take or examine the material.
    D. Before starting the talk, leave it on a table in the back of the room so that people may pick it up as they enter.

25.__

KEY (CORRECT ANSWERS)

1.	A		11.	C
2.	D		12.	B
3.	A		13.	A
4.	A		14.	B
5.	B		15.	B
6.	D		16.	C
7.	A		17.	C
8.	C		18.	A
9.	C		19.	B
10.	B		20.	D

21.	D
22.	D
23.	A
24.	A
25.	C

TEST 2

DIRECTIONS: Each question or incomplete statement is followed by several suggested answers or completions. Select the one that BEST answers the question or completes the statement. PRINT THE LETTER OF THE CORRECT ANSWER IN THE SPACE AT THE RIGHT.

1. Of the following, the FIRST step in planning an operation is to   1.____

   A. obtain relevant information
   B. identify the goal to be achieved
   C. consider possible alternatives
   D. make necessary assignments

2. A supervisor who is extremely busy performing routine tasks is MOST likely making   2.____
   INCORRECT use of what basic principle of supervision?

   A. Homogeneous Assignment   B. Span of Control
   C. Work Distribution   D. Delegation of Authority

3. Controls help supervisors to obtain information from which they can determine whether   3.____
   their staffs are achieving planned goals.
   Which one of the following would be LEAST useful as a control device?

   A. Employee diaries   B. Organization charts
   C. Periodic inspections   D. Progress charts

4. A certain employee has difficulty in effectively performing a particular portion of his rou-   4.____
   tine assignments, but his overall productivity is average.
   As the direct supervisor of this individual, your BEST course of action would be to

   A. attempt to develop the man's capacity to execute the problematical facets of his
      assignments
   B. diversify the employee's work assignments in order to build up his confidence
   C. reassign the man to less difficult tasks
   D. request in a private conversation that the employee improve his work output

5. A supervisor who uses persuasion as a means of supervising a unit would GENERALLY   5.____
   also use which of the following practices to supervise his unit?

   A. Supervise and control the staff with an authoritative attitude to indicate that he is a
      take-charge individual
   B. Make significant changes in the organizational operations so as to improve job effi-
      ciency
   C. Remove major communication barriers between himself, subordinates, and man-
      agement
   D. Supervise everyday operations while being mindful of the problems of his subordi-
      nates

6. Whenever a supervisor in charge of a unit delegates a routine task to a capable subordi-   6.____
   nate, he tells him exactly how to do it.
   This practice is GENERALLY

   A. desirable, chiefly because good supervisors should be aware of the traits of their
      subordinates and delegate responsibilities to them accordingly
   B. undesirable, chiefly because only non-routine tasks should be delegated
   C. desirable, chiefly because a supervisor should frequently test the willingness of his
      subordinates to perform ordinary tasks
   D. undesirable, chiefly because a capable subordinate should usually be allowed to
      exercise his own discretion in doing a routine job

7. The one of the following activities through which a supervisor BEST demonstrates leadership ability is by

    7.__

    A. arranging periodic staff meetings in order to keep his subordinates informed about professional developments in the field
    B. frequently issuing definite orders and directives which will lessen the need for subordinates to make decisions in handling any tasks assigned to them
    C. devoting the major part of his time to supervising subordinates so as to stimulate continuous improvement
    D. setting aside time for self-development and research so as to improve the skills, techniques, and procedures of his unit

8. The following three statements relate to the supervision of employees:

    8.__

    I. The assignment of difficult tasks that offer a challenge is more conducive to good morale than the assignment of easy tasks
    II. The same general principles of supervision that apply to men are equally applicable to women
    III. The best retraining program should cover all phases of an employee's work in a general manner

Which of the following choices list ALL of the above statements that are generally correct?

    A. II, III   B. I
    C. I, II   D. I, II, III

9. Which of the following examples BEST illustrates the application of the *exception principle* as a supervisory technique?

    9.__

    A. A complex job is divided among several employees who work simultaneously to complete the whole job in a shorter time.
    B. An employee is required to complete any task delegated to him to such an extent that nothing is left for the superior who delegated the task except to approve it.
    C. A superior delegates responsibility to a subordinate but retains authority to make the final decisions.
    D. A superior delegates all work possible to his subordinates and retains that which requires his personal attention or performance.

10. Assume that you are a supervisor. Your immediate superior frequently gives orders to your subordinates without your knowledge.
Of the following, the MOST direct and effective way for you to handle this problem is to

    10.__

    A. tell your subordinates to take orders only from you
    B. submit a report to higher authority in which you cite specific instances
    C. discuss it with your immediate superior
    D. find out to what extent your authority and prestige as a supervisor have been affected

11. In an agency which has as its primary purpose the protection of the public against fraudulent business practices, which of the following would GENERALLY be considered an *auxiliary* or *staff* rather than a *line* function?

    11.__

    A. Interviewing victims of frauds and advising them about their legal remedies
    B. Daily activities directed toward prevention of fraudulent business practices
    C. Keeping records and statistics about business violations reported and corrected
    D. Follow-up inspections by investigators after corrective action has been taken

12. A supervisor can MOST effectively reduce the spread of false rumors through the *grapevine* by

    A. identifying and disciplining any subordinate responsible for initiating such rumors
    B. keeping his subordinates informed as much as possible about matters affecting them
    C. denying false rumors which might tend to lower staff morale and productivity
    D. making sure confidential matters are kept secure from access by unauthorized employees

12.____

13. A supervisor has tried to learn about the background, education, and family relationships of his subordinates through observation, personal contact, and inspection of their personnel records.
These supervisory actions are GENERALLY

    A. *inadvisable,* chiefly because they may lead to charges of favoritism
    B. *advisable,* chiefly because they may make him more popular with his subordinates
    C. *inadvisable,* chiefly because his efforts may be regarded as an invasion of privacy
    D. *advisable,* chiefly because the information may enable him to develop better understanding of each of his subordinates

13.____

14. In an emergency situation, when action must be taken immediately, it is BEST for the supervisor to give orders in the form of

    A. direct commands which are brief and precise
    B. requests, so that his subordinates will not become alarmed
    C. suggestions which offer alternative courses of action
    D. implied directives, so that his subordinates may use their judgment in carrying them out

14.____

15. When demonstrating a new and complex procedure to a group of subordinates, it is ESSENTIAL that a supervisor

    A. go slowly and repeat the steps involved at least once
    B. show the employees common errors and the consequences of such errors
    C. go through the process at the usual speed so that the employees can see the rate at which they should work
    D. distribute summaries of the procedure during the demonstration and instruct his subordinates to refer to them afterwards

15.____

16. After a procedures manual has been written and distributed,

    A. continuous maintenance work is necessary to keep the manual current
    B. it is best to issue new manuals rather than make changes in the original manual
    C. no changes should be necessary
    D. only major changes should be considered

16.____

17. Of the following, the MOST important criterion of effective report writing is

    A. eloquence of writing style
    B. the use of technical language
    C. to be brief and to the point
    D. to cover all details

17.___

18. The use of electronic data processing

    A. has proven unsuccessful in most organizations
    B. has unquestionable advantages for all organizations
    C. is unnecessary in most organizations
    D. should be decided upon only after careful feasibility studies by individual organizations

18.___

19. The PRIMARY purpose of work measurement is to

    A. design and install a wage incentive program
    B. determine who should be promoted
    C. establish a yardstick to determine extent of progress
    D. set up a spirit of competition among employees

19.___

20. The action which is MOST effective in gaining acceptance of a study by the agency which is being studied is

    A. a directive from the agency head to install a study based on recommendations included in a report
    B. a lecture-type presentation following approval of the procedures
    C. a written procedure in narrative form covering the proposed system with visual presentations and discussions
    D. procedural charts showing the *before* situation, forms, steps, etc., to the employees affected

20.___

21. Which organization principle is MOST closely related to procedural analysis and improvement?

    A. Duplication, overlapping, and conflict should be eliminated.
    B. Managerial authority should be clearly defined.
    C. The objectives of the organization should be clearly defined.
    D. Top management should be freed of burdensome detail.

21.___

22. Which one of the following is the MAJOR objective of operational audits?

    A. Detecting fraud
    B. Determining organization problems
    C. Determining the number of personnel needed
    D. Recommending opportunities for improving operating and management practices

22.___

23. Of the following, the formalization of organization structure is BEST achieved by

    A. a narrative description of the plan of organization
    B. functional charts
    C. job descriptions together with organization charts
    D. multi-flow charts

23.___

24. Budget planning is MOST useful when it achieves   24.____

    A. cost control   B. forecast of receipts
    C. performance review   D. personnel reduction

25. GENERALLY, in applying the principle of delegation in dealing with subordinates, a   25.____
supervisor

    A. allows his subordinates to set up work goals and to fix the limits within which they
       can work
    B. allows his subordinates to set up work goals and then gives detailed orders as to
       how they are to be achieved
    C. makes relatively few decisions by himself and frames his orders in broad, general
       terms
    D. provides externalized motivation for his subordinates

_____

KEY (CORRECT ANSWERS)

1.	B		11.	C
2.	D		12.	B
3.	B		13.	D
4.	A		14.	A
5.	D		15.	A
6.	D		16.	A
7.	C		17.	C
8.	C		18.	D
9.	D		19.	C
10.	C		20.	C

21.	A
22.	D
23.	C
24.	A
25.	C

_____

EXAMINATION SECTION
TEST 1

DIRECTIONS: Each question or incomplete statement is followed by several suggested answers or completions. Select the one that *BEST* answer the question or completes the statement. *PRINT THE LETTER OF THE CORRECT ANSWER IN THE SPACE AT THE RIGHT.*

1. Although some kinds of instructions are best put in written form, a supervisor can give many instructions verbally.
   In which one of the following situations would verbal instructions be *MOST* suitable?

   A. Furnishing an employee with the details to be checked in doing a certain job
   B. Instructing an employee on the changes necessary to update the office manual used in your unit
   C. Informing a new employee where different kinds of supplies and equipment that he might need are kept
   D. Presenting an assignment to an employee who will be held accountable for following a series of steps

1._____

2. You may be asked to evaluate the organization structure of your unit.
   Which one of the following questions would you *NOT* expect to take up in an evaluation of this kind?

   A. Is there an employee whose personal problems are interfering with his or her work?
   B. Is there an up-to-date job description for each position in this section?
   C. Are related operations and tasks grouped together and regularly assigned together?
   D. Are responsibilities divided as far as possible, and. is this division clearly understood by all employees?

2._____

3. In order to distribute and schedule work fairly and efficiently, a supervisor may wish to make a work distribution study. A simple way of getting the information necessary for such a study is to have everyone for one week keep track of each task done and the time spent on each.
   Which one of the following situations showing up in such a study would *most clearly* call for corrective action?

   A. The newest employee takes longer to do most tasks than do experienced employees
   B. One difficult operation takes longer to do than most other operations carried out by the section
   C. A particular employee is very frequently assigned tasks that are not similar and have no relationship to each other
   D. The most highly skilled employee is often assigned the most difficult jobs

3._____

4. The authority to carry out a job can be delegated to a subordinate, but the supervisor remains responsible for the work of the section as a whole.
   As a supervisor, which of the following rules would be the *BEST* one for you to follow in view of the above statement?

4._____

A. Avoid assigning important tasks to your subordinates, because you will be blamed if anything goes wrong

B. Be sure each subordinate understands the specific job he has been assigned, and check at intervals to make sure assignments are done properly

C. Assign several people to every important job, so that responsibility will be spread out as much as possible

D. Have an experienced subordinate check all work done by other employees, so that there will be little chance of anything going wrong

5. The human tendency to resist change is often reflected in higher rates of turnover, absenteeism, and errors whenever an important change is made in an organization. Although psychologists do not fully understand the reasons why people resist change, they believe that the resistance stems from a threat to the individual's security, that it is a form of fear of the unknown.
In light of this statement, which one of the following approaches would probably be MOST effective in preparing employees for a change in procedure in their unit?

    5.___

A. Avoid letting employees know anything about the change until the last possible moment

B. Sympathize with employees who resent the change and let them know you share their doubts and fears

C. Promise the employees that if the change turns out to be a poor one, you will allow them to suggest a return to the old system

D. Make sure that employees know the reasons for the change and are aware of the benefits that are expected from it

6. Each of the following methods of encouraging employee participation in work planning has been used effectively with different kinds and sizes of employee groups.
Which one of the following methods would be MOST suitable for a group of four technically skilled employees?

    6.___

A. Discussions between the supervisor and a representative of the group

B. A suggestion program with semi-annual awards for outstanding suggestions

C. A group discussion summoned whenever a major problem remains unsolved for more than a month

D. Day-to-day exchange of information, opinions and experience

7. Of the following, the MOST important reason why a supervisor is given the authority to tell subordinates what work they should do, how they should do it, and when it should be done is that usually

    7.___

A. most people will not work unless there is someone with authority standing over them

B. work is accomplished more effectively if the supervisor plans and coordinates it

C. when division of work is left up to subordinates, there is constant arguing, and very little work is accomplished

D. subordinates are not familiar with the tasks to be performed

8. Fatigue is a factor that affects productivity in all work situations. However, a brief rest period will ordinarily serve to restore a person from fatigue.
According to this statement, which one of the following techniques is most likely to reduce the impact of fatigue on over-all productivity in a unit?

    8.___

A. Scheduling several short breaks throughout the day
B. Allowing employees to go home early
C. Extending the lunch period an extra half hour
D. Rotating job assignments every few weeks

9. After giving a new task to an employee, it is a good idea for a supervisor to ask specific questions to make sure that the employee grasps the essentials of the task and sees how it can be carried out. Questions which ask the employee what he thinks or how he feels about an important aspect of the task are particularly effective.
Which one of the following questions is *NOT* the type of question which would be useful in the foregoing situation?

9.____

A. "Do you feel there will be any trouble meeting the 4:30 deadline?"
B. "How do you feel about the kind of work we do here?"
C. "Do you think that combining those two steps will work all right?"
D. "Can you think of any additional equipment you may need for this process?"

10. Of the following, the *LEAST* important reason for having a *continuous* training program is that

10.____

A. employees may forget procedures that they have already learned
B. employees may develop short cuts on the job that result in inaccurate work
C. the job continues to change because of new procedures and equipment
D. training is one means of measuring effectiveness and productivity on the job

11. In training a new employee, it is usually advisable to break down the job into meaningful parts and have the new employee master one part before going on to the next.
Of the following, the *BEST* reason for using this technique is to

11.____

A. let the new employee know the reason for what he is doing and thus encourage him to remain in the unit
B. make the employee aware of the importance of the work and encourage him to work harder
C. show the employee that the work is easy so that he will be encouraged to work faster
D. make it more likely that the employee will experience success and will be encouraged to continue learning the job

12. You may occasionally find a serious error in the work of one of your subordinates.
Of the following, the *BEST* time to discuss such an error with an employee *usually* is

12.____

A. immediately after the error is found
B. after about two weeks, since you will also be able to point out some good things that the employee has accomplished
C. when you have discovered a pattern of errors on the part of this employee so that he will not be able to dispute your criticism
D. after the error results in a complaint by your own supervisor

13. For very important announcements to the staff, a supervisor should usually use both writ-   13.___
ten and oral communications. For example, when a new procedure is to be introduced,
the supervisor can more easily obtain the group's acceptance by giving his subordinates
a rough draft of the new procedure and calling a meeting of all his subordinates. The
LEAST important benefit of this technique is that it will better enable the supervisor to

    A. explain why the change is necessary
    B. make adjustments in the new procedure to meet valid staff objections
    C. assign someone to carry out the new procedure
    D. answer questions about the new procedure

14. Assume that, while you are interviewing an individual to obtain information, the individual   14.___
pauses in the middle of an answer.
The *BEST* of the following actions for you to take at that time is to

    A. correct any inaccuracies in what he has said
    B. remain silent until he continues
    C. explain your position on the matter being discussed
    D. explain that time is short and that he must complete his story quickly

15. When you are interviewing someone to obtain information, the *BEST* of the following rea-   15.___
sons for you to repeat certain of his exact words is to

    A. assure him that appropriate action will be taken
    B. encourage him to switch to another topic of discussion
    C. assure him that you agree with his point of view
    D. encourage him to elaborate on a point he has made

16. Generally, when writing a letter, the use of precise words and concise sentences is   16.___

    A. *good,* because less time will be required to write the letter
    B. *bad,* because it is most likely that the reader will think the letter is unimportant and
will not respond favorably
    C. *good,* because it is likely that your desired meaning will be conveyed to the reader
    D. *bad,* because your letter will be too brief to provide adequate information

17. In which of the following cases would it be *MOST* desirable to have *two* cards for one   17.___
individual in a *single* alphabetic file? The individual has

    A. a hyphenated surname   B. two middle names
    C. a first name with an unusual spelling
    D. a compound first name

18. Of the following, it is *MOST* appropriate to use a form letter when it is necessary to   18.___
answer many

    A. requests or inquiries from a single individual
    B. follow-up letters from individuals requesting additional information
    C. requests or inquiries about a single subject
    D. complaints from individuals that they have been unable to obtain various types of
information

19. Assume that you are asked to make up a budget for your section for the coming year, and you are told that the most important function of the budget is its "control function."
Of the following, "control" in this context implies, *most nearly,* that

19.____

    A. you will probably be asked to justify expenditures in any category when it looks as though these expenditures are departing greatly from the amount budgeted
    B. your section will probably not be allowed to spend more than the budgeted amount in any given category, although it is always permissible to spend less
    C. your section will be required to spend the exact amount budgeted in every category
    D. the budget will be filed in the Office of the Comptroller so that when the year is over the actual expenditures can be compared with the amounts in the budget

20. In writing a report, the practice of taking up the *least* important points *first* and the *most* important points *last* is a

20.____

    A. *good technique* since the final points made in a report will make the greatest impression on the reader
    B. *good technique* since the material is presented in a more logical manner and will lead directly to the conclusions
    C. *poor technique* since the reader's time is wasted by having to review irrelevant information before finishing the report
    D. *poor technique* since it may cause the reader to lose interest in the report and arrive at incorrect conclusions about the report

21. Typically, when the technique of "supervision by results" is practiced, higher management sets down, either implicitly or explicitly, certain performance standards or goals that the subordinate is expected to meet. So long as these standards are met, management interferes very little.
The *most likely* result of the use of this technique is that it will

21.____

    A. lead to ambiguity in terms of goals
    B. be successful only to the extent that close direct supervision is practiced
    C. make it possible to evaluate both employee and supervisory effectiveness
    D. allow for complete dependence on the subordinate's part

22. When making written evaluations and reviews of the performance of subordinates, it is *usually ADVISABLE* to

22.____

    A. avoid informing the employee of the evaluation if it is critical because it may create hard feelings
    B. avoid informing the employee of the evaluation whether critical or favorable because it is tension-producing
    C. to permit the employee to see the evaluation but not to discuss it with him because the supervisor cannot be certain where the discussion might lead
    D. to discuss the evaluation openly with the employee because it helps the employee understand what is expected of him

23. There are a number of well-known and respected human relations principles that successful supervisors have been using for years in building good relationships with their employees. Which of the following does *NOT* illustrate such a principle?

23.____

115

A. Give clear and complete instructions
B. Let each person know how he is getting along
C. Keep an open-door policy
D. Make all relationships personal ones

24. Assume that it is necessary for you to give an unpleasant assignment to one of your sub-   24.____
ordinates. You expect this employee to raise some objections to this assignment.
The *most appropriate of* the following actions for you to take *FIRST* is to issue the
assignment

A. *orally,* with the further statement that you will not listen to any complaints
B. *in writing,* to forestall any complaints by the employee
C. *orally,* permitting the employee to express his feelings
D. *in writing,* with a note that any comments should be submitted in writing

25. Suppose you have just announced at a staff meeting with your subordinates that a radi-   25.____
cal reorganization of work will take place next week. Your subordinates at the meeting
appear to be excited, tense, and worried.
Of the following, the *BEST* action for you to take at that time is to

A. schedule private conferences with each subordinate to obtain his reaction to the
meeting
B. close the meeting and tell your subordinates to return immediately to their work
assignments
C. give your subordinates some time to ask questions and discuss your announcement
D. insist that your subordinates do not discuss your announcement among themselves or with other members of the agency

---

KEY (CORRECT ANSWERS)

1.	C		11.	D
2.	A		12.	A
3.	C		13.	C
4.	B		14.	B
5.	D		15.	D
6.	D		16.	C
7.	B		17.	A
8.	A		18.	C
9.	B		19.	A
10.	D		20.	D

21.	C
22.	D
23.	D
24.	C
25.	C

TEST 2

DIRECTIONS: Each question or incomplete statement is followed by several suggested answers or completions. Select the one that *BEST* answer the question or completes the statement. *PRINT THE LETTER OF THE CORRECT ANSWER IN THE SPACE AT THE RIGHT.*

1. Of the following, the *BEST* way for a supervisor to increase employees' interest in their work is to   1.____

    A. allow them to make as many decisions as possible
    B. demonstrate to them that he is as technically competent as they
    C. give each employee a difficult assignment
    D. promptly convey to them instructions from higher manage-ment

2. The *one* of the following which is *LEAST* important in maintaining a high level of produc-tivity on the part of employees is the   2.____

    A. provision of optimum physical working conditions for employees
    B. strength of employees' aspirations for promotion
    C. anticipated satisfactions which employees hope to derive from their work
    D. employees' interest in their jobs

3. Of the following, the *MAJOR* advantage of group problem-solving, as compared to indi-vidual problem-solving, is that groups will *more readily*   3.____

    A. abide by their own decisions
    B. agree with agency management
    C. devise new policies and procedures
    D. reach conclusions sooner

4. The group problem-solving conference is a useful supervisory method for getting people to reach solutions to problems.
Of the following the *reason* that groups usually reach more realistic solutions than do individuals is that   4.____

    A. individuals, as a rule, take longer than do groups in reaching decisions and are therefore more likely to make an error
    B. bringing people together to let them confer impresses participants with the serious-ness of problems
    C. groups are generally more concerned with the future in evaluating organizational problems
    D. the erroneous opinions of group members tend to be corrected by the other mem-bers

5. A competent supervisor should be able to distinguish between human and technical problems.
Of the following, the *MAJOR* difference between such problems is that serious human problems, in comparison to ordinary technical problems,   5.____

    A. are remedied more quickly
    B. involve a lesser need for diagnosis
    C. are more difficult to define
    D. become known through indications which are usually the actual problem

6. Of the following, the *BEST* justification for a public agency establishing an alcoholism program for its employees is that

    A. alcoholism has traditionally been looked upon with a certain amused tolerance by management and thereby ignored as a serious illness
    B. employees with drinking problems have twice as many on-the-job accidents, especially during the early years of the problem
    C. excessive use of alcohol is associated with personality instability hindering informal social relationships among peers and subordinates
    D. the agency's public reputation will suffer despite an employee's drinking problem being a personal matter of little public concern

6.___

7. Assume you are a manager and you find a group of maintenance employees assigned to your project drinking and playing cards for money in an incinerator room after their regular working hours.
The one of the following actions it would be *BEST* for you to take is to

    A. suspend all employees immediately if there is no question in your mind as to the validity of the charges
    B. review the personnel records of those involved with the supervisor and make a joint decision on which employees should sustain penalties of loss of annual leave or fines
    C. ask the supervisor to interview each violator and submit written reports to you and thereafter consult with the supervisor about disciplinary actions
    D. deduct three days of annual leave from each employee involved if he pleads guilty in lieu of facing more serious charges

7.___

8. Assume that as a manager you must discipline a subordinate, but all of the pertinent facts necessary for a full determination of the appropriate disciplinary action to take are not yet available. However, you fear that a delay in disciplinary action may damage the morale of other employees.
The one of the following which is *MOST* appropriate for you to do in this matter is to

    A. take immediate disciplinary action as if all the pertinent facts were available
    B. wait until all the pertinent facts are available before reaching a decision
    C. inform the subordinate that you know he is guilty, issue a stern warning, and then let him wait for your further act ion
    D. reduce the severity of the discipline appropriate for the violation

8.___

9. There are two standard dismissal procedures utilized by most public agencies. The first is the "open back door" policy, in which the decision of a supervisor in discharging an employee for reasons of inefficiency cannot be cancelled by the central personnel agency. The second is the "closed back door" policy, in which the central personnel agency can order the supervisor to restore the discharged employee to his position.
Of the following, the *major DISADVANTAGE* of the "closed back door" policy as opposed to the "open back door" policy is that central personnel agencies are

    A. likely to approve the dismissal of employees when there is inadequate justification
    B. likely to revoke dismissal actions out of sympathy for employees
    C. less qualified than employing agencies to evaluate the efficiency of employees
    D. easily influenced by political, religious, and racial factors

9.___

10. The one of the following for which a formal grievance-handling system is *LEAST* useful is in

    A. reducing the frequency of employee complaints
    B. diminishing the likelihood of arbitrary action by supervisors
    C. providing an outlet for employee frustrations
    D. bringing employee problems to the attention of higher management

10.____

11. The one of the following managers whose leadership style involves the *GREATEST* delegation of authority to subordinates is the one who presents to subordinates

    A. his ideas and invites questions
    B. his decision and persuades them to accept it
    C. the problem, gets their suggestions, and makes his decision
    D. a tentative decision which is subject to change

11.____

12. Which of the following is *most likely* to cause employee productivity standards to be set too high?

    A. Standards of productivity are set by first-line supervisors rather than by higher-level managers.
    B. Employees' opinions about productivity standards are sought through written questionnaires.
    C. Initial studies concerning productivity are conducted by staff specialists.
    D. Ideal work conditions assumed in the productivity standards are lacking in actual operations.

12.____

13. The one of the following which states the *MAIN* value of an organization chart for a manager is that such charts show the

    A. lines of formal authority
    B. manner in which duties are performed by each employee
    C. flow of work among employees on the same level
    D. specific responsibilities of each position

13.____

14. Which of the following *BEST* names the usual role of a line unit with regard to the organization's programs?

    A. Seeking publicity   B. Developing
    C. Carrying out   D. Evaluating

14.____

15. Critics of promotion *from within* a public agency argue for hiring *from outside* the agency because they believe that promotion from within leads to

    A. resentment and consequent weakened morale on the part of those not promoted
    B. the perpetuation of outdated practices and policies
    C. a more complex hiring procedure than hiring from outside the agency
    D. problems of objectively appraising someone already in the organization

15.____

16. The one of the following management functions which *usually* can be handled *MOST* effectively by a committee is the

    A. settlement of interdepartmental disputes
    B. planning of routine work schedules
    C. dissemination of information
    D. assignment of personnel

16.____

17. Assume that you are serving on a committee which is considering proposals in order to recommend a new maintenance policy. After eliminating a number of proposals by unanimous consent, the committee is deadlocked on three proposals.
The one of the following which is the BEST way for the committee to reach agreement on a proposal they could recommend is to

    A. consider and vote on each proposal separately by secret ballot
    B. examine and discuss the three proposals until the proponents of two of them are persuaded they are wrong
    C. reach a synthesis which incorporates the significant features of each proposal
    D. discuss the three proposals until the proponents of each one concede those aspects of the proposals about which there is disagreement

17.___

18. A commonly used training and development method for professional staff is the case method, which utilizes the description of a situation, real or simulated, to provide a common base for analysis, discussion, and problem-solving.
Of the following, the MOST appropriate time to use the case method is when professional staff needs

    A. insight into their personality problems
    B. practice in applying management concepts to their own problems
    C. practical experience in the assignment of delegated responsibilities
    D. to know how to function in many different capacities

18.___

19. The incident process is a training and development method in which trainees are given a very brief statement of an event or of a situation presenting a job incident or an employee problem of special significance.
Of the following, it is MOST appropriate to use the incident process when

    A. trainees need to learn to review and analyze facts before solving a problem
    B. there are a large number of trainees who require the same information
    C. there are too many trainees to carry on effective discussion
    D. trainees are not aware of the effect of their behavior on others

19.___

20. The one of the following types of information about which a new clerical employee is usually LEAST concerned during the orientation process is

    A. his specific job duties   B. where he will work
    C. his organization's history   D. who his associates will be

20.___

21. The one of the following which is the MOST important limitation on the degree to which work should be broken down into specialized tasks is the point at which

    A. there ceases to be sufficient work of a specialized nature to occupy employees
    B. training costs equal the half-yearly savings derived from further specialization
    C. supervision of employees performing specialized tasks becomes more technical than supervision of general employees
    D. it becomes more difficult to replace the specialist than to replace the generalist who performs a complex set of functions

21.___

22. When a supervisor is asked for his opinion of the suitability for promotion of a subordi-   22.____
    nate, the supervisor is actually being asked to predict the subordinate's future behavior in
    a new role.
    Such a prediction is *most likely* to be accurate if the

    A. higher position is similar to the subordinate's current one
    B. higher position requires intangible personal qualities
    C. new position requires a high intellectual level of performance
    D. supervisor has had little personal association with the subordinate away from the
       job

23. In one form of the non-directive evaluation interview the supervisor communicates his   23.____
    evaluation to the employee and then listens to the employee's response without making
    further suggestions.
    The one of the following which is the *PRINCIPAL* danger of this method of evaluation is
    that the employee is most likely to

    A. develop an indifferent attitude towards the supervisor
    B. fail to discover ways of improving his performance
    C. become resistant to change in the organization's structure
    D. place the blame for his shortcomings on his co-workers

24. In establishing rules for his subordinates, a superior should be *PRIMARILY* concerned   24.____
    with

    A. creating sufficient flexibility to allow for exceptions
    B. making employees aware of the reasons for the rules and the penalties for infrac-
       tions
    C. establishing the strength of his own position in relation to his subordinates
    D. having his subordinates know that such rules will be imposed in a personal manner

25. The practice of conducting staff training sessions on a periodic basis is *generally* consid-   25.____
    ered

    A. *poor;* it takes employees away from their work assignments
    B. *poor;* all staff training should be done on an individual basis
    C. *good;* it permits the regular introduction of new methods and techniques
    D. *good;* it ensures a high employee productivity rate

KEY (CORRECT ANSWERS)

1.	A	11.	C
2.	A	12.	D
3.	A	13.	A
4.	D	14.	C
5.	C	15.	B
6.	B	16.	A
7.	C	17.	C
8.	B	18.	B
9.	C	19.	A
10.	A	20.	C

21.	A
22.	A
23.	B
24.	B
25.	C

EXAMINATION SECTION
TEST 1

DIRECTIONS: Each question or incomplete statement is followed by several suggested answers or completions. Select the one that BEST answers the question or completes the statement. *PRINT THE LETTER OF THE CORRECT ANSWER IN THE SPACE AT THE RIGHT.*

1. The one of the following which is the CHIEF reason for the difference between the administration of justice agencies and that of other units in public administration is that
    1.____

    A. correctional institutions are concerned with security
    B. some defendants are proven to be innocent after trial
    C. the administration of justice is much more complicated than other aspects of public administration
    D. correctional institutions produce services their *clients* or *customers* fail to understand or ask for

2. Of the following, the MOST important reason why employees resist change is that
    2.____

    A. they have not received adequate training in preparation for the change
    B. experience has shown that when new ideas don't work, employees get blamed and not the individuals responsible for the new ideas
    C. new ideas and methods almost always represent a threat to the security of the individuals involved
    D. new ideas often are not practical and disrupt operations unnecessarily

3. Stress situations are ideal for building up a backlog of knowledge about an employee's behavior. Not only does it inform the supervisor of many aspects of a person's behavior patterns, but it is also vitally important to have foreknowledge of how people behave under stress.
The one of the following which is NOT implied by this passage is that
    3.____

    A. a person under stress may give some indication of his unsuitability for work in an institution
    B. putting people under stress is the best means of determining their usual patterns of behavior
    C. stress situations may give important clues about performance in the service
    D. there is a need to know about a person's reaction to situations *when the chips are down*

4. There are situations requiring a supervisor to give direct orders to subordinates assigned to work under the direct control of other supervisors.
Under which of the following conditions would this shift of command responsibility be MOST appropriate?
    4.____

    A. Emergency operations require the cooperative action of two or more organizational units.
    B. One of the other supervisors is not doing his job, thus defeating the goals of the organization.
    C. The subordinates are performing their assigned tasks in the absence of their own supervisor.
    D. The subordinates ask a superior officer who is not their own supervisor how to perform an assignment given them by their supervisor.

5. The one of the following which BEST differentiates staff supervision from line supervision is that   5.___

    A. staff supervision has the authority to immediately correct a line subordinate's action
    B. staff supervision is an advisory relationship
    C. line supervision goes beyond the normal boundaries of direct supervision within a *command*
    D. line supervision does not report findings and make recommendations

6. Decision-making is a rational process calling for a *suspended judgment* by the supervisor until all the facts have been ascertained and analyzed, and the consequences of alternative courses of action studied; *then* the decision maker   6.___

    A. acts as both judge and jury and selects what he believes to be the best of the alternative plans
    B. consults with those who will be most directly involved to obtain a recommendation as to the most appropriate course of action
    C. reviews the facts which he has already analyzed, reduces his thoughts to writing, and selects that course of action which can have the fewest negative consequences if his thinking contains an error
    D. stops, considers the matter for at least a 24-hour period, before referring it to a superior for evaluation

7. Decision-making can be defined as the   7.___

    A. delegation of authority and responsibility to persons capable of performing their assigned duties with moderate or little supervision
    B. imposition of a supervisor's decision upon a work group
    C. technique of selecting the course of action with the most desired consequences, and the least undesired or unexpected consequences
    D. process principally concerned with improvement of procedures

8. A supervisor who is not well-motivated and has no desire to accept basic responsibilities will   8.___

    A. compromise to the extent of permitting poor performance for lengthy periods without correction
    B. get good performance from his work group if the employees are satisfied with their pay and other working conditions
    C. not have marginal workers in his work group if the work is interesting
    D. perform adequately as long as the work of his group consists of routine operations

9. A supervisor is more than a bond or connecting link between two levels of employees. He has joint responsibility which must be shared with both management and with the work group.
Of the following, the item which BEST expresses the meaning of this statement is:

    A. A supervisor works with both management and the work group and must reconcile the differences between them.
    B. In management, the supervisor is solely concerned with efforts directing the work of his subordinates.
    C. The supervisory role is basically that of a liaison man between management and the work force.
    D. What a supervisor says and does when confronted with day-to-day problems depends upon his level in the organization.

9.____

10. Operations research is the observation of operations in business or government, and it utilizes both hypotheses and controlled experiments to determine the outcome of decisions. In effect, it reproduces the future impact on the decision in a clinical environment suited to intensive study.
Operations research has

    A. been more promising than applied research in the ascertaining of knowledge for the purpose of decision-making
    B. never been amenable to fact analysis on the grand scale
    C. not been used extensively in government
    D. proven to be the only rational and logical approach to decision-making on long-range problems

10.____

11. Assume that a civilian makes a complaint regarding the behavior of a certain worker to the supervisor of the worker. The supervisor regards the complaint as unjustified and unreasonable.
In these circumstances, the supervisor

    A. must make a written note of the complaint and forward it through channels to the unit or individual responsible for complaint investigations
    B. should assure the complainant that disciplinary action will be appropriate to the seriousness of the alleged offense
    C. should immediately summon the worker if he is available so that the latter may attempt to straighten out the difficulty
    D. should inform the complainant that his complaint appears to be unjustified and unreasonable

11.____

12. Modern management usually establishes a personal history folder for an employee at the time of hiring. Disciplinary matters appear in such personal history folders. Employees do not like the idea of disciplinary actions appearing in their permanent personal folders.
Authorities believe that

    A. after a few years have passed since the commission of the infraction, disciplinary actions should be removed from folders
    B. disciplinary actions should remain in folders; it is not the records but the use of records that requires detailed study
    C. most personnel have not had disciplinary action taken against them and would resent the removal of disciplinary actions from such folders
    D. there is no point in removing disciplinary actions from personal history folders since employees who have been guilty of infractions should not be allowed to forget their infractions

12.____

13. While supervisors should not fear the acceptance of responsibility, they 　　　13.__

    A. generally seek out responsibility that subordinates should exercise, particularly when the supervisors do not have sufficient work to do
    B. must be on guard against the abuse of authority that often accompanies the acceptance of total responsibility
    C. should avoid responsibility that is customarily exercised by their superiors
    D. who are anxious for promotions accept responsibility but do not exercise the authority warranted by the responsibility

14. Planning is part of the decision-making process. By planning is meant the development 　　　14.__
of details of alternative plans of action.
The key to *effective* planning is

    A. careful research to determine whether a tentative plan has been tried at some time in the past
    B. participation by employees in planning, preferably those employees who will be involved in putting the selected plan into action
    C. speed; poor plans can be discarded after they are put into effect while good plans usually are not put into effect because of delays
    D. writing the plan up in considerable detail and then forwarding the plan, through channels, to the executive officer having final approval of the plan

15. Equating strict discipline with punitive measures and lax discipline with rehabilitation creates a false dichotomy. The one of the statements given below that would BEST follow from the belief expressed in this statement is that discipline 　　　15.__

    A. is important for treatment
    B. militates against treatment programs
    C. is not an important consideration in institutions where effective rehabilitation programs prevail
    D. minimizes the need for punitive measures if it is strict

16. If training starts at the lower level of command, it is like planting a seed in tilled ground but removing the sun and rain. Seeds cannot grow unless they have help from above. Of the following, the MOST appropriate conclusion to be drawn from this statement is that 　　　16.__

    A. the head of an institution may not delegate authority for the planning of an institutional training program for staff
    B. on-the-job training is better than formalized training courses
    C. regularly scheduled training courses must be planned in advance
    D. staff training is the responsibility of higher levels of command

17. The one of the following that BEST describes the meaning of *in-service staff training* is: 　　　17.__

    A. The training of personnel who are below average in performance
    B. The training given to each employee throughout his employment
    C. The training of staff only in their own specialized fields
    D. Classroom training where the instructor and employees develop a positive and productive relationship leading to improved efficiency on the job

18. All bureau personnel should be concerned about, and involved in, public relations.   18.____
    Of the following, the MOST important reason for this statement is that

    A. an institution is an agency of the government supported by public funds and
       responsible to the public
    B. institutions are places of public business and, therefore, the public is interested in
       them
    C. some personnel need publicity in order to advance
    D. personnel sometimes need publicity in order to ensure that their grievances are
       acted upon by higher authority

19. The MOST important factor in establishing a disciplinary policy in an organization is   19.____

    A. consistency of application
    B. strict supervisors
    C. strong enforcement
    D. the degree of toughness or laxity

20. The FIRST step in planning a program is to   20.____

    A. clearly define the objectives
    B. estimate the costs
    C. hire a program director
    D. solicit funds

21. The PRIMARY purpose of control in an organization is to   21.____

    A. punish those who do not do their job well
    B. get people to do what is necessary to achieve an objective
    C. develop clearly stated rules and regulations
    D. regulate expenditures

22. The UNDERLYING principle of *sound* administration is to   22.____

    A. base administration on investigation of facts
    B. have plenty of resources available
    C. hire a strong administrator
    D. establish a broad policy

23. An IMPORTANT aspect to keep in mind during the decision-making process is that   23.____

    A. all possible alternatives for attaining goals should be sought out and considered
    B. considering various alternatives only leads to confusion
    C. once a decision has been made, it cannot be retracted
    D. there is only one correct method to reach any goal

24. Implementation of accountability requires   24.____

    A. a leader who will not hesitate to take punitive action
    B. an established system of communication from the bottom to the top
    C. explicit directives from leaders
    D. too much expense to justify it

25. The CHIEF danger of a decentralized control system is that   25.___

    A. excessive reports and communications will be generated
    B. problem areas may not be detected readily
    C. the expense will become prohibitive
    D. this will result in too many *chiefs*

———

KEY (CORRECT ANSWERS)

1.	D		11.	D
2.	C		12.	A
3.	B		13.	B
4.	A		14.	B
5.	B		15.	A
6.	A		16.	D
7.	C		17.	B
8.	A		18.	A
9.	A		19.	A
10.	C		20.	A

21.	B
22.	A
23.	A
24.	B
25.	B

———

TEST 2

DIRECTIONS: Each question or incomplete statement is followed by several suggested answers or completions. Select the one that BEST answers the question or completes the statement. *PRINT THE LETTER OF THE CORRECT ANSWER IN THE SPACE AT THE RIGHT.*

1. When giving orders to his subordinates, a certain supervisor often includes information as to why the work is necessary.
   This approach by the supervisor is *generally*

   A. *inadvisable,* since it appears that he is avoiding responsibility and wishes to blame his superiors
   B. *inadvisable,* since it creates the impression that he is trying to impress the subordinates with his importance
   C. *advisable,* since it serves to motivate the subordinates by giving them a reason for wanting to do the work
   D. *advisable,* since it shows that he is knowledgeable and is in control of his assignments

   1.____

2. Some supervisors often ask capable, professional subordinates to get some work done with questions such as: *Mary, would you try to complete that work today?*
   The use of such request orders *usually*

   A. gets results which are as good as or better than results from direct orders
   B. shows the supervisor to be weak and lowers the respect of his subordinates
   C. provokes resentment as compared to the use of direct orders
   D. leads to confusion as to the proper procedure to follow when carrying out orders

   2.____

3. Assume that a supervisor, because of an emergency when time was essential, and in the absence of his immediate superior, went out of the chain of command to get a decision from a higher level.
   It would consequently be MOST appropriate for the immediate superior to

   A. reprimand him for his action, since the long-range consequences are far more detrimental than the immediate gain
   B. encourage him to use this method, since the chain of command is an outmoded and discredited system which inhibits productive work
   C. order him to refrain from any repetition of this action in the future
   D. support him as long as he informed the superior of the action at the earliest opportunity

   3.____

4. A supervisor gave instructions which he knew were somewhat complex to a subordinate. He then asked the subordinate to repeat the instructions to him.
   The supervisor's decision to have the subordinate repeat the instructions was

   A. *good practice,* mainly because the subordinate would realize the importance of carefully following instructions
   B. *poor practice,* mainly because the supervisor should have given the employee time to ponder the instructions, and then, if necessary, to ask questions
   C. *good practice,* mainly because the supervisor could see whether the subordinate had any apparent problem in understanding the instructions
   D. *poor practice,* mainly because the subordinate should not be expected to have the same degree of knowledge as the supervisor

   4.____

5. Supervisors and subordinates must successfully communicate with each other in order to work well together.
   Which of the following statements concerning communication of this type is COR-RECT?

    A. When speaking to his subordinates, a supervisor should make every effort to appear knowledgeable about all aspects of their work.
    B. Written communications should be prepared by the supervisor at his own level of comprehension.
    C. The average employee tends to give meaning to communication according to his personal interpretation.
    D. The effective supervisor communicates as much information as he has available to anyone who is interested.

    5._

6. A supervisor should be aware of situations in which it is helpful to put his orders to his subordinates in writing.
   Which of the following situations would MOST likely call for a WRITTEN order rather than an ORAL order? The order

    A. gives complicated instructions which vary from ordinary practice
    B. involves the performance of duties for which the subordinate is responsible
    C. directs subordinates to perform duties similar to those which they performed in the recent past
    D. concerns a matter that must be promptly completed or dealt with

    6._

7. Assume that a supervisor discovers that a false rumor about possible layoffs has spread among his subordinates through the grapevine.
   Of the following, the BEST way for the supervisor to deal with this situation is to

    A. use the grapevine to leak accurate information
    B. call a meeting to provide information and to answer questions
    C. post a notice on the bulletin board denying the rumor
    D. institute procedures designed to eliminate the grapevine

    7._

8. Communications in an organization with many levels becomes subject to different inter-pretations at each level and have a tendency to become distorted. The more levels there are in an organization, the greater the likelihood that the final recipient of a communica-tion will get the wrong message.
   The one of the following statements which BEST supports the foregoing viewpoint is:

    A. Substantial communications problems exist at high management levels in organi-zations.
    B. There is a relationship in an organization between the number of hierarchical levels and interference with communications.
    C. An opportunity should be given to subordinates at all levels to communicate their views with impunity.
    D. In larger organizations, there tends to be more interference with downward com-munications than with upward communications.

    8._

9. A subordinate comes to you, his supervisor, to ask a detailed question about a new agency directive; however, you do not know the answer.
   Of the following, the MOST helpful response to give the subordinate is to

   A. point out that since your own supervisor has failed to keep you informed of this matter, it is probably unimportant
   B. give the most logical interpretation you can, based on your best judgment
   C. ask him to raise the question with other supervisors until he finds one who knows the answer, then let you know also
   D. explain that you do not know and assure him that you will get the information for him

9.____

10. The traditional view of management theory is that communication in an organization should follow the table of organization. A newer theory holds that timely communication often requires bypassing certain steps in the hierarchical chain.
    However, the MAIN advantage of using formal channels of communication within an organization is that

    A. an employee is thereby restricted in his relationships to his immediate superior and his immediate subordinates
    B. information is thereby transmitted to everyone who should be informed
    C. the organization will have an appeal channel, or a mechanism by which subordinates can go over their superior's head
    D. employees are thereby encouraged to exercise individual initiative

10.____

11. It is unfair to hold subordinates responsible for the performance of duties for which they do not have the requisite authority.
    When this is done, it violates the principle that

    A. responsibility *cannot be greater* than that implied by delegated authority
    B. responsibility *should be greater* than that implied by delegated authority
    C. authority *cannot be greater* than that implied by delegated responsibility
    D. authority *should be greater* than that implied by delegated responsibility

11.____

12. Assume that a supervisor wishes to delegate some tasks to a capable subordinate.
    It would be MOST in keeping with the principles of delegation for the supervisor to

    A. ask another supervisor who is experienced in the delegated tasks to evaluate the subordinate's work from time to time
    B. monitor continually the subordinate's performance by carefully reviewing his work at every step
    C. request experienced employees to submit peer ratings of the work of the subordinate
    D. tell the subordinates what problems are likely to be encountered and specify which problems to report on

12.____

13. There are *three* types of leadership: *autocratic,* in which the leader makes the decisions   13.___
and seeks compliance from his subordinates; *democratic,* in which the leader consults
with his subordinates and lets them help set policy; and *free rein,* in which the leader acts
as an information center and exercises minimum control over his subordinates.
A supervisor can be MOST effective if he decides to

    A.   use democratic leadership techniques exclusively
    B.   avoid the use of autocratic leadership techniques entirely
    C.   employ the three types of leadership according to the situation
    D.   rely mainly on autocratic leadership techniques

14. During a busy period of work, Employee A asked his supervisor for leave in order to take   14.___
an ordinary vacation. The supervisor denied the request. The following day, Employee B
asked for leave during the same period because his wife had just gone to the hospital for
an indeterminate stay and he had family matters to tend to.
Of the following, the BEST way for the supervisor to deal with Employee B's request is
to

    A.   grant the request and give the reason to the other employee
    B.   suggest that the employee make his request to higher management
    C.   delay the request immediately since granting it would show favoritism
    D.   defer any decision until the duration of the hospital stay is determined

15. Assume that you are a supervisor and that a subordinate tells you he has a grievance.   15.___
In general, you should FIRST

    A.   move the grievance forward in order to get a prompt decision
    B.   discourage this type of behavior on the part of subordinates
    C.   attempt to settle the grievance
    D.   refer the subordinate to the personnel office

16. A supervisor may have available a large variety of rewards he can use to motivate his   16.___
subordinates. However, some supervisors choose the wrong rewards.
A supervisor is *most likely* to make such a mistake if he

    A.   appeals to a subordinate's desire to be well regarded by his co-workers
    B.   assumes that the subordinate's goals and preferences are the same as his own
    C.   conducts in-depth discussions with a subordinate in order to discover his prefer-
ence
    D.   limits incentives to those rewards which he is authorized to provide or to recom-
mend

17. Employee performance appraisal is open to many kinds of errors.   17.___
When a supervisor is preparing such an appraisal, he is *most likely* to commit an error
if

    A.   employees are indifferent to the consequences of their performance appraisals
    B.   the entire period for which the evaluation is being made is taken into consideration
    C.   standard measurement criteria are used as performance benchmarks
    D.   personal characteristics of employees which are not job-related are given weight

18. Assume that a supervisor finds that a report prepared by an employee is unsatisfactory   18.____
and should be done over. Which of the following should the supervisor do?

    A. Give the report to another employee who can complete it properly.
    B. Have the report done over by the same employee after successfully training him.
    C. Hold a meeting to train all the employees so as not to single out the employee who
performed unsatisfactorily
    D. Accept the report so as not to discourage the employee and then make the correc-
tions himself.

19. Employees sometimes wish to have personal advice and counseling, in confidence,   19.____
about their job-related problems. These problems may include such concerns as health
matters, family difficulties, alcoholism, debts, emotional disturbances, etc.
Such assistance is BEST provided through

    A. maintenance of an exit interview program to find reasons for, and solutions to, turn-
over problems
    B. arrangements for employees to discuss individual problems informally outside nor-
mal administrative channels
    C. procedures which allow employees to submit anonymous inquiries to the person-
nel department
    D. special hearing committees consisting of top management in addition to immediate
supervisors

20. An employee is always a member of some unit of the formal organization. He may also   20.____
be a member of an informal work group.
With respect to employee productivity and job satisfaction, the informal work group can
MOST accurately be said to

    A. have no influence of any kind on its members
    B. influence its members negatively only
    C. influence its members positively only
    D. influence its members negatively or positively

21. In order to encourage employees to make suggestions, many public agencies have   21.____
employee suggestion programs.
What is the MAJOR benefit of such a program to the agency as a whole? It

    A. brings existing or future problems to management's attention
    B. reduces the number of minor accidents
    C. requires employees to share in decision-making responsibilities
    D. reveals employees who have inadequate job knowledge

22. Assume that you have been asked to interview a seemingly shy applicant for a temporary   22.____
position in your department .
For you to ask the kinds of questions that begin with *What, Where, Why, When,*
Who, and How, is

    A. *good practice* ; it informs the applicant that he must conform to the requirements of
the department
    B. *poor practice;* it exceeds the extent and purpose of an initial interview
    C. *good practice;* it encourages the applicant to talk to a greater extent
    D. *poor practice;* it encourages the applicant to dominate the discussion

23. In recent years, job enlargement or job enrichment has tended to replace job simplifica-   23.__
tion.
Those who advocate job enrichment or enlargement consider it *desirable* CHIEFLY
because

    A. it allows supervisors to control closely the activities of subordinates
    B. it produces greater job satisfaction through reduction of responsibility
    C. most employees prefer to avoid work which is new and challenging
    D. positions with routinized duties are unlikely to provide job satisfaction

24. Job rotation is a training method in which an employee temporarily changes places with   24.__
another employee of equal rank.
What is usually the MAIN purpose of job rotation? To

    A. politely remove the person being rotated from an unsuitable assignment
    B. increase skills and provide broader experience
    C. prepare the person being rotated for a permanent change
    D. test the skills of the person being rotated

25. There are several principles that a supervisor needs to know if he is to deal adequately   25.__
with his training responsibilities.
Which of the following is usually NOT a principle of training?

    A. People should be trained according to their individual needs.
    B. People can learn by being told or shown how to do work, but best of all by doing
work under guidance.
    C. People can be easily trained even if they have no desire to learn.
    D. Training should be planned, scheduled, executed, and evaluated systematically.

———

KEY (CORRECT ANSWERS)

1.	C		11.	A
2.	A		12.	D
3.	D		13.	C
4.	C		14.	A
5.	C		15.	C
6.	A		16.	B
7.	B		17.	D
8.	B		18.	B
9.	D		19.	B
10.	B		20.	D

21.	A
22.	C
23.	D
24.	B
25.	C

EXAMINATION SECTION
TEST 1

DIRECTIONS: Each question or incomplete statement is followed by several suggested answers or completions. Select the one that BEST answers the question or completes the statement. *PRINT THE LETTER OF THE CORRECT ANSWER IN THE SPACE AT THE RIGHT.*

1. At times there may be a conflict between employees' needs and agency goals. A supervisor's MAIN role in motivating employees in such circumstances is to try to   1.____

   A. develop good work habits among the employees whom he supervises
   B. emphasize the importance of material rewards such as merit increases
   C. keep careful records of employees' performance for possible disciplinary action
   D. reconcile employees' objectives with those of the public agency

2. Organizations cannot function effectively without policies. However, when an organization imposes excessively detailed policy restrictions, it is MOST likely to lead to   2.____

   A. conflicts among individual employees
   B. a lack of adequate supervision
   C. a reduction of employee initiative
   D. a reliance on punitive discipline

3. The PRIMARY responsibility for establishing good employee relations in the public service USUALLY rests with   3.____

   A. employees
   B. management
   C. civil service organizations
   D. employee organizations

4. At times, certain off-the-job conduct of public employees may be of concern to management. This concern stems from the fact that   4.____

   A. agency programs could be harmed by adverse publicity if employees' conduct is considered detrimental by the public
   B. fairness to all concerned is usually the major consideration in disciplinary cases
   C. public employees must meet higher standards than employees working in private industry
   D. public employees have high ethical standards and may participate in social action programs

5. At one time or another, most employees ask for, or expect, special treatment. For a supervisor faced with this problem, the one of the following which is the MOST valid guideline is: 5.____

   A. According to the rules, a supervisor must give identical treatment to all his subordinates, regardless of the circumstances.
   B. Although all employees have equal rights, it is sometimes necessary to give an employee special treatment to meet an individual need.
   C. It would damage morale if any employee were to receive special treatment, regardless of circumstances.
   D. Since each employee has different needs, there is little reason to maintain general rules.

6. Mental health problems exist in many parts of our society and may also be found in the work setting. The BASIC role of the supervisor in relation to the mental health problems of his subordinates is to

    A. restrict himself solely to the taking of disciplinary measures, if warranted, and follow up carefully
    B. avoid involvement in personal matters
    C. identify mental health problems as early as possible
    D. resolve mental health problems through personal counseling

6.__

7. Supervisory expectation of high levels of employee performance, where such performance is possible, is MOST likely to lead to employees'

    A. expecting frequent praise and encouragement
    B. gaining a greater sense of satisfaction
    C. needing less detailed instructions then previously
    D. reducing their quantitative output

7.__

8. In public agencies, as elsewhere, supervisors sometimes compete with one another to increase their units' productivity. Of the following, the MAJOR disadvantage of such competition, from the general viewpoint of providing good public service, is that

    A. while individual employee effort will increase, unit productivity will decrease
    B. employees will be discouraged from sincere interest in their work
    C. the supervisors' competition may hinder the achievement of agency goals
    D. total payroll costs will increase as the activities of each unit increase

8.__

9. If employees are motivated primarily by material compensation, the amount of effort an individual employee will put into performing his work effectively will depend MAINLY upon how he perceives

    A. cooperation to be tied to successful effort
    B. the association between good work and increased compensation
    C. the public status of his particular position
    D. the supervisor's behavior in work situations

9.__

10. Cash awards to individual employees are sometimes used to encourage useful suggestions. However, some management experts believe that awards should involve some form of employee recognition other than cash. Which of the following reasons BEST supports opposition to using cash as a reward for worthwhile suggestions?

    A. Cash awards cause employees to expend excessive time in making suggestions.
    B. Taxpayer opposition to cash awards has increased following generous salary increases for public employees in recent years.
    C. Public funds expended on awards lead to a poor image of public employees.
    D. The use of cash awards raises the problem of deciding tne monetary value of suggestions.

10.__

11. The BEST general rule for a supervisor to follow in giving praise and criticism is to

    A. criticize and praise publicly
    B. criticize publicly and praise privately
    C. praise and criticize privately
    D. praise publicly and criticize privately

11.__

12. An important step in designing an error-control policy is to determine the maximum num- 12.____
ber of errors that can be considered acceptable for the entire organization. Of the following, the MOST important factor in making such a decision is the

    A. number of clerical staff available to check for errors
    B. frequency of errors by supervisors
    C. human and material costs of errors
    D. number of errors that will become known to the public

13. When a supervisor tries to correct a situation where errors have been widespread, he 13.____
should concentrate his efforts, and those of the employees involved, on

    A. avoiding future mistakes   B. fixing appropriate blame
    C. preparing a written report   D. determining fair penalties

14. When delegating work to a subordinate, a supervisor should ALWAYS tell the subordi- 14.____
nate

    A. each step in the procedure for doing the work
    B. how much time to expend
    C. what is to be accomplished
    D. whether reports are necessary

15. The responsibilities of all employees should be clearly defined and understood. In addi- 15.____
tion, in order for employees to successfully fulfill their responsibilities, they should also
GENERALLY be given

    A. written directives   B. close supervision
    C. corresponding authority   D. daily instructions

16. The one of the following types of training in which positive transfer of training to the 16.____
actual work situation is MOST likely to take place is

    A. conference training   B. demonstration training
    C. classroom training   D. on-the-job training

17. The type of training or instruction in which the subject matter is presented in small units 17.____
called frames is known as

    A. programmed instruction   B. reinforcement
    C. remediation   D. skills training

18. In order to bring about maximum learning in a training situation, a supervisor acting as a 18.____
trainer should attempt to create a setting in which

    A. all trainees experience a large amount of failure as an incentive
    B. all trainees experience a small amount of failure as an incentive
    C. each trainee experiences approximately the same amounts of success and failure
    D. each trainee experiences as much success and as little failure as possible

19. Assume that, in a training course given by an agency, the instructor conducts a brief quiz, on paper, toward the close of each session. From the point of view of maximizing learning, it would be BEST for the instructor to

    A. wait until the last session to provide the correct answers
    B. give the correct answers aloud immediately after each quiz
    C. permit trainees to take the questions home with them so that they can look up the answers
    D. wait until the next session to provide the correct answers

19.___

20. A supervisor, in the course of evaluating employees, should ALWAYS determine whether

    A. employees realize that their work is under scrutiny
    B. the ratings will be included in permanent records
    C. employees meet standards of performance
    D. his statements on the rating form are similar to those made by the previous supervisor

20.___

21. All of the following are legitimate objectives of employee performance reporting systems EXCEPT

    A. serving as a check on personnel policies such as job qualification requirements and placement techniques
    B. determining who is the least efficient worker among a large number of employees
    C. improving employee performance by identifying strong and weak points in individual performance
    D. developing standards of satisfactory performance

21.___

22. Studies of existing employee performance evaluation schemes have revealed a common tendency to construct guides in order to measure inferred traits. Of the following, the BEST example of an inferred trait is

    A. appearance   B. loyalty   C. accuracy   D. promptness

22.___

23. Which of the following is MOST likely to be a positive influence in promoting common agreement at a staff conference?

    A. A mature, tolerant group of participants
    B. A strong chairman with firm opinions
    C. The normal differences of human personalities
    D. The urge to forcefully support one's views

23.___

24. Before holding a problem-solving conference, the conference leader sent to each invitee an announcement on which he listed the names of all invitees. His action in listing the names was

    A. *wise*, mainly because all invitees will know who has been invited, and can, if necessary, plan a proper approach
    B. *unwise*, mainly because certain invitees could form factions prior to the conference
    C. *unwise*, mainly because invitees might come to the conference in a belligerent mood if they had had interpersonal conflicts with other invitees
    D. *wise*, mainly because invitees who are antagonistic to each other could decide not to attend

24.___

140

25. Methods analysis is a detailed study of existing or proposed work methods for the pur-   25.____
    pose of improving agency operations. Of the following, it is MOST accurate to say that
    this type of study

    A.   can sometimes be made informally by the experienced supervisor who can identify
    problems and suggest solutions
    B.   is not suitable for studying the operations of a public agency
    C.   will be successfully accomplished only if an outside organization reviews agency
    operations
    D.   usually costs more to complete than is justified by the potential economies to be
    realized

————

KEY (CORRECT ANSWERS)

1.	D		11.	D
2.	C		12.	C
3.	B		13.	A
4.	A		14.	C
5.	B		15.	C
6.	C		16.	D
7.	B		17.	A
8.	C		18.	D
9.	B		19.	B
10.	D		20.	C

21.	B
22.	B
23.	A
24.	A
25.	A

————

TEST 2

DIRECTIONS: Each question or incomplete statement is followed by several suggested answers or completions. Select the one that BEST answers the question or completes the statement. *PRINT THE LETTER OF THE CORRECT ANSWER IN THE SPACE AT THE RIGHT.*

1. Present-day managerial practices advocate that adequate hierarchical levels of communication be maintained among all levels of management. Of the following, the BEST way to accomplish this is with   1.__

   A. interdepartmental memoranda only
   B. interdepartmental memoranda only
   C. periodic staff meetings, interdepartmental and interdepartmental memoranda
   D. interdepartmental and interdepartmental memoranda

2. It is generally agreed upon that it is important to have effective communications in the unit so that everyone knows exactly what is expected of him. Of the following, the communications system which can assist in fulfilling this objective BEST is one which consists of   2.__

   A. written policies and procedures for administrative functions and verbal policies and procedures for professional functions
   B. written policies and procedures for professional and administrative functions
   C. verbal policies and procedures for professional and administrative functions
   D. verbal policies and procedures for professional functions

3. If a department manager wishes to build an effective department, he MOST generally must   3.__

   A. be able to hire and fire as he feels necessary
   B. consider the total aspects of his job, his influence and the effects of his decisions
   C. have access to reasonable amounts of personnel and money with which to build his programs
   D. attend as many professional conferences as possible so that he can keep up-to-date with all the latest advances in the field

4. Of the following, the factor which generally contributes MOST effectively to the performance of the unit is that the supervisor   4.__

   A. personally inspect the work of all employees
   B. fill orders at a faster rate than his subordinates
   C. have an exact knowledge of theory
   D. implement a program of professional development for his staff

5. Administrative policies relate MOST closely to   5.__

   A. control of commodities and personnel
   B. general policies emanating from the central office
   C. fiscal management of the department only
   D. handling and dispensing of funds

6. Part of being a good supervisor is to be able to develop an attitude towards employees which will motivate them to do their best on the job. The GOOD supervisor, therefore, should

    A. take an interest in subordinates, but not develop an all-consuming attitude in this area
    B. remain in an aloof position when dealing with employees
    C. be as close to subordinates as possible on the job
    D. take a complete interest in all the activities of subordinates, both on and off the job

6._____

7. The practice of a supervisor assigning an experienced employee to train new employees instead of training them himself, is, GENERALLY, considered

    A. *undesirable*; the more experienced employee will resent being taken away from his regular job
    B. *desirable*; the supervisor can then devote more time to his regular duties
    C. *undesirable*; the more experienced employee is not working at the proper level to train new employees
    D. *desirable*; the more experienced employee is probably a better trainer than the supervisor

7._____

8. It is generally agreed that on-the-job training is MOST effective when new employees are

    A. provided with study manuals, standard operating procedures and other written materials to be studied for at least two weeks before the employees attempt to do the job
    B. shown how to do the job in detail, and then instructed to do the work under close supervision
    C. trained by an experienced worker for at least a week to make certain that the employees can do the job
    D. given work immediately which is checked at the end of each day

8._____

9. Employees sometimes form small informal groups, commonly called cliques. With regard to the effect of such groups on processing of the workload, the attitude a supervisor should take towards these cliques is that of

    A. *acceptance*, since they take the employees' minds off their work without wasting too much time
    B. *rejection*, since those workers inside the clique tend to do less work than the outsiders
    C. *acceptance*, since the supervisor is usually included in the clique
    D. *rejection*, since they are usually disliked by higher management

9._____

10. Of the following, the BEST statement regarding rules and regulations in a unit is that they

    A. are "necessary evils" to be tolerated by those at and above the first supervisory level only
    B. are stated in broad, indefinite terms so as to allow maximum amount of leeway in complying with them
    C. must be understood by all employees in the unit
    D. are primarily for management's needs since insurance regulations mandate them

10._____

11. It is sometimes considered desirable for a supervisor to survey the opinions of his employees before taking action on decisions affecting them. Of the following, the greatest DISADVANTAGE of following this approach is that the employees might   11.___

   A. use this opportunity to complain rather than to make constructive suggestions
   B. lose respect for their supervisor whom they feel cannot make his own decisions
   C. regard this as an attempt by the supervisor to get ideas for which he can later claim credit
   D. be resentful if their suggestions are not adopted

12. Of the following, the MOST important reason for keeping statements of duties of employees up-to-date is to   12.___

   A. serve as a basis of information for other governmental jurisdictions
   B. enable the department of personnel to develop job-related examinations
   C. differentiate between levels within the occupational groups
   D. enable each employee to know what his duties are

13. Of the following, the BEST way to evaluate the progress of a new subordinate is to   13.___

   A. compare the output of the new employee from week to week as to quantity and quality
   B. obtain the opinions of the new employee's co-workers
   C. test the new employee periodically to see how much he has learned
   D. hold frequent discussions with the employee focusing on his work

14. Of the following, a supervisor is LEAST likely to contribute to good morale in the unit if he   14.___

   A. encourages employees to increase their knowledge and proficiency in their work on their own time
   B. reprimands subordinates uniformly when infractions are committed
   C. refuses to accept explanations for mistakes regardless of who has made them or how serious they are
   D. compliments subordinates for superior work performance in the presence of their peers

15. The practice of promoting supervisors from within a given unit only, rather than from within the entire agency, may BEST be described as   15.___

   A. *desirable*, because the type of work in each unit generally is substantially different from all other units
   B. *undesirable*, since it will severely reduce the number of eligibles from which to select a supervisor
   C. *desirable*, since it enables each employee to know in advance the precise extent of promotion opportunities in his unit
   D. *undesirable*, because it creates numerous administrative and budgetary difficulties

16. Of the following, the BEST way for a supervisor to make assignments GENERALLY is to   16.___

   A. give the easier assignments to employees with greater seniority
   B. give the difficult assignments to the employees with greater seniority
   C. make assignments according to the ability of each employee
   D. rotate the assignments among the employees

17. Assume that a supervisor makes a proposal through appropriate channels which would delegate final authority and responsibility to a subordinate employee for a major control function within the agency. According to current management theory, this proposal should be

    A. *adopted*, since this would enable the supervisor to devote more time to non-routine tasks

    B. *rejected*, since final responsibility for this high-level assignment may not properly be delegated to a subordinate employee

    C. *adopted*, since the assignment of increased responsibility to subordinate employees is a vital part of their development and training

    D. *rejected*, since the morale of the subordinate employees not selected for this assignment would be adversely affected

17.____

18. If it becomes necessary for a supervisor to improve the performance of a subordinate to assure the achievement of results according to plans, the BEST course of action, of the following, generally, would be to

    A. emphasize the subordinate's strengths and try to motivate the employee to improve on those factors

    B. emphasize the subordinate's weak areas of performance and try to bring them up to an acceptable standard

    C. issue a memorandum to all employees warning that if performance does not improve, disciplinary measures will be taken

    D. transfer the subordinate to another section engaged in different work

18.____

19. A supervisor who specifies each phase of a job in detail, supervises closely and permits very little discretion in performance of tasks, GENERALLY

    A. provides motivation for his staff to produce more work

    B. finds that his subordinates make fewer mistakes than those with minimal supervision

    C. finds that his subordinates have little or no incentive to work any harder than necessary

    D. provides superior training opportunities for his employees

19.____

20. Assume that you supervise two employees who do not get along well with each other. Their relationship has been continuously deteriorating. You decide to take steps to solve this problem by first determining the reason for their inability to get along well with each other. This course of action is

    A. *desirable*, because their work is probably adversely affected by their differences

    B. *undesirable*, because your inquiries might be is-interpreted by the employees and cause resentment

    C. *desirable*, because you could then learn who is at fault for causing the deteriorating relationship and take appropriate disciplinary measures

    D. *undesirable*, because it is best to let them work their differences out between themselves

20.____

21. Routine procedures that have worked well in the past should be reviewed periodically by a supervisor MAINLY because

    A. they may have become outdated or in need of revision
    B. employees may dislike the procedures even though they have proven successful in the past
    C. these reviews are the main part of a supervisor's job
    D. this practice serves to give the supervisor an idea of how productive his subordinates are

    21.___

22. Assume that an employee tells his supervisor about a grievance he has against a co-worker. The supervisor assures the employee that he will immediately take action to eliminate the grievance. The supervisor's attitude should be considered

    A. *correct*; because a good supervisor is one who can come to a quick decision
    B. *incorrect*; because the supervisor should have told the employee that he will investigate the grievance and then determine a future course of action
    C. *correct*; because the employee's morale will be higher, resulting in greater productivity
    D. *incorrect*; because the supervisor should remain uninvolved and let the employees settle grievances between themselves

    22.___

23. If an employee's work output is low and of poor quality due to faulty work habits, the MOST constructive of the following ways for a supervisor to correct this situation, GENERALLY, is to

    A. discipline the employee
    B. transfer the employee to another unit
    C. provide additional training
    D. check the employee's work continuously

    23.___

24. Assume that it becomes necessary for a supervisor to ask his staff to work overtime. Which one of the following techniques is MOST likely to win their willing cooperation to do this?

    A. Point out that this is part of their job specification entitled "performs related work"
    B. Explain the reason it is necessary for the employees to work overtime
    C. Promise the employees special consideration regarding future leave matters
    D. Warn that if the employees do not work overtime, they will face possible disciplinary action

    24.___

25. If an employee's work performance has recently fallen below established minimum standards for quality and quantity, the threat of demotion or other disciplinary measures as an attempt to improve this employee's performance would probably be the MOST acceptable and effective course of action

    A. *only* after other more constructive measures have failed
    B. *if* applied uniformly to all employees as soon as performance falls below standard
    C. *only* if the employee understands that the threat will not actually be carried out
    D. *if* the employee is promised that, as soon as his work performance improves, he will be reinstated to his previous status

    25.___

KEY (CORRECT ANSWERS)

1.	C		11.	D
2.	B		12.	D
3.	B		13.	A
4.	D		14.	C
5.	A		15.	B
6.	A		16.	C
7.	B		17.	B
8.	B		18.	B
9.	A		19.	C
10.	C		20.	A

21.	A
22.	B
23.	C
24.	B
25.	A

———

TEST 3

DIRECTIONS: Each question or incomplete statement is followed by several suggested answers or completions. Select the one that BEST answers the question or completes the statement. *PRINT THE LETTER OF THE CORRECT ANSWER IN THE SPACE AT THE RIGHT.*

1. If, as a supervisor, it becomes necessary for you to assign an employee to supervise your unit during your vacation, it would generally be BEST to select the employee who

    A. is the best technician on the staff
    B. can get the work out smoothly, without friction
    C. has the most seniority
    D. is the most popular with the group

    1.___

2. Assume that, as a supervisor, your own work has accumulated to the point where you decide that it is desirable for you to delegate in order to meet your deadlines. The one of the following tasks which would be MOST appropriate to delegate to a subordinate is

    A. checking the work of the employees for accuracy
    B. attending a staff conference at which implementation of a new departmental policy will be discussed
    C. preparing a final report including a recommendation on purchase of expensive new laboratory equipment
    D. preparing final budget estimates for next year's budget

    2.___

3. Of the following actions, the one LEAST appropriate for you to take during an *initial* interview with a new employee is to

    A. find out about the experience and education of the new employee
    B. attempt to determine for what job in your unit the employee would best be suited
    C. tell the employee about his duties and responsibilities
    D. ascertain whether the employee will make good promotion material

    3.___

4. If it becomes necessary to reprimand a subordinate employee, the BEST of the following ways to do this is to

    A. ask the employee to stay after working hours and then reprimand him
    B. reprimand the employee immediately after the infraction has been committed
    C. take the employee aside and speak to him privately during regular working hours
    D. write a short memo to the employee warning that strict adherence to departmental policy and procedures is required of all employees

    4.___

5. If you, as a supervisor, believe that one of your subordinate employees has a serious problem, such as alcoholism or an emotional disturbance, which is adversely affecting his work, the BEST way to handle this situation *initially* would be to

    A. urge him to seek proper professional help before he is dismissed from his job
    B. ignore it and let the employee work out the problem himself
    C. suggest that the employee take an extended leave of absence until he can again function effectively
    D. frankly tell the employee that unless his work improves, you will take disciplinary measures against him

    5.___

6. Of the following, the BEST way to develop a subordinate's potential is to 6._____

    A. give him a fair chance to learn by doing
    B. assign him more than his share of work
    C. criticize only his work
    D. urge him to do his work rapidly

7. During a survey, an employee from another agency asks you to assist him on a job which would require a full day of your time. Of the following, the BEST immediate action for you to take is to 7._____

    A. refuse to assist him
    B. ask for compensation before doing it
    C. assist him promptly
    D. notify his department head

8. Of the following, the BEST way to handle an overly talkative subordinate is to 8._____

    A. have your superior talk to him about it
    B. have a subordinate talk to him about it
    C. talk to him about it in a group conference
    D. talk to him about it in private

9. While you are making a survey, a citizen questions you about the work you are doing. Of the following, the BEST thing to do is to 9._____

    A. answer the questions tactfully
    B. refuse to answer any questions
    C. advise him to write a letter to the main office
    D. answer the questions in double-talk

10. Respect for a supervisor is MOST likely to increase if he is 10._____

    A. morose   B. sporadic   C. vindictive   D. zealous

11. A subordinate who continuously bypasses his immediate supervisor for technical information should be 11._____

    A. reprimanded by his immediate supervisor
    B. ignored by his immediate supervisor
    C. given more difficult work to do
    D. given less difficult work to do

12. Complicated instructions should NOT be written 12._____

    A. accurately   B. lucidly   C. factually   D. verbosely

13. Of the following, the MOST important reason for checking a report is to 13._____

    A. check accuracy   B. eliminate unnecessary sections
    C. catch mistakes   D. check for delineation

14. Two subordinates under your supervision dislike each other to the extent that production   14.___
is cut down. Your BEST action as a supervisor is to

    A.   ignore the matter and hope for the best
    B.   transfer the more aggressive man
    C.   cut down on the work load
    D.   talk to them together about the matter

15. One of the following characteristics which a supervisor should NOT display while explain-   15.___
ing a job to a subordinate is

    A.   enthusiasm   B.   confidence
    C.   apathy   D.   determination

16. Of the following, for BEST production of work, it should be assigned according to a per-   16.___
son's

    A.   attitude toward the work   B.   ability to do the work
    C.   salary   D.   seniority

17. You receive an anonymous written complaint from a citizen about a subordinate who   17.___
used abusive language. Of the following, your BEST course of action is to

    A.   ignore the letter
    B.   report it to your supervisor
    C.   discuss the complaint with the subordinate privately
    D.   keep the subordinate in the office

18. A supervisor should recognize that the way to get the BEST results from his instructions   18.___
and assignments to the staff is to use

    A.   a suggestive approach after he has decided exactly what is to be done and how
    B.   the willing and cooperative staff members and avoid the hard-to-handle people
    C.   care to select the persons most capable of carrying out the assignments
    D.   an authoritative, non-nonsense tone when issuing instructions or giving assign-
        ments

19. As the supervisor of a unit, you find that you are spending too much of your time on rou-   19.___
tine tasks and not enough on coordinating the work of the staff or preparing necessary
reports. Of the following, it would be MOST advisable for you to

    A.   discard a great portion of the routine jobs done in the unit
    B.   give some of the routine jobs to other members of the staff
    C.   postpone the routine jobs and concentrate on coordinating the work of the staff
    D.   delegate the job of coordinating the work to the most capable member of the staff

20. At times a supervisor may be called upon to train new employees. Suppose that you are   20.___
giving such training in several sessions to be held on different days. During the first session, a trainee interrupts everal times to ask questions at key points in your discussion.
Of the following, the BEST way to handle this trainee is to

    A.   advise him to pay closer attention so he can avoid asking too many questions
    B.   tell him to listen without interrupting and he'll hear his questions answered

C. answer his questions to show him that you know your field, but make a mental note that this trainee is a troublemaker
D. answer each question fully and make certain he understands the answers

21. Employee errors can be reduced to a minimum by effective supervision and by training. Which of the following approaches used by a supervisor would usually be MOST effective in handling an employee who has made an avoidable and serious error for the first time?

    A. Tell the worker how other employees avoid making errors
    B. Analyze with the employee the situation leading to the error and then take whatever administrative or training steps are needed to avoid such errors
    C. Use this error as the basis for a staff meeting at which the employee's error is disclosed and discussed in an effort to improve the performance
    D. Urge the employee to modify his behavior in light of his mistake

21.____

22. Suppose that a particular staff member, formerly one of your most regular workers, has recently fallen into the habit of arriving a bit late to work several times a week. You feel that such a habit can grow consistently worse and spread to other staff members unless it is checked. Of the following, the BEST action for you to take, as the supervisor in charge of the unit, is to

    A. go immediately to your own supervisor, present the facts, and have this employee disciplined
    B. speak privately to this tardy employee, advise him of the need to improve his punctuality, and inform him that he'll be disciplined if late again
    C. talk to the co-worker with whom this late employee is most friendly and ask the friend to help him solve his tardiness problem
    D. speak privately with this employee, and try to discover and deal with the reasons for the latenesses

22.____

23. A supervisor may make an assignment in the form of a request, a command, or a call for volunteers. It is LEAST desirable to make an assignment in the form of a request when

    A. an employee does not like the particular kind of assignment to be given
    B. the assignment requires working past the regular closing day
    C. an emergency has come up
    D. the assignment is not particularly pleasant for anybody

23.____

24. When you give a certain task that you normally perform yourself to one of your employees, it is MOST important that you

    A. lead the employee to believe that he has been chosen above others to perform this job
    B. describe the job as important even though it is merely a routine task
    C. explain the job that needs to be accomplished, but always let the employee decide how to do it
    D. tell the employee why you are delegating the job to him and explain exactly what he is to do

24.____

25. A supervisor when instructing new trainees in the routine of his unit should include a description of the department's overall objectives and programs in order to

25._

A. insure that individual work assignments will be completed satisfactorily
B. create a favorable impression of his supervisory capabilities
C. develop a better understanding of the purposes behind work assignments
D. produce an immediate feeling of group cooperation

KEY (CORRECT ANSWERS)

1.	B		11.	A
2.	A		12.	D
3.	D		13.	C
4.	C		14.	D
5.	A		15.	C
6.	A		16.	B
7.	A		17.	C
8.	D		18.	C
9.	A		19.	B
10.	D		20.	D

21.	B
22.	D
23.	A
24.	D
25.	C

TEST 4

DIRECTIONS: Each question or incomplete statement is followed by several suggested answers or completions. Select the one that BEST answers the question or completes the statement. *PRINT THE LETTER OF THE CORRECT ANSWER IN THE SPACE AT THE RIGHT.*

1. An integral part of every supervisor's job is getting his ideas or instructions across to his staff. The extent of his success, if he has a reasonably competent staff, is PRIMARILY dependent on the

    A.   interest of the employee
    B.   intelligence of the employee
    C.   reasoning behind the ideas or instructions
    D.   presentation of the ideas or instructions

1._____

2. Generally, what is the FIRST action the supervisor should take when an employee approaches him with a complaint?

    A.   Review the employee's recent performance with him
    B.   Use the complaint as a basis to discuss improvement of procedures
    C.   Find out from the employee the details of the complaint
    D.   Advise the employee to take his complaint to the head of the department

2._____

3. Of the following, which is NOT usually considered one of the purposes of counseling an employee after an evaluation of his performance?

    A.   Explaining the performance standards used by the supervisor
    B.   Discussing necessary disciplinary action to be taken
    C.   Emphasizing the employee's strengths and weaknesses
    D.   Planning better utilization of the employee's strengths

3._____

4. Assume that a supervisor, when reviewing a decision reached by one of his subordinates, finds the decision incorrect. Under these circumstances, it would be MOST desirable for the supervisor to

    A.   correct the decision and inform the subordinate of this at a staff meeting
    B.   correct the decision and suggest a more detailed analysis in the future
    C.   help the employee find the reason for the correct decision
    D.   refrain from assigning this type of a problem to the employee

4._____

5. An IMPORTANT characteristic of a good supervisor is his ability to

    A.   be a stern disciplinarian
    B.   put off the settling of grievances
    C.   solve problems   D.   find fault in individuals

5._____

6. A new supervisor will BEST obtain the respect of the men assigned to him if he

    A.   makes decisions rapidly and sticks to them, regardless of whether they are right or wrong
    B.   makes decisions rapidly and then changes them just as rapidly if the decisions are wrong
    C.   does not make any decisions unless he is absolutely sure that they are right
    D.   makes his decisions after considering carefully all available information

6._____

7. A newly appointed worker is operating at a level of performance below that of the other   7.___
employees. In this situation, a supervisor should FIRST

    A. lower the acceptable standard for the new man
    B. find out why the new man cannot do as well as the others
    C. advise the new worker he will be dropped from the payroll at the end of the proba-
       tionary period
    D. assign another new worker to assist the first man

8. Assume that you have to instruct a new man on a specific departmental operation. The   8.___
new man seems unsure of what you have said. Of the following, the BEST way for you to
determine whether the man has understood you is to

    A. have the man explain the operation to you in his own words
    B. repeat your explanation to him slowly
    C. repeat your explanation to him, using simpler wording
    D. emphasize the important parts of the operation to him

9. A supervisor realizes that he has taken an instanteous dislike to a new worker assigned   9.___
to him. The BEST course of action for the supervisor to take in this case is to

    A. be especially observant of the new worker's actions
    B. request that the new worker be reassigned
    C. make a special effort to be fair to the new worker
    D. ask to be transferred himself

10. A supervisor gives detailed instructions to his men as to how a certain type of job is to be   10.___
done. One ADVANTAGE of this practice is that this will

    A. result in a more flexible operation
    B. standardize operations
    C. encourage new men to learn
    D. encourage initiative in the men

11. Of the following, the one that would MOST likely be the result of poor planning is: 11.___

    A. Omissions are discovered after the work is completed.
    B. During the course of normal inspection, a meter is found to be inaccessible.
    C. An inspector completes his assignments for that day ahead of schedule.
    D. A problem arises during an inspection and prevents an inspector from completing
       his day's assignments.

12. Of the following, the BEST way for a supervisor to maintain good employee morale is for   12.___
the supervisor to

    A. avoid correcting the employee when he makes mistakes
    B. continually praise the employee's work even when it is of average quality
    C. show that he is willing to assist in solving the employee's problems
    D. accept the employee's excuses for failure even though the excuses are not valid

13. A supervisor takes time to explain to his men why a departmental order has been issued. 13.____
This practice is

    A. *good*, mainly because without this explanation the men will not be able to carry out the order
    B. *bad*, mainly because time will be wasted for no useful purpose
    C. *good*, because understanding the reasons behind an order will lead to more effective carrying out of the order
    D. *bad*, because men will then question every order that they receive

14. Of the following, the MOST important responsibility of a supervisor in charge of a section 14.____
is to

    A. establish close personal relationships with each of his subordinates in the section
    B. insure that each subordinate in the section knows the full range of his duties and responsibilities
    C. maintain friendly relations with his immediate supervisor
    D. protect his subordinates from criticism from any source

15. The BEST way to get a good work output from employees is to 15.____

    A. hold over them the threat of disciplinary action or removal
    B. maintain a steady, unrelenting pressure on them
    C. show them that you can do anything they can do faster and better
    D. win their respect and liking, so they want to work for you

---

KEY (CORRECT ANSWERS)

1.	A	6.	D
2.	C	7.	B
3.	A	8.	A
4.	C	9.	C
5.	C	10.	B

11.	A
12.	C
13.	C
14.	B
15.	D

SUPERVISION, ADMINISTRATION, MANAGEMENT AND ORGANIZATION
EXAMINATION SECTION
TEST 1

DIRECTIONS: Each question or incomplete statement is followed by several suggested answers or completions. Select the one that BEST answers the question or completes the statement. *PRINT THE LETTER OF THE CORRECT ANSWER IN THE SPACE AT THE RIGHT.*

1. The one of the following practices by a supervisor which is *most likely* to lead to confusion and inefficiency is for him to   1._____

   A. give orders verbally directly to the man assigned to the job
   B. issue orders only in writing
   C. follow up his orders after issuing them
   D. relay his orders to the men through co-workers

2. If you are given an oral order by a supervisor which you do not understand completely, you should   2._____

   A. use your own judgment
   B. discuss the order with your men
   C. ask your superior for a further explanation
   D. carry out that part of the order which you do understand and then ask for more information

3. An orientation program for a group of new employees should NOT *ordinarily* include a   3._____

   A. review of the organizational structure of the agency
   B. detailed description of the duties of each new employee
   C. description of the physical layout of the repair shop
   D. statement of the rules pertaining to sick leave, vacation, and holidays

4. The MOST important rule to follow with regard to discipline is that a man should be disciplined   4._____

   A. after everyone has had time to "cool off"
   B. as soon as possible after the infraction of rules
   C. only for serious rule violations
   D. before he makes a mistake

5. If the men under your supervision continue to work effectively even when you are out sick for several days, it would *most probably* indicate that   5._____

   A. the men are merely trying to show you up
   B. the men are in constant fear of you and are glad you are away
   C. you have trained your men properly and have their full cooperation
   D. you are serving no useful purpose since the men can get along without you

6. When evaluating subordinates, the employee who should be rated HIGHEST by his supervisor is the one who   6.___

    A. never lets the supervisor do heavy lifting
    B. asks many questions about the work
    C. makes many suggestions on work procedures
    D. listens to instructions and carries them out

7. Of the following, the factor which is *generally* MOST important to the conduct of success-ful training is   7.___

    A. time   B. preparation   C. equipment   D. space

8. One of the MAJOR disadvantages of "on-the-job" training is that it   8.___

    A. requires a long training period for instructors
    B. may not be progressive
    C. requires additional equipment
    D. may result in the waste of supplies

9. For a supervisor to train workers in several trades which involve various skills, presents many training problems. The one of the following which is NOT true in such a training sit-uation is that   9.___

    A. less supervision is required
    B. greater planning for training is required
    C. rotation of assignments is necessary
    D. less productivity can be expected

10. For a supervisor of repair workers to have each worker specialize in learning a single trade is, *generally,*   10.___

    A. *desirable*; each worker will become expert in his assigned trade
    B. *undesirable*; there is less flexibility of assignments possible when each worker has learned only a single trade
    C. *desirable*; the training responsibility of the supervisor is simplified when each worker is required to learn a single trade
    D. *undesirable*; workers lose interest quickly when they know they are expected to learn a single trade

11. An IMPORTANT advantage of standardizing work procedures is that it   11.___

    A. develops all-around skills
    B. makes the work less monotonous
    C. provides an incentive for good work
    D. enables the work to be done with less supervision

12. Generally, the GREATEST difficulty in introducing new work methods is due to the fact that   12.___

    A. men become set in their ways
    B. the old way is generally better
    C. only the department will benefit from changes
    D. explaining new methods is time consuming

13. Assume that you are required to transmit an order, with which you do not agree, to your   13.____
    subordinates. In this case, it would be BEST for you to

    A. ask one of your superiors to transmit the order
    B. refuse to transmit an order with which you do not agree
    C. transmit the order but be sure to explain that you do not agree with it
    D. transmit the order and enforce it to the best of your ability

14. The MAIN reason for written orders is that   14.____

    A. proper blame can be placed if the order is not carried out
    B. the order will be carried out faster
    C. the order can be properly analyzed as to its meaning
    D. there will be no doubt as to what the order says

15. You have been informed unofficially by another shop manager that some of the men   15.____
    under your supervision are loafing on the job. This situation can be BEST handled by

    A. telling the man to mind his own business
    B. calling the men together and reprimanding them
    C. having the men work under your direct supervision
    D. arranging to make spot checks at more frequent intervals

16. Suggestions on improving methods of doing work, when submitted by a new employee,   16.____
    should be

    A. examined for possible merit because the new man may have a fresh viewpoint
    B. ignored because it would make the old employees resentful
    C. disregarded because he is too unfamiliar with the work
    D. examined only for the purpose of judging the new man

17. One of your employees often slows down the work of his crew by playing practical jokes.   17.____
    The BEST way to handle this situation is to

    A. arrange for his assignment to more than his share of unpleasant jobs
    B. warn him that he must stop this practice at once
    C. ignore this situation for he will soon tire of it
    D. ask your superior to transfer him

18. One of your men is always complaining about working conditions, equipment, and his fel-   18.____
    low workers. The BEST action for you to take in this situation is to

    A. have this man work alone if possible
    B. consider each complaint on its merits
    C. tell him bluntly that you will not listen to any of his complaints
    D. give this man the worst jobs until he quits complaining

19. It is generally agreed that men who are interested in their work will do the best work. A   19.____
    supervisor can *least* stimulate this interest by

    A. complimenting men on good work
    B. correcting men on their working procedures
    C. striving to create overtime for his men
    D. recommending merit raises for excellent work

20. If you, as a supervisor, have criticized one of your men for making a mistake, you should 20.__

    A. remind the man of his error from time to time to keep him on his toes
    B. overlook any further errors which this man may make, otherwise he may feel he is a victim of discrimination
    C. give the man the opportunity to redeem himself
    D. impress the man with the fact that all his work will be closely checked from then on

21. In his efforts to maintain standards of performance, a shop manager uses a system of close supervision to detect or catch errors. An *opposite* method of accomplishing the *same* objective is to employ a program which 21.__

    A. instills in each employee a pride of workmanship to do the job correctly the first time
    B. groups each job according to the importance to the overall objectives of the program
    C. makes the control of quality the responsibility of an inspector
    D. emphasizes that there is a "one" best way for an employee to do a specific job

22. Assume that after taking over a repair shop, a shop manager feels that he is taking too much time maintaining records. He should 22.__

    A. temporarily assign this job to one of his senior repair crew chiefs
    B. get together with his supervisor to determine if all these records are needed
    C. stop keeping those records which he believes are unnecessary
    D. spend a few additional hours each day until his records are current

23. In order to apply performance standards to employees engaged in repair shop activities, a shop manager must FIRST 23.__

    A. allow workers to decide for themselves the way to do the job
    B. determine what is acceptable as satisfactory work
    C. separate the more difficult tasks from the simpler tasks
    D. stick to an established work schedule

24. Of the following actions a shop manager can take to determine whether the vehicles used in his shop are being utilized properly, the one which will give him the *least* meaningful information is 24.__

    A. conducting an analysis of vehicle assignments
    B. reviewing the number of miles travelled by each vehicle with and without loads
    C. recording the unloaded weights of each vehicle
    D. comparing the amount of time vehicles are parked at job sites with the time required to travel to and from job sites

25. For a shop manager, the MOST important reason that equipment which is used infrequently should be considered for disposal is that 25.__

    A. the time required for its maintenance could be better used elsewhere
    B. such equipment may cause higher management to think that your shop is not busy
    C. the men may resent having to work on such equipment
    D. such equipment usually has a higher breakdown rate in operation

KEY (CORRECT ANSWERS)

1.	D		11.	D
2.	C		12.	A
3.	B		13.	D
4.	B		14.	D
5.	C		15.	D
6.	D		16.	A
7.	B		17.	B
8.	B		18.	B
9.	A		19.	C
10.	B		20.	C

21. A
22. B
23. B
24. C
25. A

TEST 2

DIRECTIONS: Each question or incomplete statement is followed by several suggested answers or completions. Select the one that BEST answers the question or completes the statement. *PRINT THE LETTER OF THE CORRECT ANSWER IN THE SPACE AT THE RIGHT.*

1. Assume that one of your subordinates approaches you with a grievance concerning working conditions. Of the following, the BEST action for you to take *first* is to

    A. "soft-soap" him, since most grievances are imaginary
    B. settle the grievance to his satisfaction
    C. try to talk him out of his complaint
    D. listen patiently and sincerely to the complaint

1._

2. Of the following, the BEST way for a supervisor to help a subordinate learn a new skill which requires the use of tools is for him to give this subordinate

    A. a list of good books on the subject
    B. lectures on the theoretical aspects of the task
    C. opportunities to watch someone using the tools
    D. opportunities to practice the skill, under close supervision

2._

3. A supervisor finds that his own work load is excessive because several of his subordinates are unable to complete their assignments.
Of the following, the BEST action for him to take to improve this situation is to

    A. discipline these subordinates
    B. work overtime
    C. request additional staff
    D. train these subordinates in more efficient work methods

3._

4. The one of the following situations which is MOST likely to be the result of *poor* morale is a(n)

    A. high rate of turnover
    B. decrease in number of requests by subordinates for transfers
    C. increase in the backlog of work
    D. decrease in the rate of absenteeism

4._

5. As a supervisor, you find that several of your subordinates are not meeting their deadlines because they are doing work assigned to them by one of your fellow supervisors without your knowledge.
Of the following, the BEST course of action for you to take in this situation is to

    A. tell the other supervisors to make future assignments through you
    B. assert your authority by publicly telling the other supervisors to stop issuing orders to your workers
    C. go along with this practice; it is an effective way to fully utilize the available manpower
    D. take the matter directly to your immediate supervisor without delay

5._

6. If a supervisor of a duplicating section in an agency hears a rumor concerning a change   6.____
in agency personnel policy through the "grapevine," he should

    A. repeat it to his subordinates so they will be informed
    B. not repeat it to his subordinates before he determines the facts because, as super-visor, his work may give it unwarranted authority
    C. repeat it to his subordinates so that they will like him for confiding in them
    D. not repeat it to his subordinates before he determines the facts because a duplicat-ing section is not concerned with matters of policy

7. When teaching a new employee how to operate a machine, a supervisor should FIRST   7.____

    A. let the employee try to operate the machine by himself, since he can learn only by his mistakes
    B. explain the process to him with the use of diagrams before showing him the machine
    C. have him memorize the details of the operation from the manual
    D. explain and demonstrate the various steps in the process, making sure he under-stands each step

8. If a subordinate accuses you of always giving him the least desirable assignments, you   8.____
should *immediately*

    A. tell him that it is not true and you do not want to hear any more about it
    B. try to get specific details from him, so that you can find out what his impressions are based on
    C. tell him that you distribute assignments in the fairest way possible and he must be mistaken
    D. ask him what current assignment he has that he does not like, and assign it to someone else

9. Suppose that the production of an operator under your supervision has been unsatisfac-   9.____
tory and you have decided to have a talk with him about it.
During the interview, it would be BEST for you to

    A. discuss *only* the subordinate's weak points so that he can overcome them
    B. discuss *only* the subordinate's strong points so that he will not become discour-aged
    C. compare the subordinate's work with that of his co-workers so that he will know what is expected of him
    D. discuss *both* his weak and strong points so that he will get a view of his overall per-formance

10. Suppose that an operator under your supervision makes a mistake in color on a 2,000-   10.____
page job and runs it on white paper instead of on blue paper.
Of the following, your BEST course in these circumstances would be to point out the error to the operator *and*

    A. have the operator rerun the job immediately on blue paper
    B. send the job to the person who ordered it without comment
    C. send the job to the person who ordered it and tell him it could not be done on blue paper
    D. ask the person who ordered the job whether the white paper is acceptable

11. Assuming that all your subordinates have equal technical competence, the BEST policy 11.__
for a supervisor to follow when making assignments of undesirable jobs would be to

    A. distribute them as evenly as possible among his subordinates
    B. give them to the subordinate with the poorest attendance record
    C. ask the subordinate with the least seniority to do them
    D. assign them to the subordinate who is least likely to complain

12. To get the BEST results when training a number of subordinates at the *same* time, a 12.__
supervisor should

    A. treat all of them in an identical manner to avoid accusations of favoritism
    B. treat them all fairly, but use different approaches in dealing with people of different
personality types
    C. train only one subordinate, and have him train the others, because this will save a
lot of the supervisor's time
    D. train first the subordinates who learn quickly so as to make the others think that the
operation is easy to learn

13. Assume that, after a week's vacation, you return to find that one of your subordinates has 13.__
produced a job which is unsatisfactory.
Your BEST course of action at *that* time would be to

    A. talk to your personnel department about implementing disciplinary action
    B. discuss unsatisfactory work in the unit at a meeting with all of your subordinates
    C. discuss the job with the subordinate to determine why he was unable to do it prop-
erly
    D. ignore the matter, because it is too late to correct the mistake

14. Suppose that an operator under your supervision informs you that Mr. Y, a senior admin- 14.__
istrator in your agency, has been submitting for copying many papers which are
obviously personal in nature. The operator wants to know what to do about it, since the
duplication of personal papers is against agency rules.
Your BEST course in these circumstances would be to

    A. tell the operator to pretend not to notice the content of the material and continue to
copy whatever is given to him
    B. tell the operator that Mr. Y, as a senior administrator, must have gotten special per-
mission to have personal papers duplicated
    C. have the operator refer Mr. Y to you and inform Mr. Y yourself that duplication of
personal papers is against agency rules
    D. call Mr. Y's superior and tell him that Mr. Y has been having personal papers dupli-
cated, which is against agency rules

15. Assume that you are teaching a certain process to an operator under your supervision. 15.__
In order to BEST determine whether he is *actually* learning what you are teaching, you
should ask questions which

    A. can easily be answered by a "yes" or "no"
    B. require or encourage guessing
    C. require a short description of what has been taught
    D. are somewhat ambiguous so as to make the learner think about the procedures in
question

16. If an employee is chronically late or absent, as his supervisor, it would be BEST for you to

   A. let his work pile up so he can see that no one else will do it for him
   B. discuss the matter with him and stress the importance of finding a solution
   C. threaten to enter a written report on the matter into his personnel file
   D. work out a system with him so he can have a different work schedule than the other employees

17. Assume that you have a subordinate who has just finished a basic training course in the operation of a machine. Giving him a large and difficult *first* assignment would be

   A. *good,* because it would force him to "learn the ropes"
   B. *bad,* because he would probably have difficulty in carrying it out, discouraging him and resulting in a waste of time and supplies
   C. *good,* because how he handles it would give you an excellent basis for judging his competence
   D. *bad,* because he would probably assume that you are discriminating against him

18. After putting a new employee under your supervision through an initial training period, assigning him to work with a more experienced employee for a while would be a

   A. *good idea,* because it would give him the opportunity to observe what he had been taught and to participate in production himself
   B. *bad idea,* because he should not be required to work under the direction of anyone who is not his supervisor
   C. *good idea,* because it would raise the morale of the more experienced employee who could use him to do all the unpleasant chores
   D. *bad idea,* because the best way for him to learn would be to give him full responsibility for assignments right away

19. Assume that a supervisor is responsible for ordering supplies for the duplicating section in his agency.
    Which one of the following actions would be MOST helpful in determining *when* to place orders so that an adequate supply of materials will be on hand at all times?

   A. Taking an inventory of supplies on hand at least every two months
   B. Asking his subordinvtes to inform him when they see that supplies are low
   C. Checking the inventory of supplies whenever he has time
   D. Keeping a running inventory of supplies and a record of estimated needs

20. Routine procedures that have worked well in the past should be reviewed periodically by a supervisor MAINLY because

   A. they may have become outdated or in need of revision
   B. employees might dislike the procedures even though they have proven successful in the past
   C. these reviews are the main part of a supervisor's job
   D. this practice serves to give the supervisor an idea of how productive his subordinates are

21. Assume that an employee tells his supervisor about a grievance he has against a co-worker. The supervisor assures the employee that he will immediately take action to eliminate the grievance.
The supervisor's attitude should be considered

    A. *correct*; because a good supervisor is one who can come to a quick decision
    B. *incorrect*; because the supervisor should have told the employee that he will investigate the grievance and then determine a future course of action
    C. *correct*; because the employee's morale will be higher, resulting in greater productivity
    D. *incorrect*; because the supervisor should remain uninvolved and let the employees settle grievances between themselves

21.__

22. If an employee's work output is low and of poor quality due to faulty work habits, the MOST constructive of the following ways for a supervisor to correct this situation, *generally*, is to

    A. discipline the employee
    B. transfer the employee to another unit
    C. provide additional training
    D. check the employee's work continuously

22.__

23. Assume that it becomes necessary for a supervisor to ask his staff to work overtime. Which one of the following techniques is MOST likely to win their willing cooperation to do this?

    A. Explain that this is part of their job specification entitled, "performs related work"
    B. Explain the reason it is necessary for the employees to work overtime
    C. Promise the employees special consideration regarding future leave matters
    D. Explain that if the employees do not work overtime, they will face possible disciplinary action

23.__

24. If an employee's work performance has recently fallen below established minimum standards for quality and quantity, the threat of demotion or other disciplinary measures as an attempt to improve this employee's performance would *probably* be the MOST acceptable and effective course of action

    A. *only* after other more constructive measures have failed
    B. *if* applied uniformly to all employees as soon as performance falls below standard
    C. *only* if the employee understands that the threat will not actually be carried out
    D. *if* the employee is promised that as soon as his work performance improves, he will be reinstated to his previous status

24.__

25. If, as a supervisor, it becomes necessary for you to assign an employee to supervise your unit during your vacation, it would *generally* be BEST to select the employee who

    A. is the best technician on the staff
    B. can get the work out smoothly, without friction
    C. has the most seniority
    D. is the most popular with the group

25.__

KEY (CORRECT ANSWERS)

1.	D	11.	A
2.	D	12.	B
3.	D	13.	C
4.	A	14.	C
5.	A	15.	C
6.	B	16.	B
7.	D	17.	B
8.	B	18.	A
9.	D	19.	D
10.	D	20.	A

21.	B
22.	C
23.	B
24.	A
25.	B

TEST 3

DIRECTIONS: Each question or incomplete statement is followed by several suggested answers or completions. Select the one that BEST answers the question or completes the statement. *PRINT THE LETTER OF THE CORRECT ANSWER IN THE SPACE AT THE RIGHT.*

1. An employee under your supervision has demonstrated a deep-seated personality problem that has begun to affect his work. This situation should be   1.__

   A. *ignored*; mainly because such problems usually resolve themselves
   B. *handled*; mainly because the employee should be assisted in seeking professional help
   C. *ignored*; mainly because the employee will consider any advice as interference
   D. *handled*; mainly because supervisors should be qualified to resolve deep-seated personality problems

2. Of the following, a supervisor will usually be MOST successful in maintaining employee morale while providing effective leadership if he   2.__

   A. takes prompt disciplinary action every time it is needed
   B. gives difficult assignments only to those workers who ask for such work
   C. promises his workers anything reasonable they request
   D. relies entirely on his staff for decisions

3. When a supervisor makes an assignment to his subordinates, he should include a clear statement of what results are expected when the assignment is completed.
   Of the following, the BEST reason for following this procedure is that it will   3.__

   A. make it unnecessary for the supervisor to check on the progress of the work
   B. stimulate initiative and cooperation on the part of the more responsible workers
   C. give the subordinates a way to judge whether their work is meeting the requirements
   D. give the subordinates the feeling that they have some freedom of action

4. Assume that, on a new employee's first day of work, his supervisor gives him a good orientation by telling him the general regulations and procedures used in the office and introducing him to his department head and fellow employees. For the remainder of the day, it would be BEST for the supervisor to   4.__

   A. give him steady instruction in all phases of his job, while stressing its most important aspects
   B. have him observe a fellow employee perform the duties of the job
   C. instruct him in that part of the job which he would prefer to learn first
   D. give him a simple task which requires little instruction and allows him to familiarize himself with the surroundings

5. When it becomes necessary to criticize subordinates because several errors in the unit's work have been discovered, the supervisor should *usually*   5.__

   A. focus on the job operation and avoid placing personal blame
   B. make every effort to fix blame and admonish the person responsible

   C.   include in the criticism those employees who recognize and rectify their own mis-
       takes

   D.   repeat the criticism at regular intervals in order to impress the subordinates with
       the seriousness of their errors

6.   If two employees under your supervision are continually bickering and cannot get along   6.____
     together, the FIRST action that you should take is to

   A.   investigate possible ways of separating them
   B.   ask your immediate superior for the procedure to follow in this situation
   C.   determine the cause of their difficulty
   D.   develop a plan and tell both parties to try it

7.   In general, it is appropriate to recommend the transfer of an employee for all of the fol-   7.____
     lowing reasons EXCEPT

   A.   rewarding him
   B.   providing him with a more challenging job
   C.   remedying an error in initial placement
   D.   disciplining him

8.   Of the following, the MAIN *disadvantage* of basing a training and development program   8.____
     on a series of lectures is that the lecture technique

   A.   does not sufficiently involve trainees in the learning process
   B.   is more costly than other methods of training
   C.   cannot be used to facilitate the understanding of difficult information
   D.   is time consuming and inefficient

9.   A supervisor has been assigned to train a new employee who is properly motivated but   9.____
     has made many mistakes.
     In the interview between the supervisor and employee about this problem, the
     employee should FIRST be

   A.   asked if he can think of anything that he can do to improve his work
   B.   complimented sincerely on some aspect of his work that is satisfactory
   C.   asked to explain why he made the mistakes
   D.   advised that he may be dismissed if he continues to be careless

10.   In training subordinates for more complex work, a supervisor must be aware of the   10.____
     progress that the subordinates are making.
     Determinination of the results that have been accomplished by training is a concept
     commonly known as

   A.   reinforcement   B.   feedback
   C.   cognitive dissonance   D.   the halo effect

11.   Assume that one of your subordinates loses interest in his work because he feels that   11.____
     your recent evaluation of his performance was unfair.
     The one of the following which is the BEST way to help him is to

   A.   establish frequent deadlines for his work
   B.   discuss his feelings and attitude with him

C. discuss with him only the positive aspects of his performance
D. arrange for his transfer to another unit

12. Informal organizations often develop at work.   12.___
Of the following, the supervisor should realize that these groups will USUALLY

A. determine work pace through unofficial agreements
B. restrict vital communication channels
C. lower morale by providing a chance to spread grievances
D. provide leaders who will substitute for the supervisor when he is absent

13. Assume that you, the supervisor, have called to your office a subordinate whom, on sev-   13.___
eral recent occasions, you have seen using the office telephone for personal use.
In this situation, it would be MOST appropriate to *begin* the interview by

A. discussing the disciplinary action that you believe to be warranted
B. asking the subordinate to explain the reason for his personal use of the office telephone
C. telling the subordinate about other employees who were disciplined for the same
offense
D. informing the subordinate that he is not to use the office telephone under any circumstances until further notice

14. Of the following, the success of any formal training program depends PRIMARILY upon   14.___
the

A. efficient and thorough preparation of materials, facilities, and procedures for
instruction
B. training program's practical relevance to the on-the-job situation
C. scheduling of training sessions so as to minimize interference with normal job
responsibilities
D. creation of a positive initial reception on the part of the trainees

15. All of the following are legitimate purposes for regularly evaluating employee perfor-   15.___
mance EXCEPT

A. stimulating improvement in performance
B. developing more accurate standards to be used in future ratings
C. encouraging a spirit of competition
D. allowing the employee to set realistic work goals for himself

16. A certain supervisor is very conscientious. He wants to receive personally all reports,   16.___
correspondence, etc., and to be completely involved in all of the unit's operations. However, he is having difficulty in keeping up with the growing amount of paperwork.
Of the following, the MOST desirable course of action for him to take is to

A. put in more hours on the job
B. ask for additional office help
C. begin to delegate more of his work
D. inquire of his supervisor if the paper work is really necessary

17. Assume that you are a supervisor. One of the workers under your supervision expresses   17._____
his need to speak to you about a client who has been particularly uncooperative in providing information.
The MOST appropriate action for you to take FIRST would be to

    A. agree to see the client for the worker in order to get the information
    B. advise the worker to try several more times to get the information before he asks
you for help
    C. tell the worker you will go with him to see the client in order to observe his tech-
nique
    D. ask the worker some questions in order to determine the type of help he needs in
this situation

18. The supervisor who is MOST likely to achieve a high level of productivity from the profes-   18._____
sional employees under his supervision is the one who

    A. watches their progress continuously
    B. provides them with just enough information to carry out their assigned tasks
    C. occasionally pitches in and helps them with their work
    D. shares with them responsibility for setting work goals

19. Assume that there has been considerable friction for some time among the workers of a   19._____
certain unit. The supervisor in charge of this unit becomes aware that the problem is getting serious as shown by increased absenteeism and lateness, loud arguments, etc.
Of the following, the BEST course of action for the supervisor to take FIRST is to

    A. have a staff discussion about objectives and problems
    B. seek out and penalize the apparent trouble-makers
    C. set up and enforce stricter formal rules
    D. discipline the next subordinate who causes friction

20. Assume that an employee under your supervision asks you for some blank paper and   20._____
pencils to take home to her young grandson who, she says, delights in drawing.
The one of the following actions you SHOULD take is to

    A. give her the material she wants and refrain from any comment
    B. refuse her request and tell her that the use of office supplies for personal reasons
is not proper
    C. give her the material but suggest that she buy it next time
    D. tell her to take the material herself since you do not want to know anything about
this matter

21. A certain supervisor is given a performance evaluation by his superior.   21._____
In it he is commended for his method of "delegation," a term that USUALLY refers to
the action of

    A. determining the priorities for activities which must be completed
    B. assigning to subordinates some of the duties for which he is responsible
    C. standardizing operations in order to achieve results as close as possible to estab-
lished goals
    D. dividing the activities necessary to achieve an objective into simple steps

22. A supervisor is approached by a subordinate who complains that a fellow worker is not assuming his share of the workload and is, therefore, causing more work for others in the office.
Of the following, the MOST appropriate action for the supervisor to take in response to this complaint is to tell the subordinate

    A. that he will look into the matter
    B. to concentrate on his own job and not to worry about others
    C. to discuss the matter with the other worker
    D. that not everyone is capable of working at the same pace

22._

23. Aside from the formal relationships established by management, informal and unofficial relationships will be developed among the personnel within an organization.
Of the following, the MAIN importance of such informal relationships to the operations of the formal organization is that they

    A. reinforce the basic goals of the formal organization
    B. insure the interchangeability of the personnel within the organization
    C. provide an additional channel of communications within the formal organization
    D. insure predictability and control of the behavior of members of the organization

23._

24. The most productive worker in a unit frequently takes overly-long coffee breaks and lunch hours while maintaining his above-average rate of productivity.
Of the following, it would be MOST advisable for the supervisor to

    A. reprimand him, because rules must be enforced equally regardless of the merit of an individual's job performance
    B. ignore the infractions because a superior worker should be granted extra privileges for his efforts
    C. take no action unless others in the unit complain, because a reprimand may hurt the superior worker's feelings and cause him to produce less
    D. tell other members of the unit that a comparable rate of productivity on their part will be rewarded with similar privileges

24._

25. A supervisor has been asked by his superior to choose an employee to supervise a special project.
Of the following, the MOST significant factor to consider in making this choice is the employee's

    A. length of service
    B. ability to do the job
    C. commitment to the goals of the agency
    D. attitude toward his fellow workers

25._

KEY (CORRECT ANSWERS)

1.	B		11.	B
2.	A		12.	A
3.	C		13.	B
4.	D		14.	B
5.	A		15.	C
6.	C		16.	C
7.	D		17.	D
8.	A		18.	D
9.	B		19.	A
10.	B		20.	B

21. B
22. A
23. C
24. A
25. B

———

TEST 4

DIRECTIONS: Each question or incomplete statement is followed by several suggested answers or completions. Select the one that BEST answers the question or completes the statement. *PRINT THE LETTER OF THE CORRECT ANSWER IN THE SPACE AT THE RIGHT.*

1. Assume that you are a newly appointed supervisor. Your MOST important responsibility is to

    A. make certain that all of the employees under your supervision are treated equally
    B. reduce disciplinary situations to a minimum
    C. insure an atmosphere of mutual trust between your workers and yourself
    D. see that the required work is done properly

1.__

2. In order to make sure that work is completed on time, the supervisor should

    A. pitch in and do as much of the work herself as she can
    B. schedule the work and control its progress
    C. not assign more than one person to any one task
    D. assign the same amount of work to each subordinate

2.__

3. Assume that you are a supervisor in charge of a number of workers who do the same kind of work and who each produce about the same volume of work in a given period of time. When their performance is evaluated, the worker who should be rated as the MOST accurate is the one

    A. whose errors are the easiest to correct
    B. whose errors involve the smallest amount of money
    C. who makes the fewest errors in her work
    D. who makes fewer errors as she becomes more experienced

3.__

4. As a supervisor, you have been asked by the manager to recommend whether the work of the bookkeeping office requires a permanent increase in bookkeeping office staff. Of the following questions, the one whose answer would be MOST likely to assist you in making your recommendation is:

    A. Are temporary employees hired to handle seasonal fluctuations in work loads?
    B. Are some permanent employees working irregular hours because they occasionally work overtime?
    C. Are the present permanent employees keeping the work of the bookkeeping office current?
    D. Are employees complaining that the work is unevenly divided?

4.__

5. Assume that you are a supervisor. One of your subordinates tells you that he is dissatisfied with his work assignment and that he wishes to discuss the matter with you. The employee is obviously very angry and upset. Of the following, the course of action that you should take FIRST in this situation is to

    A. promise the employee that you will review all the work assignments in the office to determine whether any changes should be made
    B. have the employee present his complaint, correcting him whenever he makes what seems to be an erroneous charge against you

5.__

C. postpone discussion of the employee's complaint, explaining to him that the matter can be settled more satisfactorily if it is discussed calmly

D. permit the employee to present his complaint in full, withholding your comments until he has finished making his complaint

6. Assume that you are a supervisor. You find that you are spending too much time on routine tasks, and not enough time on supervision of the work of your subordinates. It would be *advisable* for you to

    6.____

A. assign some of the routine tasks to your subordinates

B. postpone the performance of routine tasks until you have completed your supervisory tasks

C. delegate the supervisory work to a capable subordinate

D. eliminate some of the supervisory tasks that you are required to perform

7. Assume that you are a supervisor. You discover that one of your workers has violated an important rule. The FIRST course of action for you as the supervisor to take would be to

    7.____

A. call a meeting of the entire staff and discuss the matter generally without mentioning any employee by name

B. arrange to supervise the offending worker's activities more closely

C. discuss the violation privately with the worker involved

D. discuss the matter with the worker within hearing of the entire staff so that she will feel too ashamed to commit this violation in the future

8. As a supervisor, you are to prepare a vacation schedule for the bookkeeping office employees. The one of the following that is the LEAST important factor for you to consider in setting up this schedule is

    8.____

A. seniority

B. vacation preferences of employees

C. average producivity of the office

D. workload

9. In assigning a complicated task to a group of subordinates, a certain supervisor does not indicate the specific steps to be followed in performing the assignment, nor does he designate which subordinate is to be responsible for seeing that the task is done on time. This supervisor's method of assigning the task is MOST likely to result in

    9.____

A. confusion among subordinates with consequent delays in work

B. greater individual effort and self-reliance

C. assumption of authority by capable subordinates

D. loss of confidence by subordinates in their ability

10. While you are explaining a new procedure to an employee, she asks you a question about the procedure which you cannot answer. The MOST appropriate action for you to take is to

    10.____

A. admit your inability to answer the question and promise to obtain the information

B. point out the unlikelihood of a situation arising which would require an answer to the question

C. ask the worker to give her reason for asking the question before you give any further reply
D. tell her to inform you immediately, should a situation arise requiring an answer to her question

---

KEY (CORRECT ANSWERS)

1.	D		6.	A
2.	B		7.	C
3.	C		8.	C
4.	C		9.	A
5.	D		10.	A

SUPERVISION, ADMINISTRATION, MANAGEMENT AND ORGANIZATION

EXAMINATION SECTION
TEST 1

DIRECTIONS: Each question or incomplete statement is followed by several suggested answers or completions. Select the one that BEST answers the question or completes the statement. *PRINT THE LETTER OF THE CORRECT ANSWER IN THE SPACE AT THE RIGHT.*

1. A supervisor scheduled an interview with a subordinate in order to discuss his unsatisfactory performance during the previous several weeks. The subordinate's work contained an excessive number of careless errors.
   After the interview, the supervisor, reviewing his own approach for self-examination, listed three techniques he had used in the interview, as follows:
      I. Specifically pointed out to the subordinate where he had failed to meet the standards expected.
      II. Shared the blame for certain management errors that had irritated the subordinate.
      III. Agreed with the subordinate on specific targets to be met during the period ahead.
   Of the following statements the one that is MOST acceptable concerning the above 3 techniques is that

   A. all 3 techniques are correct
   B. techniques I and II are correct; III is not correct
   C. techniques II and III are correct; I is not correct
   D. techniques I and III are correct; II is not correct

1.____

2. Assume that the performance of an employee is not satisfactory. Of the following, the MOST effective way for a supervisor to attempt to improve the performance of the employee is to meet with him *and* to

   A. order him to change his behavior
   B. indicate the actions that are unsatisfactory and the penalties for them
   C. show him alternate ways of behaving and a method for him to evaluate his attempts at change
   D. suggest that he use the behavior of the supervisor as a model of acceptable conduct

2.____

3. Training employees to be productive workers is based on four fundamental principles:
      I. Demonstrate how the job should be done by telling and showing the correct operations step-by-step
      II. Allow the employee to get some of the feel of the job by allowing him to try it a bit
      III. Put him on the job while continuing to check his performance
      IV. Let him know why the job is important and why it must be done right.
   The MOST logical order for these training steps is:

   A. I, III, II, IV   B. I, IV, II, III
   C. II, I, III, IV   D. IV, I, II, III

3.____

4. Sometimes a supervisor is faced with the need to train under-educated new employees. 4.___
The following five statements relate to training such employees.
    I.   Make the training general rather than specific
    II. Rely upon demonstrations and illustrations whenever possible
    III. Overtrain rather than undertrain by erring on the side of imparting a little
       more skill than is absolutely necessary
    IV. Provide lots of follow-up on the job
    V. Reassure and recognize frequently in order to increase self-confidence
Which of the following choices lists *all* the above statements that are generally COR-
RECT?

  A. II, II, and IV
  C. I, II, and V
                     B. II, III, IV, and V
                     D. I, II, IV, and V

5. One of the ways in which some supervisors train subordinates is to discuss the subordi- 5.___
nate's weaknesses with them. Experts who have explored the actual feelings and reactions of subordinates in such situations have come to the conclusion that such interviews
usually

  A. are seen by subordinates as a threat to their self-esteem
  B. give subordinates a feeling of importance which leads to better learning
  C. convince subordinates to accept the opinion of the supervisor
  D. result in the development of better supervision

6. The one of the following which BEST describes the rate at which a trainee learns depart- 6.___
mental procedures is that he *probably* will learn

  A. at the same rate throughout if the material to be learned is complex
  B. slowly in the beginning and then learning will accelerate steadily
  C. quickly for a while, than slow down temporarily
  D. at the same rate if the material to be learned is lengthy

7. Which of the following statements concerning the delegation of work to subordinate 7.___
employees is *generally* CORRECT?

  A. A supervisor's personal attitude toward delegation has a minimal effect on his skill
      in delegating.
  B. A willingness to let subordinates make mistakes has a place in work delegation.
  C. The element of trust has little impact on the effectiveness of work delegation.
  D. The establishment of controls does not enhance the process of delegation.

8. Assume that you are the chairman of a group that has been formed to discuss and solve 8.___
a particular problem. After a half-hour of discussion, you feel that the group is wandering
off the point and is no longer discussing the problem.
In this situation, it would be BEST for you to

  A. wait to see whether the group will get back on the track by itself
  B. ask the group to stop and to try a different approach
  C. ask the group to stop, decide where they are going, and then to decide how to con-
      tinue
  D. ask the group to stop, decide where they are going, and then to continue in a differ-
      ent direction

9. One method of group decision-making is the use of committees. Following are four statements concerning committees.

    I.   Considering the value of each individual member's time, committees are costly.

    II.   One result of committee decisions is that no one may be held responsible for the decision.

    III.   Committees will make decisions more promptly then individuals.

    IV.   Committee decisions tend to be balanced and to take different viewpoints into account.

Which of the following choices lists *all* of the above statements that are generally CORRECT?

    A. I and II   B. II and III   C. I, II, IV   D. II, III, IV

10. Assume that an employee bypasses his supervisor and comes directly to you, the superior officer, to ask for a short leave of absence because of a pressing personal problem. The employee did not first consult with his immediate supervisor because he believes that his supervisor is unfavorably biased against him.
Of the following, the MOST desirable way for you to handle this situation is to

    A. instruct the employee that it is not appropriate for him to go over the head of his supervisor regardless of their personal relationship

    B. listen to a brief description of his problem and then tactfully suggest that he take the matter up with his supervisor before coming to you

    C. request that both the employee and his supervisor meet jointly with you in order to discuss the employee's problem and to get at the reasons behind their apparent difficulty

    D. listen carefully to the employee's problem and then, without committing yourself one way or the other, promise to discuss it with his supervisor

11. Which of the following statements concerning the motivation of subordinates is generally INCORRECT? The

    A. authoritarian approach as the method of supervision is likely to result in the setting of minimal performance standards for themselves by subordinates

    B. encouragement of competition among subordinates may lead to deterioration of teamwork

    C. granting of benefits by a supervisor to subordinates in order to gain their gratitide will result in maximum output by the subordinates

    D. opportunity to achieve job satisfaction has an important effect on motivating subordinates

12. Of the following, the MOST serious disadvantage of having a supervisor evaluate subordinates on the basis of measurable performance goals that are set jointly by the supervisor and the subordinates is that this results-oriented appraisal method

    A. focuses on past performance rather than plans for the future

    B. fails to provide sufficient feedback to help subordinates learn where they stand

    C. encourages the subordinates to conceal poor performance and set low goals

    D. changes the primary task of the supervisor from helping subordinates improve to criticizing their performance

13. A supervisor can BEST provide on-the-job satisfaction for his subordinates by   13.___

    A. providing rewards for good performance
    B. allowing them to decide when to do the assigned work
    C. motivating them to perform according to accepted procedures
    D. providing challenging work that achieves departmental objectives

14. Which of the following factors *generally* contributes MOST to job satisfaction among   14.___
supervisory employees?

    A. Autonomy and independence on the job
    B. Job security
    C. Pleasant physical working conditions
    D. Adequate economic rewards

15. Large bureaucracies typically exhibit certain characteristics.   15.___
Of the following, it would be CORRECT to state that such bureaucracies *generally*

    A. tend to oversimplify communications
    B. pay undue attention to informal organizations
    C. develop an attitude of "group-think" and conformity
    D. emphasize personal growth among employees

16. When positive methods fail to achieve conformity with accepted standards of conduct or   16.___
performance, a negative type of action, punitive in nature, usually must follow.
The one of the following that is *usually* considered LEAST important for the success of
such punishment or negative discipline is that it be

    A. certain   B. swift   C. severe   D. consistent

17. Assume that you are a supervisor. Philip Smith, who is under your supervision, informs   17.___
you that James Jones, who is also your subordinate, has been creating antagonism and
friction within the unit because of his unnecessarily gruff manner in dealing with his co-
workers. Smith's remarks confirm your own observations of Jones' behavior and its
effects. In handling this situation, the one of the following procedures which will *probably*
be MOST effective is to

    A. ask Smith to act as an informal counselor to Jones and report the results to you
    B. counsel the other employees in your unit on methods of changing attitudes of peo-
ple
    C. interview Jones and help him to understand this problem
    D. order Jones to carry out his responsibilities with greater consideration for the feel-
ings of his co-workers

18. The PRINCIPLE relating to the number of subordinates who can be supervised effec-   18.___
tively by one supervisor is *commonly* known as

    A. span of control   B. delegation of authority
    C. optimum personnel assignment   D. organizational factor

19. Ascertaining and improving the level of morale in a public agency is one of the responsi-   19._____
    bilities of a conscientious supervisor.
    The one of the following aspects of subordinates' behavior which is NOT an indication
    of low morale is

    A. lower-level employees participating in organizational decision-making
    B. careless treatment of equipment
    C. general deterioration of personal appearance
    D. formation of cliques

20. Employees may resist changes in agency operations even though such changes are   20._____
    often necessary. If you, as a supervisor, are attempting to introduce a necessary change,
    you should *first* fully explain the reasons for it to your staff. Your NEXT step should be to

    A. set specific goals and outline programs for all employees
    B. invite employee participation in effectuating the change by asking for suggestions
       to accomplish it
    C. discuss the need for improved work performance by city employees
    D. point out the penalties for non-cooperation without singling out any employee by
       name

21. A supervisor should *normally* avoid giving orders in an offhand or casual manner   21._____
    MAINLY because his subordinates

    A. are like mot people and may resent being treated lightly
    B. may attach little importance to these orders
    C. may work best if given the choice of work methods
    D. are unlikely to need instructions in most matters

22. Assume that, as a supervisor, you have just praised a subordinate. While he expresses   22._____
    satisfaction at your praise, he complains that it does not help him get promoted even
    though he is on a promotion eligible list, since there is no current vacancy.
    In these circumstances, it would be BEST for you to

    A. minimize the importance of advancement and emphasize the satisfaction in the
       work itself
    B. follow up by pointing out some errors he has committed in the past
    C. admit that the situation exists, and express the hope that it will improve
    D. tell him that, until quite recently, advancement was even slower

23. Departmental policies are usually broad rules or guides for action. It is important for a   23._____
    supervisor to understand his role with respect to policy implementation.
    Of the following, the MOST accurate description of this role is that a supervisor should

    A. be apologetic toward his subordinates when applying unpopular policies to them
    B. act within policy limits, although he can attempt to influence policy change by mak-
       ing his thoughts and observations known to his superior
    C. arrange his activities so that he is able to deal simultaneously with situations that
       involve several policy matters
    D. refrain as much as possible from exercising permissible discretion in applying pol-
       icy to matters under his control

24. A supervisor should be aware that *most* subordinates will ask questions at meetings or group discussions *in order to*   24.___

    A. stimulate other employees to express their opinions
    B. discover how they may be affected by the subjects under discussion
    C. display their knowledge of the topics under discussion
    D. consume time in order to avoid returning to their normal tasks

25. Don't assign responsibilities with conflicting objectives to the same work group. For example, to require a unit to monitor the quality of its own work is a bad practice. This practice is *most likely* to be bad because   25.___

    A. the chain of command will be unnecessarily lengthened
    B. it is difficult to portray mixed duties accurately on an organization chart
    C. employees may act in collusion to cover up poor work
    D. the supervisor may delegate responsibilities which he should retain

---

KEY (CORRECT ANSWERS)

1. A			11. C
2. C			12. C
3. D			13. D
4. B			14. A
5. A			15. C
6. C			16. C
7. B			17. C
8. C			18. A
9. C			19. A
10. D			20. B

21. B
22. C
23. B
24. B
25. C

TEST 2

DIRECTIONS: Each question or incomplete statement is followed by several suggested answers or completions. Select the one that BEST answers the question or completes the statement. *PRINT THE LETTER OF THE CORRECT ANSWER IN THE SPACE AT THE RIGHT.*

1. Some supervisors use an approach in which each phase of the job is explained in broad terms supervision is general, and employees are allowed broad discretion in performing their job duties.
   Such a supervisory approach *usually* affects employee motivation by

   A. improving morale and providing an incentive to work harder
   B. providing little or no incentive to work harder than the minimum required
   C. creating extra pressure, usually resulting in decreased performance
   D. reducing incentive to work and causing employees to feel neglected, particularly in performing complex tasks

   1.____

2. An employee complains to a superior officer that he has been treated unfairly by his supervisor, stating that other employees have been given less work to do and shown other forms of favoritism.
   Of the following, the BEST thing for the superior officer to do FIRST in order to handle this problem is to

   A. try to discover whether the subordinate has a valid complaint or if something else is the real problem
   B. ask other employees whether they feel that their treatment is consistent and fair
   C. ask his supervisor to explain the charges
   D. see that the number of cases assigned to this employee is reduced

   2.____

3. Of the following, the MOST important condition needed to help a group of people to work well together and get the job done is

   A. higher salaries and a better working environment
   B. enough free time to relieve the tension
   C. good communication among everyone involved in the job
   D. assurance that everyone likes the work

   3.____

4. A supervisor realizes that a subordinate has called in sick for three Mondays out of the past four. These absences have interfered with staff performance and have been part of the cause of the unit's "behind schedule" condition.
   In order to correct this situation, it would be BEST for the supervisor to

   A. order the subordinate to explain his abuse of sick leave
   B. discuss with the subordinate the penalties for abusing sick leave
   C. discuss the matter with his own supervisor
   D. ask the subordinate in private whether he has a problem about coming to work

   4.____

5. Of the following, the MOST effective way for a supervisor to minimize undesirable rumors about new policies in the units under his supervision is to

   A. bypass the supervisor and communicate directly with the individual members of the units
   B. supply immediate and accurate information to everyone who is supposed to be informed

   5.____

C. play down the importance of the rumors
D. issue all communications in written form

6. Which of the following is an *indication* that a superior officer is delegating authority PROPERLY?

    6.___

  A. The superior officer closely checks the work of experienced subordinates at all stages in order to maintain standards.
  B. The superior officer gives overlapping assignments to insure that work is completed on time.
  C. The work of his subordinates can proceed and be completed during the superior officer's absence.
  D. The work of each supervisor is reviewed by him more than once in order to insure quality.

7. Of the following supervisory practices, the one which is *MOST LIKELY* to foster employee morale is for the supervisor to

    7.___

  A. take an active interest in subordinates' personal lives
  B. ignore mistakes
  C. give praise when justified
  D. permit rules to go unenforced occasionally

8. As the supervisor who is responsible for the implementation of a new paperwork procedure, you note that the workers often do not follow the stipulated procedure.
Before taking action, it would be ADVISABLE to realize that

    8.___

  A. unconscious behavior, such as failure to adapt to change, is largely uncontrollable
  B. new procedures sometimes have to be modified and adapted after being tried out
  C. threats of disciplinary action will encourage approval of change
  D. procedures that fail should be abandoned and replaced

9. The one of the following which is *generally* considered to be the MOST significant criticism of the modern practice of effective human relations in management of large organizations is that human relations

    9.___

  A. weakens management authority over employees
  B. gives employees control of operations
  C. can be used to manipulate and control employees
  D. weakens unions

10. Of the following, the MOST important reason why the supervisor should promote *good* supervisor-subordinate relations is to encourage his staff to

    10.___

  A. feel important   B. be more receptive to control
  C. be happy in their work   D. meet production performance levels

11. A superior officer decides to assign a special report directly to an employee, bypassing his supervisor.
In general, this practice is

    11.___

  A. *advisable*, chiefly because it broadens the superior officer's span of authority
  B. *inadvisable*, chiefly because it undermines the authority of the supervisor in the eyes of his subordinates

    C. *advisable,* chiefly because it reduces the number of details the supervisor must know
    D. *inadvisable,* chiefly because it gives too much work to the employee

12. Many supervisors make it a practice to solicit suggestions from their subordinates and to encourage their participation in decision making.
The success of this type of supervision *usually* depends MOST directly upon the

    A. quality of leadership provided by the supervisor
    B. number of the supervisor's immediate subordinates
    C. availability of opportunities for employee advancement
    D. degree to which work assignments cause problems

12.____

13. Small informal groups or "cliques" often appear in a work setting.
The one of the following which is generally an *advantage* of such groups, from an administrative point of view, is that they

    A. are not influenced by the administrative set-up of the office
    B. encourage socializing after working hours
    C. develop leadership roles among the office staff
    D. provide a "steam valve" for release of tension and fatigue

13.____

14. Assume that you are a superior officer in charge of several supervisors, who, in turn, are in charge of a number of employees. The employees who are supervised by Jones (a supervisor) come as a group to you and indicate several resons why Jones is incompetent and "has to go."
Of the following, your *best* course of action to take FIRST is to

    A. direct the employees to see Jones about the matter
    B. suggest to the employees that they should attempt to work with Jones until he can be transferred
    C. discuss the possibility of terminating Jones with *your* superior
    D. ask Jones about the comments of the employees after they depart

14.____

15. Of the following, the MAIN effect which the delegation of authority can have on the efficiency of an organization is to

    A. reduce the risk of decision-making errors
    B. produce uniformity of policy and action
    C. facilitate speedier decisions and actions
    D. enable closer control of operations

15.____

16. Of the following, the main DISADVANTAGE of temporarily transferring a newly appointed worker to another unit because of an unexpected vacancy is that the temporary nature of his assignment will, *most likely,*

    A. undermine his incentive to orient himself to his new job
    B. interfere with his opportunities for future advancement
    C. result in friction between himself and his new co-workers
    D. place his new supervisor in a difficult and awkward position

16.____

17. Assume that you, as a supervisor, have decided to raise the quality of work produced by your subordinates.
The BEST of the following procedures for you to follow is to

    A. develop mathematically precise standards
    B. appoint a committee of subordinates to set firm and exacting guidelines, including penalties for deviations
    C. modify standards developed by supervisors in other organizations
    D. provide consistent evaluation of subordinates' work, furnishing training whenever advisable

17.____

18. Assume that a supervisor under your supervision strongly objects whenever changes are proposed which would improve the efficiency of his unit.
Of the following, the MOST desirable way for you to *change* his attitude is to

    A. involve him in the planning and formulation of changes
    B. promise to recommend him for a more challenging assignment if he accepts changes
    C. threaten to have him transferred to another unit if he does not accept changes
    D. ask him to go along with the changes on a tentative, trial basis

18.____

19. Work goals may be defined in terms of units produced or in terms of standards of performance.
Which of the following statements concerning work goals is CORRECT?

    A. Workers who have a share in establishing goals tend to set a fairly high standard for themselves, but fail to work toward it.
    B. Workers tend to produce according to what they believe are the goals actually expected of them.
    C. Since workers usually produce less than the established goals, management should set goals higher than necessary.
    D. The individual differences of workers can be minimized by using strict goals and invariable procedures.

19.____

20. Of the following, the type of employee who would respond BEST to verbal instructions given in the form of a suggestion or wish is the

    A. experienced worker who is eager to please
    B. sensitive and emotional worker
    C. hostile worker who is somewhat lazy
    D. slow and methodical worker

20.____

21. As a supervisor, you note that the output of an experienced staff member has dropped dramatically during the last two months. In addition, his error rate is significantly above that of other staff members. When you ask the employee the reason for his poor performance, he says, "Well, it's rather personal and I would rather not talk about it if you don't mind."
At this point, which of the following would be the BEST reply?

    A. Tell him that you will give him two weeks to improve or you will discuss the matter with your own supervisor
    B. Insist that he tell you the reason for his poor work and assure him that anything personal will be kept confidential

21.____

C. Say that you don't want to interfere, but, at the same time, his work has deterio-
rated, and that you're concerned about it

D. Explain in a friendly manner that you are going to place a warning letter in his personnel folder that states he has one month in which to improve

22. Research studies have shown that employees who are strongly interested in achievment   22.____
and advancement on the job *usually* want assignments where the chance of success is

A. *low,* and desire frequent supervisory evaluation of their performance
B. *high,* and desire general supervisory evaluation of their performance
C. *high,* and desire infrequent supervisory evaluation of their performance
D. *moderate,* and desire specific supervisory evaluation of their performance

23. Of the following, a function of the supervisor that concerns itself with the process of   23.____
determining a course of action from alternatives is *usually* referred to as

A. decentralization
B. planning
C. controlling
D. input

24. Favorable working conditions are an important variable in producing an effective work   24.____
unit.
Which of the following would be LEAST conducive in providing a favorable work situation?

A. Applying a job enrichment program to a routine clerical position
B. Setting practical goals for the work unit which are consistent with the overall objective of the agency
C. Assigning individuals to positions which require a higher level of educational
achievement than that which they possess
D. Establishing a communications system which distributes information and provides
feedback to all organizational levels

25. Every supervisor within an organization should know to whom he reports and who   25.____
reports to him.
Within the organization this will *most likely* insure

A. unity of command
B. confidentiality of sensitive issues
C. excellent morale
D. the elimination of the grapevine

KEY (CORRECT ANSWERS)

1.	A		11.	B
2.	A		12.	A
3.	C		13.	D
4.	D		14.	D
5.	B		15.	C
6.	C		16.	A
7.	C		17.	D
8.	B		18.	A
9.	C		19.	B
10.	D		20.	A

21.	C
22.	D
23.	B
24.	C
25.	A

TEST 3

DIRECTIONS: Each question or incomplete statement is followed by several suggested answers or completions. Select the one that BEST answers the question or completes the statement. *PRINT THE LETTER OF THE CORRECT ANSWER IN THE SPACE AT THE RIGHT.*

1. In trying to improve the motivation of his subordinates, a supervisor can achieve the BEST results by taking action based upon the assumption that *most* employees

   A. have an inherent dislike of work
   B. wish to be closely directed
   C. are more interested in security than in assuming responsibility
   D. will exercise self-direction without coercion

   1.____

2. Supervisors in public departments have many functions.
   Of the following, the function which is LEAST appropriate for a supervisor is to

   A. serve as a deputy for the administrator within his own unit
   B. determine needs within his unit and plan programs to meet these needs
   C. supervise, train, and evaluate all personnel assigned to his unit
   D. initiate and carry out fund-raising projects, such as bazaars and carnivals, to buy needed equipment

   2.____

3. When there are conflicts or tensions between top management and lower-level employees in any public department, the supervisor should FIRST attempt to

   A. represent and enforce the mangement point of view
   B. act as the representative of the workers to get their ideas across to management
   C. serve as a two-way spokesman, trying to interpret each side to the other
   D. remain neutral, but keep informed of changes in the situation

   3.____

4. A probationary period for new employees is usually provided in public agencies.
   The MAJOR purpose of such a period is *usually* to

   A. allow a determination of employee's suitability for the position
   B. obtain evidence as to employee's ability to perform in a higher position
   C. conform to requirements that ethnic hiring goals be met for all positions
   D. train the new employee in the duties of the position

   4.____

5. An effective program of orientation for new employees usually includes *all* the following EXCEPT

   A. having the supervisor introduce the new employee to his job, outlining his responsibilities and how to carry them out
   B. permitting the new worker to tour the facility or department, so he can observe all parts of it in action
   C. scheduling meetings for new employees, at which the job requirements are explained to them and they are given personnel manuals
   D. testing the new worker on his skills, and sending him to a centralized in-service workshop

   5.____

6. In-service training is an important responsibility of supervisors.
   The MAJOR reason for such training is to

   6.____

    A.   avoid future grievance procedures, because employees might say they were not prepared to carry out their jobs
    B.   maximize the effectiveness of the department by helping each employee perform at his full potential
    C.   satisfy inspection teams from central headquarters of the department
    D.   help prevent disagreements with members of the community

7.   There are many forms of useful in-service training.   7.___
    Of the following, the training method which is NOT an appropriate technique for leadership development is to

    A.   provide special workshops or clinics in activity skills
    B.   conduct pre-season institutes to familiarize new workers with the program of the department and with their roles
    C.   schedule team meetings for problem-solving, including both supervisors and leaders
    D.   have the leader rate himself on an evaluation form periodically

8.   Of the following techniques of evaluating work training programs, the one that is BEST is to   8.___

    A.   pass out a carefully designed questionnaire to the trainees at the completion of the program
    B.   test the knowledge that trainees have both at the beginning of training and at its completion
    C.   interview the trainees at the completion of the program
    D.   evaluate performance before and after training for both a control group and an experimental group

9.   Assume that a new supervisor is having difficulty making his instructions to subordinates clearly understood. The one of the following which is the FIRST step he should take in dealing with this problem is to   9.___

    A.   set up a training workshop in communication skills
    B.   determine the extent and nature of the communication gap
    C.   repeat both verbal and written instructions several times
    D.   simplify his written and spoken vocabulary

10.   Discipline of employees is usually a supervisor's responsibility. There may be several useful forms of disciplinary action in public employment.   10.___
    Of the following, the form that is LEAST appropriate is the

    A.   written reprimand or warning
    B.   involuntary transfer to another work setting
    C.   demotion or suspension
    D.   assignment of added hours of work each week

11.   Of the following, the MOST effective means of dealing with employee disciplinary problems is to   11.___

    A.   give personality tests to individuals to identify their psychological problems
    B.   distribute and discuss a policy manual containing exact rules governing employee behavior

C. establish a single, clear penality to be imposed for all wrongdoing irrespective of degree

D. have supervisors get to know employees well through social mingling

12. A recently developed technique for appraising work performance is to have the supervisor record on a continual basis all significant incidents in each subordinate's behavior that indicate unsuccessful action and those that indicate poor behavior.
Of the following, a major DISADVANTAGE of this method of performance appraisal is that it

12.____

A. often leads to overly close supervision
B. results in competition among those subordinates being evaluated
C. tends to result in superficial judgments
D. lacks objectivity for evaluating performance

13. Assume that you are a supervisor and have observed the performance of an employee during a period of time. You have concluded that his performance needs improvement. In order to improve his performance, it would, therefore, be BEST for you to

13.____

A. note your findings in the employee's personnel folder so that his behavior is a matter of record
B. report the findings to the personnel officer so he can take prompt action
C. schedule a problem-solving conference with the employee
D. recommend his transfer to simpler duties

14. When an employee's absences or latenesses seem to be nearing excessiveness, the supervisor should speak with him to find out what the problem is.
Of the following, if such a discussion produces no reasonable explanation, the discussion *usually* BEST serves to

14.____

A. affirm clearly the supervisor's adherence to proper policy
B. alert other employees that such behavior is unacceptable
C. demonstrate that the supervisor truly represents higher management
D. notify the employee that his behavior is being observed and evaluated

15. Assume that an employee willfully and recklessly violates an important agency regulation. The nature of the violation is of such magnitude that it demands immediate action, but the facts of the case are not entirely clear. Further assume that the supervisor is free to make any of the following recommendations.
The MOST appropriate action for the supervisor to take is to recommend that the employee be

15.____

A. discharged
C. forced to resign
B. suspended
D. transferred

16. Although employees' titles may be identical, each position in that title may be considerably different.
Of the following, a supervisor should carefully assign each employee to a specific position based PRIMARILY on the employee's

16.____

A. capability   B. experience   C. education   D. seniority

17. The one of the following situations where it is MOST appropriate to transfer an employee   17.___
to a *similar* assignment is one in which the employee

    A. lacks motivation and interest
    B. experiences a personality conflict with his supervisor
    C. is negligent in the performance of his duties
    D. lacks capacity or ability to perform assigned tasks

18. The one of the following which is LEAST likely to be affected by improvement in the   18.___
morale of personnel is employee

    A. skill   B. absenteeism   C. turnover   D. job satisfaction

19. The one of the following situations in which it is LEAST appropriate for a supervisor to   19.___
delegate authority to subordinates is where the supervisor

    A. lacks confidence in his own abilities to perform certain work
    B. is overburdened and cannot handle all his responsibilities
    C. refers all disciplinary problems to his subordinate
    D. has to deal with an emergency or crisis

20. Of the following, the BEST attitude toward the use of volunteers in programs is that vol-   20.___
unteers should be

    A. discouraged, since they cannot be depended upon to show up regularly
    B. employed as a last resort when paid personnel are unavailable
    C. seen as an appropriate means of providing leadership, when effectively recruited
       and supervised
    D. eliminated to raise the professionalism of personnel

21. A supervisor finds that he is spending too much time on routine tasks, and not enough   21.___
time on coordinating the work of his employees.
It would be MOST advisable for this supervisor to

    A. delegate the task of work coordination to a capable subordinate
    B. eliminate some of the routine tasks that the unit is required to perform
    C. assign some of the routine tasks to his subordinates
    D. postpone the performance of routine tasks until he has achieved proper coordina-
       tion of his employees' work

22. Of the following, the MOST important reason for having an office manual in looseleaf   22.___
form rather than in permanent binding is that the looseleaf form

    A. facilitates the addition of new material and the removal of obsolete material
    B. permits several people to use different sections of the manual at the same time
    C. is less expensive to prepare than permanent binding
    D. is more durable than permanent binding

23. In his first discussion with a newly appointed employee, the LEAST important of the fol-   23.___
lowing topics for a supervisor of a unit to include is the

    A. duties the subordinate is expected to perform on the job
    B. functions of the unit
    C. methods of determining standards of performance
    D. nature and duration of the training the subordinate will receive on the job

24. A supervisor has just been told by a subordinate, Mr. Jones, that another employee, Mr.   24.____
Smith, deliberately disobeyed an important rule of the department by taking home some
confidential departmental material.
Of the following courses of action, it would be MOST advisable for the supervisor *first*
to

   A. discuss the matter privately, with both Mr. Jones and Mr. Smith at the same time
   B. call a meeting of the enture staff and discuss the matter generally without mention-
   ing any employee by name
   C. arrange to supervise Mr. Smith's activities more closely
   D. discuss the matter privately with Mr. Smith

25. The one of the following actions which would be MOST effificient and economical for a   25.____
supervisor to take to minimize the effect of seasonal fluctuations in the work load of his
unit is to

   A. increase his permanent staff until it is large enough to handle the work of the busy
   season
   B. request the purchase of time and labor saving equipment to be used primarily during the busy season
   C. lower, temporarily, the standards for quality of work performance during peak loads
   D. schedule for the slow season work that it is not essential to perform during the
   busy season

KEY (CORRECT ANSWERS)

1.	D		11.	B
2.	D		12.	A
3.	C		13.	C
4.	A		14.	D
5.	D		15.	B
6.	B		16.	A
7.	D		17.	B
8.	D		18.	A
9.	B		19.	C
10.	D		20.	C

21.	C
22.	A
23.	C
24.	D
25.	D

193

TEST 4

DIRECTIONS: Each question or incomplete statement is followed by several suggested answers or completions. Select the one that BEST answers the question or completes the statement. *PRINT THE LETTER OF THE CORRECT ANSWER IN THE SPACE AT THE RIGHT.*

1. Assume that, while instructing a worker on a new procedure, the instructor asks, at frequent intervals, whether there are any questions. His asking for questions is a 　　　　1.___

   A. *good practice,* because it affords the worker an opportunity to participate actively in the lesson
   B. *good practice,* because it may reveal points that are not understood by the worker
   C. *poor practice,* because workers generally find it embarrassing to ask questions
   D. *poor practice,* because it may result in wasting time on irrelevant matters

2. Any person thoroughly familiar with the specific steps in a particular type of work is well-qualified to serve as a training course instructor in the work.
   This statement is *erroneous* CHIEFLY because 　　　　2.___

   A. a qualified instructor cannot be expected to have detailed information about many specific fields
   B. a person who knows a field thoroughly may not be good at passing his knowledge along to others
   C. it is practically impossible for any instructor to be acquainted with all the specific steps in a particular type of work
   D. what is true of one type of work is not necessarily true of other types of work

3. Of the following traits, the one that is LEAST essential for the "ideal" supervisor is that she 　　　　3.___

   A. be consistent in her interpretation of the rules and policies of the agency for which she works
   B. is able to judge a person's ability at her first meeting with that person
   C. know her own job thoroughly
   D. appreciate and acknowledge honest effort and above-average work

4. The one of the following which is generally the basic reason for using standard procedures is to 　　　　4.___

   A. serve as a basis for formulating policies
   B. provide the sequence of steps for handling recurring activities
   C. train new employees in the policies and objectives
   D. facilitate periodic review of standard practices,

5. An employee, while working at the bookkeeping machine, accidentally kicks off the holdup alarm system. She notifies the supervisor that she can hear the holdup alarm bell ringing, and requests that the holdup alarm system be reset.
   After the holdup alarm system has been reset, the supervisor should notify the manager that the alarm 　　　　5.___

   A. is in proper wdrking order
   B. should be shut off while the employee is working the bookkeeping machine to avoid another such accident

C.   kick-plate should be moved away from the worker's reception window so that it cannot be set off accidentally

D.   should be relocated so that it cannot be heard in the bookkeeping office

6.   A supervisor who spends a considerable amount of time correcting subordinates' procedural errors should consider FIRST the possibility of

6._____

A.   disciplining those who make errors consistently
B.   instituting refresher training sessions
C.   redesigning work forms
D.   requesting that the requirements for entry-level jobs be changed

7.   A supervisor has a subordinate who has been late the past four mornings.
Of the following, the MOST important action for the supervisor to take FIRST is to

7._____

A.   read the rules concerning lateness to the employee in an authoritative manner
B.   give the subordinate a chance to explain the reason for his lateness
C.   tell the employee he must come in on time the next day
D.   ask the friends of the employee whether they can tell him the reason for the employee's lateness

8.   During a conversation, a subordinate tells his supervisor about a family problem.
For the supervisor to give EXPLICIT advice to the subordinate would be

8._____

A.   *desirable*, primarily because a happy employee is more likely to be productive
B.   *undesirable*, primarily because the supervisor should not allow a subordinate to discuss personal problems
C.   *desirable*, primarily because their personal relations will show a marked improvement
D.   *undesirable*, primarily because a supervisor should not take responsibility for handling a subordinate's personal problem

9.   As a supervisor, you have received instructions for a drastic change in the procedure for processing cases.
Of the following, the approach which is MOST likely to result in acceptance of the change by your subordinates is for you to

9._____

A.   inform all subordinates of the change by written memo so that they will have guidelines to follow
B.   ask your superior to inform the unit members about the change at a staff meeting
C.   recruit the most experienced employee in the unit to give individual instruction to the other unit members
D.   discuss the change and the reasons for it with the staff so that they understand their role in its implementation

10.   Of the following, the principle which should GENERALLY guide: a supervisor in the training of employees under his supervision is that

10._____

A.   training of employees should be delegated to more experienced employees in the same title
B.   primary emphasis should be placed on training for future assignments
C.   the training process should be a highly individual matter
D.   training efforts should concentrate on employees who have the greatest potential

KEY (CORRECT ANSWERS)

1. B
2. B
3. B
4. B
5. D

6. B
7. B
8. D
9. D
10. C

———————

BASIC FUNDAMENTALS OF WRITTEN COMMUNICATION

CONTENTS	Page

BASIC FUNDAMENTALS OF WRITTEN COMMUNICATION

INSTRUCTIONAL OBJECTIVES

1. Ability to write legibly.
2. Ability to fill out forms and applications correctly.
3. Ability to take messages and notes accurately.
4. Ability to write letters effectively.
5. Ability to write directions and instructions clearly.
6. Ability to outline written and spoken information.
7. Ability to persuade or teach others through written communication.
8. Ability to write effective overviews and summaries.
9. Ability to make smooth transitions within written communications.
10. Ability to use language forms appropriate for the reader.
11. Ability to prepare effective informational reports.

CONTENT

INTRODUCTION

Public-service employees are required to prepare written communications for a variety of purposes. Written communication is a fundamental tool, not only for the public-service occupations, but throughout the world of work. Many public-service occupations require written communication with ordinary citizens of diverse backgrounds, so the trainee should develop the ability to write in simple, nontechnical language that the ordinary citizen will understand.

This unit is designed to develop the student's ability to communicate effectively in writing for a number of different purposes and in a number of different formats. Whatever the particular purpose or format, how·· ever, effective writing will require the writer:

- to have a clear idea of his purpose and his audience;
- to organize his thoughts and information in an orderly way;
- to express himself concisely, accurately, and concretely;
- to report relevant facts;
- to explain and summarize ideas clearly; and
- to evaluate the effectiveness of his communication.

1. **BUSINESS WRITING**
   Several forms of written communication tend to recur frequently in most public-service agencies, including:
   - letters
   - forms
   - memoranda
   - minutes of meetings
   - short reports
   - telegrams and cables
   - news releases
   - and many others

   The public-service employee should be familiar with the principles of writing in these forms, and should be able to apply them in preparing effective communications.

Letters

Every letter sent from a public-service agency should be considered an ambassador of goodwill. The impression it creates may mean the difference between favorable public attitudes or unfavorable ones. It may mean the difference between creating a friend or an enemy for the agency. Every public-service employee has a responsibility to serve the public effectively and to provide services in an efficient and courteous manner. The letters an agency sends out reflect its attitudes toward the public.

The impression a letter creates depends upon both its appearance and its tone. A letter which shows erasures and pen written corrections gives an impression that the sending agency is slovenly. Similarly, a rude or impersonal letter creates the impression that the agency is insensitive or unfeeling. In preparing letters, the employee should apply principles of style and tone which will serve to create the most favorable impression.

Select the Letter Type. The two most common types of business letters are letters of inquiry and letters of response - that is, "asking" letters and "answering" letters. Whichever type of letter the employee is asked to write, the following guidelines will simplify the task and help to achieve a style and tone which will create a favorable impression on the reader.

Select the Right Format. Several styles of letter format are in common use today, including:

- the indented format,
- the block format, and
- the semi-block format.

Modified forms of these are also in use in some offices. The student should become familiar with the formats preferred for usage in his office, and be able to use whichever form the employer requests.

Know the Letter Elements. Every letter includes certain basic elements, such as:

- the letterhead, which identifies the name and address of the sender.
- the date on which the letter was transmitted.
- the inside address, with the name, street, city, and state of the addressee.
- the salutation, greeting the addressee.
- the body, containing the message.
- the complimentary close, the "good-bye" of the business letter.
- the signature, handwritten by the sender.
- the typed signature, the typewritten name and title of the sender.

In addition, several other elements are occasionally found in business letters:

- the *attention line,* directing the letter to the attention of a particular individual or his representative.
- the *subject line,* informing the reader at a glance of the subject of the letter.

- the *enclosure notation,* noting items enclosed with the letter.
- the *copy notation,* listing other persons who receive copies of the letter.
- the *postscript,* an afterthought sometimes (but not normally) added following the last typed line of the letter.

Be *Brief.* Use only the words which help to say what is needed in a clear and straightforward manner. Do not repeat information already known to the reader, or contained elsewhere in the letter. Likewise, do not repeat information contained in the letter being answered. Rather than repeat the content of a previous letter, one can say something like, "Please refer to our letter dated March 5:"

An employee can shorten his letters by using single words that serve the same function as longer phrases. Many commonly used phrases can be replaced by single words. For example,

Phrase	Single word
in order to	to
in reference to in	about
the amount of	for, of
in a number of cases	some
in view of	because
with regard to	about, in

Similarly, avoid the use of adjectives and nouns that are formed from verbs. If the root verbs are used instead, the writing will be more concise and more vivid. For example,

Noun form	Verb form
We made an adjustment on our books	We adjusted our books
We are sorry we cannot make a replacement of	We are sorry we cannot replace
Please make a correction in our order	Please correct our order

Be on the lookout for unnecessary adjectives and adverbs which tend to clutter letters without adding information or improving style. Such unnecessary words tend to distract the reader and make it more difficult for him to grasp the main points. Observe how the superfluous words, italicized in the following example, obscure the meaning: "You may be *very much* disappointed to learn that the *excessively large* demand for our *highly popular recent* publication, 'Your Income Taxes,' has led to an *unexpected* shortage of this *attractive* publication and we *sadly* expect they will not be replenished until *quite* late this year."

Summarizing, then, a *good letter is simple and clear, with short, simple words, sentences, and paragraphs. Related parts of sentences and paragraphs are kept together and placed in an order which makes it easy for the reader to follow the main thoughts.*

<u>Be Natural</u>. Whenever possible, use a human touch. Use names and personal pronouns to let the reader know the letter was written by a person, not an institution. Instead of saying, "It is the policy of this agency to contact its clients once each year to confirm their status," try this: "Our policy, Mr. Jones, is to confirm your status once each year."

<u>Use Concrete Nouns</u>. Avoid using abstract words and generalizations. Use names of objects, places, and persons rather than abstractions.

<u>Use Active verbs</u>. The passive voice gives a motionless, weak tone to most writing. Instead of "The minutes were taken by Mrs. Smith," say, "Mrs. Smith took the minutes." Instead of "The plans were prepared by the banquet committee," say, "The banquet committee prepared the plans."

<u>Use a Natural Tone</u>. Many people tend to become hard, cold, and unnatural the moment they write a letter. *Communicating by letter should have the same natural tone of conversation used in everyday speech.* One way to achieve a natural and personal tone in the majority of letters is through the use of personal pronouns. Instead of saying, "Referring to your letter of March 5, reporting the non-receipt of goods ordered last February 15, please be advised that the goods were shipped as requested," say, "I am sorry to hear that you failed to receive the items you ordered last February 15. We shipped them the same day we received your letter."

<u>Forms</u>

In most businesses and public service agencies, repetitive work is simplified by the use of *forms*. Forms exist for nearly every purpose imaginable: for ordering supplies, preparing invoices, applying for jobs, applying for insurance, paying taxes, recording inventories, and so on. While the forms encountered in different agencies may differ widely, several principles should be applied in completing any form:

- <u>Legibility</u>. Entries on forms should be clear and legible. Print or type wherever possible. When space provided is insufficient, attach a supplementary sheet to the form.

- <u>Completeness</u>. Make an entry in every space provided on the form. If a particular space does not apply to the applicant, enter there the term "N/A" (for "not applicable"). The reader of the completed form will then know that the applicant did not simply overlook that space.

- <u>Conciseness</u>. Forms are intended to elicit a maximum amount of information in the least possible space. When completing a form, it is usually not necessary to write complete sentences. Provide the necessary information in the least possible words.

- *Accuracy.* Be sure the information provided on the form is accurate. If the entry is a number, such as a social security number or an address, double-check the correctness of the number. Be sure of the spelling of names, No one appreciates receiving a communication in which his name is misspelled.

Memoranda

The written communications passing between offices or departments are usually transmitted in a form known as *"interoffice memorandum."* The headings most often used on such "memos" are:

- TO: identifying the addressee,
- FROM: identifying the sender or the originating office,
- SUBJECT: identifying briefly the subject of the memo,
- DATE: identifying the date the memo was prepared.

Larger agencies may also use headings such as FILE or REFERENCE NO. to aid in filing and retrieving memoranda.

In writing a memo, many of the same rules for letter-writing may be applied. Both the appearance and tone of the memo should create a pleasing impression. The format should be neat and follow the standards set by the originating office. The tone should be friendly, courteous, and considerate. The language should be clear, concise, and complete.

Memos usually dispense with salutations, complimentary closings, and signatures of the writers. In most other respects, however, the memorandum will follow the rules of good letter-writing.

Minutes of Meetings

Most formal public-service organization conduct meetings from time to time at which group decisions are made about agency policies, procedures, and work assignments. The records of such meetings are called *minutes.*

Minutes should be written as clearly and simply as possible, summarizing only the essential facts and decisions made at the meeting. While some issue may have been discussed at great length, only the final decision or resolution made of it should be recorded in the minutes. Information of this sort is usually included:

- Time and place of the call to order,
- Presiding officer and secretary,
- Voting members present (with names, if a small organization),

- Approval and corrections of previous minutes,
- Urgent business,
- Old business,
- New business,
- Time of adjournment,
- Signature of recorder.

Minutes should be written in a factual and objective style. The opinions of the recorder should not be in evidence. Every item of business coming up before a meeting should be included in the minutes, together with its disposition. For example:

- "M/S/P (Moved, seconded, passed) that Mr. Thomas Jones take responsibility for rewriting the personnel procedures manual."
- "Discussion of the summer vacation schedule was tabled until the next meeting."
- "M/S/P, a resolution that no client of the agency should be kept waiting more than 20 minutes for an interview."

Note that considerable discussion may have surrounded each of the above items in the minutes, but that only the topic and its resolution are recorded.

Short Reports

The public-service employee often is called upon to prepare a short report gathering and interpreting information on a single topic. Reports of this kind are sometimes prepared so that all the relevant information may be assembled in one place to aid the organization in making certain decisions. Such reports may be read primarily by the staff of the organization or by others closely related to the decision-making process.

Reports may be prepared at other times for distribution to the public or to other agencies and institutions. These reports may serve the purpose of informing public opinion or persuading others on matters of public policy.

Whatever the purpose of the short report, its physical appearance and style of presentation should be designed to create a favorable impression on the reader. Even if the report is distributed only within the writer's own unit, an attractive, clear, thorough report will reflect the writer's dedication to his assignment and the pride he takes in his work.

Some guidelines which will assist the trainee in preparation of effective short reports include use of the following:

- A good quality paper;
- Wide and even margins, allowing binding room;

- An accepted standard style of typing;
- A title page;
- A table of contents (for more lengthy reports only);
- A graphic numbering or outlining system, if needed for clarity;
- Graphics and photos to clarify meaning when useful;
- Footnotes, used sparingly, and only when they contribute to the report;
- A bibliography of sources, using a standard citation style.

A discussion of the organization of content for informational reports follows later in this document.

News Releases

From time to time, the public-service employees may be called upon to prepare a news release for his agency. Whenever the activities of the agency are newsworthy or of interest to the public, the agency has an obligation to report such activities to the press. The most common means for such reporting is by using the press release. Most newspapers and broadcasting stations are initially informed of agencies' activities by news releases distributed by the agencies themselves. Thus, the news release is a basic tool for communicating with the public served by the agency.

The news release is written in news style, with these basic characteristics:

- Sentences are short and simple.

- Paragraphs are short (one or two sentences) and relate to a single item of information.

- Paragraphs are arranged in *inverted order*—the most important in information appears first.

- The first or *lead* paragraph summarizes the entire story. If the reader went no further, he would have the essential information.

- Subsequent paragraphs provide further details, the most important occurring first.

- Reported information is attributed to sources; that is, the source of the news is reported in the story.

- The expression of the writer's opinions is scrupulously avoided.

- The 5 W's (who, what, why, where, when) are included.

News releases should be typed double spaced on standard 8 1/2 x 11 paper, with generous margins and at least 2" of open space above the lead paragraph. Do not write headlines - that is the editor's job. At the top of the first page of the release include the name of the agency releasing the story and the name and phone number of the person to contact if more information is needed. If the release runs more than one page, end each page with the word "-more-" to indicate that more copy follows. End the release with the symbols "###" to indicate that the copy ends at that point.

Accuracy and physical appearance are essential characteristics of the news release. Typographical errors, or errors of fact, such as misspelled names, lead editors to doubt the reliability of the story. Great care should be taken to assure the accuracy and reliability of a news release.

2. ## REPORTING ON A TOPIC

    At one time or another, most public-service employees will be asked to prepare a report on some topic. Usually the need for the report grows out of some policy decision contemplated by the agency for which full information must be considered. For example:

    - Should the agency undertake some new project or service?
    - Should working conditions be changed?
    - Are new specialists needed on the staff?
    - Or should a branch office be opened up?

    Or any of a hundred other such decisions which the agency must make from time to time.

    When called upon to prepare such a report, the employee should have a model to follow which will guide his collection of information and will help him to prepare an effective and useful report.

    As with other forms of written communication, both the physical appearance and content of the report are important to create a favorable impression and to engender confidence. The physical appearance of such reports has been discussed earlier; additional suggestions for reports are given in Unit 3. Basic guidelines follow below for organizing and preparing the content.

    ### Preparation for the Report

    What is the Purpose of the Report? The preparer of the report should have clearly in mind <u>why</u> the report is needed:

    - What is the decision being contemplated by the agency?
    - To what use will the report be put?

    Before beginning to prepare the report, the writer should discuss its purpose fully with the decision-making staff to articulate the purpose the report is intended to serve. If the employee is himself initiating the report, it would be well to discuss its purpose with colleagues to assure that its purpose is clear in his own mind.

    What Questions Should the Report Answer? Once the purpose of the report is clear, the questions the report must answer may begin to become clear. For example, if the decision faced by the agency is whether or not to offer a new service, questions may be asked such as these:

    - What persons would be served by the new service?

- What would the new service cost?
- What new staff would be needed?
- What new equipment and facilities would be needed?
- What alternative ways exist for offering the service?
- How might the new service be administered?

And so on. Unless the purpose of the report is clear, it is difficult to decide what specific questions need to be answered. Once the purpose is clear, these questions can be specified.

Where Can the Relevant Information be Obtained? Once the questions are clear in the writer's mind, he can identify the information he will need to answer them. Information may usually be obtained from two general sources:

- *Relevant documents.* Records, publications, and other reports are often useful in locating the information needed to answer particular questions. These may be in the files of the writer's own agency, in other agencies, or in libraries.

- *Personal contacts.* Persons in a position to know the needed information may be contacted in person, by phone, or by letter. Such contacts are especially important in obtaining firsthand accounts of previous experience.

The Text of the Report

What are the Answers to the Questions? Once the relevant in-formation is in hand, the answers to the questions may be assembled.

- What does the information reveal? This activity amounts to summarizing the information obtained. It often helps to organize this summary around the specific questions asked by the report. For example, if the report asks in one part, "What are the costs of the new service likely to be?" one section of the report should summarize the information gathered to answer this question.

Organizing the Report. The organization of a report into main and sub-sections depends upon the nature of the report. Reports will differ widely in their organization and treatment. In general, however, the report should generally follow the pattern previously discussed. That is, reports which generally include the following subjects in order will be found to be clear in their intent and to communicate effectively:

- *Description of problem or purpose.* Example: "One problem facing our agency is whether or not we should extend our hours of operation to better serve the public. This report is intended to examine the problem and make recommendations."

- *Questions to be answered.* Example: "In examining this problem, answers were sought to the following questions: What persons would be served? What would it cost? What staff would be needed?"

- *Information sources.* Example: "To answer these questions, letters of complaint for the past three years were examined. Interviews with clients were conducted by phone and in person, phone interviews were conducted with the agency directors in Memphis, Philadelphia, and Chicago,"

- *Summary of findings.* Example: "At least 25 percent of the agency's clients would be served better by evening or Saturday service. The costs of operating eight hours of extended service would be negligible, since the service could be provided by rescheduling work assignments. The present staff report they would be inconvenienced by evening and Saturday work assignments."

The Writer's Responsibilities. It is the writer's responsibility to address finally the original purpose of the report. Once the questions have been answered, an informed judgment can be made as to the decision facing the agency. It is at this stage that the writer attempts to draw conclusions from the information he has gathered and summarized. For example, if the original purpose of the report was to help make a decision about whether or not the agency should offer a new service, the writer should draw conclusions from the information and recommend either for or against the new service.

Conclusions and Recommendations. Example: "It appears that operating during extended hours would better serve a significant number of clients. The writer recommends that the agency offer this new service. The present staff should be given temporary assignments to cover the extended hours. As new staff are hired to replace separating persons, they should be hired specifically to cover the extended hours."

3. PERSUASIVE WRITING

Often in life, people are called upon to persuade individuals and groups to adopt ideas believed to be good, or attitudes favorable to ideas thought to be worthwhile or behavior believed to be beneficial. The public service employee may find he must persuade the staff of his own agency, his superiors, the clients of the agency, or the general public in his community.

Persuading others by means of written and other forms of communication is a difficult task and requires much practice. Some principles have emerged from the study of persuasion which may provide some guidelines for developing a model for persuasive writing.

General Guidelines for Writing Persuasively

Know the Credibility of the Source. People are more likely to be persuaded by a message they perceive originates from a trustworthy source. Their trust is enhanced if the source is seen as authoritative, or knowledgeable on the issue discussed in the message. Their trust is increased also if the source appears to have nothing to gain either way, has no vested interest in the final decision. Then, the assertions made in persuasive writing should be backed up by referencing trustworthy and disinterested information sources.

Avoid Overemotional Appeals. Appealing to the common emotions of man—love, hate, tear, sex, etc.—can have a favorable effect on the outcome of a persuasive message. But care should be taken because, if the appeal is too strong, it can lead to a reverse effect. For example, if an agency wanted to persuade the public to get chest X-rays, it would have much greater chance of success if it adopted a positive and helpful attitude rather than trying to frighten them into this action. For instance, appealing mildly to the sense of well-being which accompanies knowledge of one's own good health, instead of shocking the public by showing horror pictures of patients who died from lack of timely X-rays.

Consider the Other Man's Point of View. To persuade another to one's own point of view, should the writer include information and arguments <u>contrary</u> to his own position? Or should he argue <u>only</u> for his own side?

Generally, it depends on where most of the audience stand in the first place. If most of the audience already favor the position being advocated, then the writer will probably do better including only information favorable to his position. However, if the greater part of the audience are likely to oppose this position, then the writer would probably be better off including their arguments also. In this case, he may be helping his cause by rebutting the opposing arguments as he introduces them into the writing.

An example of this technique might occur in arguing for such an idea as a four-day, forty-hour workweek. Thus: "Many people feel that the ten-hour day is too long and that they would arrive home too late for their regular dinner hour. But think! If you have dinner a littler later each night, you'll have a three-day weekend every week. More days free to go fishing, or camping. More days with your wife and children." That is good persuasive writing!

Interpersonal Communications

The important role of interpersonal communication in persuading others—face-to-face and person-to-person communications—has been well documented. Mass mailings or printed messages will likely have less effect than personal letters and conversations between persons already known to each other. In any persuasion campaign the personal touch is very important.

An individual in persuading a large number of persons will likely be more effective if he can organize a letter-writing campaign of persuasive messages written by persons favorable to his position to their friends and acquaintances, than if his campaign is based upon sending out a mass mailing of a printed message.

Conditions for Persuading. In order for an audience of one or many to be persuaded in the manner desired, these conditions must be met:

- the audience must be _exposed_ to the message,
- members of the audience must _perceive_ the intent of the message,
- they must _remember_ the message afterwards,
- each member must _decide_ whether or not to adopt the ideas.

Each member of the audience will respond to a message differently. While every person may receive the message, not everyone will read it. Even among those who read it, not everyone will perceive it in the same way. Some will remember it longer than others. Not everyone will decide to adopt the ideas. These effects are called _selective exposure, selective perception, selective retention,_ and _selective decision._

The Persuasion Campaign. How can one counteract these selective effects in persuading others? One thing that is known is that _people tend to be influenced by persuasive messages which they are already predisposed to accept._ This means a person is more likely to persuade people a little than to persuade them a lot.

In planning a persuasion campaign, therefore, the messages should be tailored to the audiences. Success will be more likely if one starts with people who believe _almost_ as the writer wants to persuade them to believe—people who are most likely to agree with the position advocated.

The writer also wants to use arguments based on values the particular audience already accepts. For example, in advocating a new teen-age job program, he might argue with business men that the program will help business; with parents, that it will build character; with teachers, that it is educational; with taxpayers, that it will reduce future taxes; and so on.

The idea is to find some way to make sure that each member of the particular audiences reached can see an advantage for himself, and for the writer to then tailor the messages for those audiences.

4. INSTRUCTIONAL WRITING

Another task that the public-service employee may expect to face from time to time is the instruction of some other person in the performance of a task. This may sometimes involve preparing written instructions to other employees in the unit, or preparing a training manual for new employees.

It may sometimes involve preparing instructional manuals for clients of the unit, such as "How to Apply for a Real Estate License," "How to Bathe your Baby," or "How to Recognize the Symptoms of Heart Disease."

Whatever the purpose or the audience, certain principles of instruction may be applied which will help make more effective these instructional or training communications. These are: *advance organizers, practice, errorless learning,* and *feedback.*

Advance Organizers

At or near the beginning of an instructional communication, it helps the learner if he is provided with what can be called an "advance organizer." This element of the communication performs two functions:

- it provides a framework or "map" for the leader to organize the information he will encounter,
- it helps the learner perceive his purpose in learning the tasks which will follow.

The first paragraphs in this section, for example, serve together as an advance organizer. The trainee is informed that he may be called upon to perform these tasks in his job *(perceived purpose),* and that he will be instructed in advance organizers, practice, errorless learning, and feedback *(framework, or "map").*

Practice

The notion of *practice makes perfect* is a sound instructional principle. When trying to teach someone to perform a task by means of written communication, the writer should build in many opportunities for practicing the task, or parts of it. This built-in practice should be both appropriate and active:

- *Appropriate practice* is practice which is directly related to learning the tasks at hand.

- *Active practice* is practice in actually performing the task at hand or parts of it, rather than simply reading about the task, or thinking about it.

By inserting questions into the text of the communication, by giving practice quizzes, exercises, or field work, one can build into his instructional communication the kind of practice necessary for the reader to readily learn the task.

Errorless Learning

The practice given learners should be easy to do. That is, they should not be asked to practice a task if they are likely to make a lot of mistakes. When a mistake is practiced it is likely to recur again and again, like spelling "demons," which have been spelled wrong so often it's difficult to recall the way they should be spelled. Because it is better to practice a task right from the first, it is important that learners do not make errors in practice.

- One method for encouraging correct practice is to give the reader hints, or *prompts,* to help him practice correctly.

- Another method is to instruct him in a logical sequence a little bit at a time. Don't try to teach everything at once. Break the task down into small parts and teach each part of the task in order. Then give the learner practice in each part of the task before giving him practice in the whole thing.

- A third way of encouraging errorless learning is to build in practice and review throughout the communication. The learner may forget part of the task if the teacher doesn't review it with him from time to time.

Remember, people primarily learn from what they do, so build in to the instructional communication many opportunities for the learner to practice correctly all of the parts of the task required for learning, first separately and then all together.

Feedback

The reader, or learner, can't judge how well he is learning the task unless he is informed of it. In a classroom situation, the teacher usually confirms that the learner has been successful, or points out the errors he made, and provides additional instruction. An instructional communication can also help learners in the same way, by providing *feedback* to the learner.

Following practice, the writer should include in his instructional communication information which will let the reader know whether he performed the task correctly. In case he didn't, the writer should also include some further information which will help the reader perform it correctly next time. This feedback, then, performs two functions:

- it helps the learner confirm that his practice was done correctly, and

- it helps him correct his performance of the task in case he made any errors.

Feedback will be most helpful to the learner if it occurs immediately following practice. The learner should be brought to know of his success or his errors just as soon as possible after practice.

STUDENT LEARNING ACTIVITIES

- Write "asking" and "answering" letters, and answer a letter of complaint, using the format assigned by the teacher.

- Write memoranda to other "offices" in a fictitious organization. Plan a field trip using only memos to communicate with other students in the class.

- Take minutes of a small group meeting. Or attend a meeting of the school board and take minutes.

- Write a short report on a public service occupation of special interest to you.

- Write a 15-word telegram reserving a single room at a hotel and asking to be picked up at the airport.

- Write a news release announcing a new service offered to the public by your agency.

- Based upon hearing a reading or pretaping of a report, summarize the report in news style.

- View films on effective communication, for example, *Getting the Facts, Words that Don't Inform,* and *A Message to No One.*

- For a given problem or purpose, compile a list of specific questions you would need to answer to write a report on the topic.

- For a given list of questions, discuss and compile a list of information sources relevant to the questions.

- As a member of a group, consider the problem of "What field trip should the class take to help students learn how to write an effective news release?" What questions will you need to answer? Where will you obtain your information?

- As a member of a group, gather the information and prepare a short report based on it for presentation to the class.

- Write a report on a problem assigned by your teacher.

- Write a brief persuasive letter to a friend on a given topic. Assume he does not already agree with you. Apply principles of source credibility, emotional appeals, and one or both sides of the issue to persuade him.

- Plan a persuasive campaign to persuade a given segment of your community to take some given action.

- Write a short instructional communication on a verbal learning task assigned by your teacher.

- Write a short instructional communication on a learning task which involves the operation of equipment.

- Try your instructional communications with a fellow student to check for errors during practice.

TEACHER MANAGEMENT ACTIVITIES

- Have students practice letter writing. Assign letters of "asking" and "answering." Read them a letter of complaint and ask them to write an answering letter. Establish common rules of format and style for each assignment. Change the rules from time to time to give practice in several styles.

- Have small groups plan an event, such as a field trip, assigning the various tasks to one another using only memoranda. Evaluate the effectiveness of each group's memo writing by the speed and completeness of their planning.

- Have the class attend a public meeting. Assign each the task of taking the minutes. Evaluate the minutes for brevity and completeness.

- Encourage each student to prepare a short report on a public service occupation of special interest to himself.

- Give the students practice in writing 15-word telegrams.

- Have the students prepare a news release announcing some new service offered to the public, such as "Taxpayers can now obtain help from the Internal Revenue Service in completing their income tax forms as a result of a new service now being offered by the agency."

- Give the students practice in summarizing and writing leads by giving them the facts of a news event and asking them to write a one or two-sentence lead summarizing the significant facts of the event.

- Read a speech or a story. Have students write a summary and a report of the speech or story in news style.

- Show films on effective communication, for example, *Getting the Facts, Words that Don't Inform,* and *A Message to No One.*

- State a general problem and have each student prepare a list of the specific questions implied by the problem.

- State a list of specific questions and discuss with the class the sources of information which might bear upon each of the questions.

- Have small groups consider and write short reports jointly on the general problem, "What field trip should the class take to help students learn how to write an effective news release?" Have each group identify the specific questions to be answered, with sources for needed information.

- Have each student identify and prepare a short report on a general problem of interest.

- Assign students to work in groups of three or four to draft a letter to a friend to persuade him to make a contribution to establish a new city art museum.

- Assign the students to groups of five or six, each group to map out a persuasive campaign on a given topic. Some topics are "Give Blood," "Get Chest X-Ray," "Quit Smoking," "Don't Litter," "Inspect Your House Wiring," etc.

- Have each student identify a simple verbal learning task and prepare an instructional communication to teach that task to another student not familiar with the task.

- Have each student prepare an instructional manual designed to train someone to operate some simple piece of equipment, such as an adding machine, a slide projector, a tape recorder, or something of similar complexity.

- Have each student try his instructional communication out on another student, unfamiliar with the task. He should observe the activities and responses of the trial student to identify errors made in practice. He should revise the communication, adding practice, review, and prompts wherever needed to reduce errors in practice.

EVALUATION QUESTIONS

Written Communications

1. Which type of letter would be correct for a public service worker to send?   1.____

   A. A letter containing erasures
   B. A letter reflecting goodwill
   C. A rude letter
   D. An impersonal letter

2. Memos usually leave out: 2.____

   A. Complimentary closings
   B. The name of the sender
   C. The name of the addressee
   D. The date the memo was sent

3. A good business letter would not contain: 3.____

   A. Short, simple words, sentences, and paragraphs
   B. Information contained in the letter being answered
   C. Concrete nouns and active verbs
   D. Orderly placed paragraphs

4. In writing business letters it is important to: 4.____

   A. Use a conversational tone
   B. Use a hard, cold tone
   C. Use abstract words
   D. Use a passive tone

5. Messages between departments in an agency are usually sent by: 5.____

   A. Letter
   B. Memo
   C. Telegram
   D. Long reports

6. Repetitive work can be simplified by the use of: 6.____

   A. Memos
   B. Telegrams
   C. Forms
   D. Reports

7. In filling out forms and applications, it is important to be: 7.____

   A. Legible
   B. Complete
   C. Accurate
   D. All of the above

8. Memos should be:
8.__

    A. Clear
    B. Brief
    C. Complete
    D. All of the above

9. Minutes of meetings should not include:
9.__

    A. The opinions of the recorder
    B. The approval of previous minutes
    C. The corrections of previous minutes
    D. The voting members present

10. Reports are written by public service workers to:
10.__

    A. Assemble information in one place
    B. Aid the organization in making decisions
    C. Inform the public and other agencies
    D. All of the above

11. News releases should include:
11.__

    A. A lead paragraph summarizing the story
    B. Long paragraphs about many topics
    C. The writer's opinion
    D. All of the above

12. Readers of news releases and reports are influenced by the:
12.__

    A. Content of the material
    B. Accuracy of the material
    C. Physical appearance of the material
    D. All of the above

13. The contents of a report should include:
13.__

    A. A description of the problem
    B. The questions to be answered
    C. Unimportant information
    D. A summary of findings

14. People tend to be influenced easier if:
14.__

    A. They can see something in the position that would be advantageous to them
    B. They are almost ready to agree anyhow
    C. The appeal to the emotions is not overly strong
    D. All of the above

KEY (CORRECT ANSWERS)

1. B
2. A
3. B
4. A
5. B

6. C
7. D
8. D
9. A
10. D

11. A
12. D
13. C
14. D

SUPERVISION STUDY GUIDE

Social science has developed information about groups and leadership in general and supervisor-employee relationships in particular. Since organizational effectiveness is closely linked to the ability of supervisors to direct the activities of employees, these findings are important to executives everywhere.

IS A SUPERVISOR A LEADER?

First-line supervisors are found in all large business and government organizations. They are the men at the base of an organizational hierarchy. Decisions made by the head of the organization reach them through a network of intermediate positions. They are frequently referred to as part of the management team, but their duties seldom seem to support this description.

A supervisor of clerks, tax collectors, meat inspectors, or securities analysts is not charged with budget preparation. He cannot hire or fire the employees in his own unit on his say-so. He does not administer programs which require great planning, coordinating, or decision making.

Then what is he? He is the man who is directly in charge of a group of employees doing productive work for a business or government agency. If the work requires the use of machines, the men he supervises operate them. If the work requires the writing of reports, the men he supervises write them. He is expected to maintain a productive flow of work without creating problems which higher levels of management must solve. But is he a leader?

To carry out a specific part of an agency's mission, management creates a unit, staffs it with a group of employees and designates a supervisor to take charge of them. Management directs what this unit shall do, from time to time changes directions, and often indicates what the group should not do. Management presumably creates status for the supervisor by giving him more pay, a title, and special priviledges.

Management asks a supervisor to get his workers to attain organizational goals, including the desired quantity and quality of production. Supposedly, he has authority to enable him to achieve this objective. Management at least assumes that by establishing the status of the supervisor's position it has created sufficient authority to enable him to achieve these goals -- not his goals, nor necessarily the group's, but management's goals.

In addition, supervision includes writing reports, keeping records of membership in a higher-level administrative group, industrial engineering, safety engineering, editorial duties, housekeeping duties, etc. The supervisor as a member of an organizational network, must be responsible to the changing demands of the management above him. At the same time, he must be responsive to the demands of the work group of which he is a member. He is placed in the difficult position of communicating and implementing new decisions, changed programs and revised production quotas for his work group, although he may have had little part in developing them.

It follows, then, that supervision has a special characteristic: achievement of goals, previously set by management, through the efforts of others. It is in this feature of the supervisor's job that we find the role of a leader in the sense of the following definition: *A leader is that person who <u>most</u> effectively influences group activities toward goal setting and goal achievements.*

This definition is broad. It covers both leaders in groups that come together voluntarily and in those brought together through a work assignment in a factory, store, or government agency. In the natural group, the authority necessary to attain goals is determined by the group membership and is granted by them. In the working group, it is apparent that the establishment of a supervisory position creates a predisposition on the part of employees to accept the authority of the occupant of that position. We cannot, however, assume that mere occupancy confers authority sufficient to assure the accomplishment of an organization's goals.

Supervision is different, then, from leadership. The supervisor is expected to fulfill the role of leader but without obtaining a grant of authority from the group he supervises. The supervisor is expected to influence the group in the achieving of goals but is often handicapped by having little influence on the organizational process by which goals are set. The supervisor, because he works in an organizational setting, has the burdens of additional organizational duties and restrictions and requirements arising out of the fact that his position is subordinate to a hierarchy of higher-level supervisors. These differences between leadership and supervision are reflected in our definition: *Supervision is basically a leadership role, in a formal organization, which has as its objective the effective influencing of other employees.*

Even though these differences between supervision and leadership exist, a significant finding of experimenters in this field is that supervisors <u>must</u> be leaders to be successful.

The problem is: How can a supervisor exercise leadership in an organizational setting? We might say that the supervisor is expected to be a natural leader in a situation which does not come about naturally. His situation becomes really difficult in an organization which is more eager to make its supervisors into followers rather than leaders.

LEADERSHIP: NATURAL AND ORGANIZATIONAL

Leadership, in its usual sense of *natural* leadership, and supervision are not the same. In some cases, leadership embraces broader powers and functions than supervision; in other cases, supervision embraces more than leadership. This is true both because of the organization and technical aspects of the supervisor's job and because of the relatively freer setting and inherent authority of the natural leader.

The natural leader usually has much more authority and influence than the supervisor. Group members not only follow his command but prefer it that way. The employee, however, can appeal the supervisor's commands to his union or to the supervisor's superior or to the personnel office. These intercessors represent restrictions on the supervisor's power to lead.

The natural leader can gain greater membership involvement in the group's objectives, and he can change the objectives of the group. The supervisor can attempt to gain employee support only for management's objectives; he cannot set other objectives. In these instances leadership is broader than supervision.

The natural leader must depend upon whatever skills are available when seeking to attain objectives. The supervisor is trained in the administrative skills necessary to achieve management's goals. If he does not possess the requisite skills, however, he can call upon management's technicians.

A natural leader can maintain his leadership, in certain groups, merely by satisfying members' need for group affilation. The supervisor must maintain his leadership by directing and organizing his group to achieve specific organizational goals set for him and his group by management. He must have a technical competence and a kind of coordinating ability which is not needed by many natural leaders.

A natural leader is responsible only to his group which grants him authority. The supervisor is responsible to management, which employs him, and, also, to the work group of which he is a member. The supervisor has the exceedingly difficult job of reconciling the demands of two groups frequently in conflict. He is often placed in the untenable position of trying to play two antagonisic roles. In the above instances, supervision is broader than leadership.

ORGANIZATIONAL INFLUENCES ON LEADERSHIP

The supervisor is both a product and a prisoner of the organization wherein we find him. The organization which creates the supervisor's position also obstructs, restricts, and channelizes the exercise of his duties. These influences extend beyond prescribed functional relationships to specific supervisory behavior. For example, even in a face-to-face situation involving one of his subordinates, the supervisor's actions are controlled to a great extent by his organization. His behavior must conform to the organization policy on human relations, rules which dictate personnel procedures, specific prohibitions governing conduct, the attitudes of his own superior, etc. He is not a free agent operating within the limits of his work group. His freedom of action is much more circumscribed than is generally admitted. The organizational influences which limit his leadership actions can be classified as structure, prescriptions, and proscriptions.

The organizational structure places each supervisor's position in context with other designated positions. It determines the relationships between his position and specific positions which impinge on his. The structure of the organization designates a certain position to which he looks for orders and information about his work. It gives a particular status to his position within a pattern of statuses from which he perceives that (1) certain positions are on a par, organizationally, with his, (2) other positions are subordinate, and (3) still others are superior. The organizational structure determines those positions to which he should look for advice and assistance, and those positions to which he should give advice and assistance.

For instance, the organizational structure has predetermined that the supervisor of a clerical processing unit shall report to a supervisory position in a higher echelon. He shall have certain relationships with the supervisors of the work units which transmit work to and receive work from his unit. He shall discuss changes and clarification of procedures with certain staff units, such as organization and methods, cost accounting, and personnel. He shall consult supervisors of units which provide or receive special work assignments.

The organizational structure, however, establishes patterns other than those of the relationships of positions. These are the patterns of responsibility, authority, and expectations.

The supervisor is responsible for certain activities or results; he is presumably invested with the authority to achieve these. His set of authority and responsibility is interwoven with other sets to the end that all goals and functions of the organization are parceled out in small, manageable lots. This, of course, establishes a series of expectations: a single supervisor can perform his particular set of duties only upon the assumption that preceding or contiguous sets of duties have been, or are being, carried out. At the same time, he is aware of the expectations of others that he will fulfill his functional role.

The structure of an organization establishes relationships between specified positions and specific expectations for these positions. The fact that these relationships and expectations are established is one thing; whether or not they are met is another.

PRESCRIPTIONS AND PROSCRIPTIONS

But let us return to the organizational influences which act to restrict the supervisor's exercise of leadership. These are the prescriptions and proscriptions generally in effect in all organizations, and those peculiar to a single organization. In brief these are the *thous shalt's* and the *thou shalt not's.*

Organizations not only prescribe certain duties for individual supervisory positions, they also prescribe specific methods and means of carrying out these duties and maintaining management-employee relations. These include rules, regulations, policy, and. tradition. It does no good for the supervisor to say, *This seems to be the best way to handle such-and such,* if the organization has established a routine for dealing with problems. For good or bad, there are rules that state that firings shall be executed in such a manner, accompanied by a certain notification; that training shall be conducted, and in this manner. Proscriptions are merely negative prescriptions: you may not discriminate against any employee because of politics or race; you shall not suspend any employee without following certain procedures and obtaining certain approvals.

Most of these prohibitions and rules apply to the area of interpersonal relations, precisely the area which is now arousing most interest on the part of administrators and managers. We have become concerned about the contrast between formally prescribed relationships and interpersonal relationships, and this brings us to the often discussed informal organization.

FORMAL AND INFORMAL ORGANIZATIONS

As we well know, the functions and activities of any organization are broken down into individual units of work called positions. Administrators must establish a pattern which will link these positions to each other and relate them to a system of authority and responsibility. Man-to-man are spelled out as plainly as possible for all to understand. Managers, then, build an official structure which we call the formal organization.

In these same organizations employees react individually and in groups to institutionally determined roles. John, a worker, rides in the same car pool as Joe, a foreman. An unplanned communication develops. Harry, a machinist, knows more about highspeed machining than his foreman or anyone else in his shop. An unofficial tool boss comes into being. Mary, who fought with Jane is promoted over her. Jane now ignores Mary's directions. A planned relationship fails to develop. The employees have built a structure which we call the informal organization.

Formal organization is a system of management-prescribed relations between positions in an organization.

Informal organization is a network of unofficial relations between people in an organization.

These definitions might lead us to the absurd conclusion that positions carry out formal activities and that employees spend their time in unofficial activities. We must recognize that organizational activities are in all cases carried out by people. The formal structure provides a needed framework within which interpersonal relations occur. What we call informal organization is the complex of normal, natural relations among employees. These personal relationships may be negative or positive. That is, they may impede or aid the achievement of organizational, goals. For example, friendship between two supervisors greatly increases the probability of good cooperation and coordination between their sections. On the other hand, *buck passing* nullifies the formal structure by failure to meet a prescribed and expected responsibility.

It is improbable that an ideal organization exists where all activities are acarried out in strict conformity to a formally prescribed pattern of functional roles. Informal organization arises because of the incompleteness and ambiguities in the network of formally prescribed relationships, or in response to the needs or inadequacies of supervisors or managers who hold prescribed functional roles in an organization. Many of these relationships are not prescribed by the organizational pattern; many cannot be prescribed; many should not be prescribed.

Management faces the problem of keeping the informal organization in harmony with the mission of the agency. One way to do this is to make sure that all employees have a clear understanding of and are sympathetic with that mission. The issuance of organizational charts, procedural manuals, and functional descriptions of the work to be done by divisions and sections helps communicate management's plans and goals. Issuances alone, of course, cannot do the whole job. They should be accompanied by oral discussion and explanation. Management must ensure that there is mutual understanding and acceptance of charts and procedures. More important is that management acquaint itself with the attitudes, activities, and peculiar brands of logic which govern the informal organization. Only through this type of knowledge can they and supervisors keep informal goals consistent with the agency mission.

SUPERVISION, STATUS, AND FUNCTIONAL ROLE

A well-established supervisor is respected by the employees who work with him. They defer to his wishes. It is clear that a superior-subordinate relationship has been established. That is, status of the supervisor has been established in relation to other employees of the same work group. This same supervisor gains the respect of employees when he behaves in a certain manner. He will be expected generally, to follow the customs of the group in such matters as dress, recreation, and manner of speaking. The group has a set of expectations as to his behavior. His position is a functional role which carries with it a collection of rights and obligations.

The position of supervisor usually has a status distinct from the individual who occupies it: it is much like a position description which exists whether or not there is an incumbent. The status of a supervisory position is valued higher than that of an employee position both because of the functional role of leadership which is assigned to it and because of the status symbols of titles, rights, and privileges which go with it.

Social ranking, or status, is not simple because it involves both the position and the man. An individual may be ranked higher than others because of his education, social background, perceived leadership ability, or conformity to group customs and ideals. If such a man is ranked higher by the members of a work group than their supervisor, the supervisor's effectiveness may be seriously undermined.

If the organization does not build and reinforce a supervisor's status, his position can be undermined in a different way. This will happen when managers go around rather than through the supervisor or designate him as a straw boss, acting boss, or otherwise not a real boss.

Let us clarify this last point. A role, and corresponding status, establishes a set of expectations. Employees expect their supervisor to do certain things and to act in certain ways. They are prepared to respond to that expected behavior. When the supervisor's behavior does not conform to their expectations, they are surprised, confused, and ill-at-ease. It becomes necessary for them to resolve their confusion, if they can. They might do this by turning to one of their own members for leadership. If the confusion continues, or their attempted solutions are not satisfactory, they will probably become a poorly motivated, non-cohesive group which cannot function very well.

COMMUNICATION AND THE SUPERVISOR

In a recent survey railroad workers reported that they rarely look to their supervisors for information about the company. This is startling, at least to us, because we ordinarily think of the supervisor as the link between management and worker. We expect the supervisor to be the prime source of information about the company. Actually, the railroad workers listed the supervisor next to last in the order of their sources of information. Most suprising of all, the supervisors, themselves, stated that rumor and unofficial contacts were their principal sources of information. Here we see one of the reasons why supervisors may not be as effective as management desires.

The supervisor is not only being bypassed by his work group, he is being ignored, and his position weakened, by the very organization which is holding him responsible for the activities of his workers. If he is management's representative to the employee, then management has an obligation to keep him informed of its activities. This is necessary if he is to carry out his functions efficiently and maintain his leadership in the work group. The supervisor is expected to be a source of information; when he is not, his status is not clear, and employees are dissatisfied because he has not lived up to expectations.

By providing information to the supervisor to pass along to employees, we can strengthen his position as leader of the group, and increase satisfaction and cohesion within the group. Because he has more information than the other members, receives information sooner, and passes it along at the proper times, members turn to him as a source and also provide him with information in the hope of receiving some in return. From this we can see an increase in group cohesiveness because:

o   Employees are bound closer to their supervisor because he is *in the know*

o   there is less need to go outside the group for answers

o   employees will more quickly turn to the supervisor for enlightenment.

The fact that he has the answers will also enhance the supervisor's standing in the eyes of his men. This increased sta,tus will serve to bolster his authority and control of the group and will probably result in improved morale and productivity.

The foregoing, of course, does not mean that all management information should be given out. There are obviously certain policy determinations and discussions which need not or cannot be transmitted to all supervisors. However, the supervisor must be kept as fully informed as possible so that he can answer questions when asked and can allay needless fears and anxieties. Further, the supervisor has the responsibility of encouraging employee questions and submissions of information. He must be able to present information to employees so that it is clearly understood and accepted. His attitude and manner should make it clear that he believes in what he is saying, that the information is necessary or desirable to the group, and that he is prepared to act on the basis of the information.

SUPERVISION AND JOB PERFORMANCE

The productivity of work groups is a product; employees' efforts are multiplied by the supervision they receive. Many investigators have analyzed this relationship and have discovered elements of supervision which differentiate high and low production groups. These researchers have identified certain types of supervisory practices which they classify as *employee-centered* and other types which they classify as *production centered*.

The difference between these two kinds of supervision lies not in specific practices but in the approach or orientation to supervision. The employee-centered supervisor directs most of his efforts toward increasing employee motivation. He is concerned more with realizing the potential energy of persons than with administrative and technological methods of increasing efficiency and productivity. He is the man who finds ways of causing employees to want to work harder with the same tools. These supervisors emphasize the personal relations between their employees and themselves.

Now, obviously, these pictures are overdrawn. No one supervisor has all the virtues of the ideal type of employee-centered supervisor. And, fortunately, no one supervisor has all the bad traits found in many production-centered supervisors. We should remember that the various practices that researchers have found which distinguish these two kinds of supervision represent the many practices and methods of supervisors of all gradations between these extremes. We should be careful, too, of the implications of the labels attached to the two types. For instance, being production-centered is not necessarily bad, since the principal responsibility of any supervisor is maintaining the production level that is expected of his work group. Being employee-centered may not necessarily be good, if the only result is a happy, chuckling crew of loafers. To return to the researchers's findings, employee-centered supervisors:

- o   Recommend promotions, transfers, pay increases

- o   Inform men about what is happening in the company

- o   Keep men posted on how well they are doing

- o   Hear complaints and grievances sympathetically

- o   Speak up for subordinates

Production-centered supervisors, on the other hand, don't do those things. They check on employees more frequently, give more detailed and frequent instructions, don't give reasons for changes, and are more punitive when mistakes are made. Employee-centered supervisors were reported to contribute to high morale and high production, whereas production-centered supervision was associated with lower morale and less production.

More recent findings, however, show that the relationship between supervision and productivity is not this simple. Investigators now report that high production is more frequently associated with supervisory practices which combine employee-centered behavior with concern for production. (This concern is not the same, however, as anxiety about production, which is the hallmark of our production-centered supervisor.) Let us examine these apparently contradictory findings and the premises from which they are derived.

SUPERVISION AND MORALE

Why do supervisory activities cause high or low production? As the name implies, the activities of the employee-centered supervisor tend to relate him more closely and satisfactorily to his workers. The production-centered supervisor's practices tend to separate him from his group and to foster antagonism. An analysis of this difference may answer our question.

Earlier, we pointed out that the supervisor is a type of leader and that leadership is intimately related to the group in which it occurs. We discover, now, that an employee-centered supervisor's primary activities are concerned with both his leadership and his group membership. Such a supervisor is a member of a group and occupies a leadership role in that group.

These facts are sometimes obscured when we speak of the supervisor as management's representative, or as the organizational link between management and the employee, or as the end of the chain of command. If we really want to understand what it is we expect of the supervisor, we must remember that he is the designated leader of a group of employees to whom he is bound by interaction and interdependence.

Most of his actions are aimed, consciously or unconsciously, at strengthening membership ties in the group. This includes both making members more conscious that he is a member of their group) and causing members to identify themselves more closely with the group. These ends are accomplished by:

making the group more attractive to the worker: they
find satisfaction of their needs for recognition,
friendship, enjoyable work, etc.;

maintaining open communication: employees can express
their views and obtain information about the organization.

giving assistance: members can seek advice on
personal problems as well as their work; and
acting as a buffer between the group and management:
he speaks up for his men and explains the reasons
for management's decisions.

Such actions both strengthen group cohesiveness and solidarity and affirm the supervisor's leadership position in the group.

DEFINING MORALE

This brings us back to a point mentioned earlier. We had said that employee-centered supervisors contribute to high morale as well as to high production. But how can we explain units which have low morale and high productivity, or vice versa? Usually production and morale are considered separately, partly because they are measured against different criteria and partly because, in some instances, they seem to be independent of each other.

Some of this difficulty may stem from confusion over definitions of morale. Morale has been defined as, or measured by, absences from work, satisfaction with job or company, dissension among members of work groups, productivity, apathy or lack of interest, readiness to help others, and a general aura of happiness as rated by observers. Some of these criteria of morale are not subject to the influence of the supervisor, and some of them are not clearly related to productivity. Definitions like these invite findings of low morale coupled with high production.

Both productivity and morale can be influenced by environmental factors not under the control of group members or supervisors. Such things as plant layout, organizational structure and goals, lighting, ventilation, communications, and management planning may have an adverse or desirable effect.

We might resolve the dilemma by defining morale on the basis of our understanding of the supervisor as leader of a group; morale is the degree of satisfaction of group members with their leadership. In this light, the supervisor's employee-centered activities bear a clear relation to morale. His efforts to increase employee identification with the group and to strengthen his leadership lead to greater satisfaction with that leadership. By increasing group cohesiveness and by demonstrating that his influence and power can aid the group, he is able to enhance his leadership status and afford satisfaction to the group.

SUPERVISION, PRODUCTION, AND MORALE

There are factors within the organization itself which determine whether increased production is possible:

Are production goals expressed in terms understandable to employees and are they realistic?

Do supervisors responsible for production respect the agency mission and production goals?

If employees do not know how to do the job well, does management provide a trainer-- often the supervisor--who can teach efficient work methods?

There are other factors within the work group which determine whether increased production will be attained:

Is leadership present which can bring about the desired level of production?

Are production goals accepted by employees as reasonable and attainable?

If group effort is involved, are members able to coordinate their efforts?

Research findings confirm the view that an employee-centered supervisor can achieve higher morale than a production-centered supervisor. Managers may well ask what is the relationship between this and production?

Supervision is production-oriented to the extent that it focuses attention on achieving organizational goals, and plans and devises methods for attaining them; it is employee-centered to the extent that it focuses attention on employee attitudes toward those goals, and plans and works toward maintenance of employee satisfaction.

High productivity and low morale result when a supervisor plans and organizes work efficiently but cannot achieve high membership satisfaction. Low production and high morale result when a supervisor, though keeping members satisfied with his leadership, either has not gained acceptance of organizational goals or does not have the technical competence to achieve them.

The relationship between supervision, morale, and productivity is an interdependent one, with the supervisor playing an integrating role due to his ability to influence productivity and morale independently of each other.

A supervisor who can plan his work well has good technical knowledge, and who can install better production methods can raise production without necessarily increasing group satisfaction. On the other hand, a supervisor who can motivate his employees and keep them satisfied with his leadership can gain high production in spite of technical difficulties and environmental obstacles.

CLIMATE AND SUPERVISION

Climate, the intangible environment of an organization made up of attitudes, beliefs, and traditions, plays a large part in morale, productivity, and supervision. Usually when we speak of climate and its relationship to morale and productivity, we talk about the merits of *democratic* versus *authoritarian* climate. Employees seem to produce more and have higher morale in a democratic climate, whereas in an authoritarian climate, the reverse seems to be true or so the researchers tell us. We would do well to determine what these terms mean to supervision.

Perhaps most of our difficulty in understanding and applying these concepts comes from our emotional reactions to the words themselves. For example, authoritarian climate is usually painted as the very blackest kind of dictatorship. This not surprising, because we are usually expected to believe that it is invariably bad. Conversely, democratic climate is drawn to make the driven snow look impure by comparison.

Now these descriptions are most probably true when we talk about our political processes, or town meetings, or freedom of speech. However the same labels have been used by social scientists in other contexts and have also been applied to government and business organizations, without, it seems, any recognition that the meanings and their social values may have changed somewhat .

For example, these labels were used in experiments conducted in an informal class room setting using 11 year old boys as subjects. The descriptive labels applied to the climate of the setting as well as the type of leadership practiced. When these labels were transferred to a management setting it seems that many presumed that they principally meant the king of leadership rather than climate. We can see that there is a great difference between the experimental and management settings and that leadership practices for one might be inappropriate for the other.

It is doubtful that formal work organizations can be anything but authoritarian, in that goals are set by management and a hierarchy exists through which decisions and orders from the top are transmitted downward. Organizations are authoritarian by structure and need: direction and control are placed in the hands of a few in order to gain fast and efficient decision making. Now this does not mean to describe a dictatorship. It is merely the recognition of the fact that direction of organizational affairs comes from above. It should be noted that leadership in some natural groups is, in this sense, authoritarian.

Granting that formal organizations have this kind of authoritarian leadership, can there be a democratic climate? Certainly there can be, but we would want to define and delimit this term. A more realistic meaning of democratic climate in organizations is, the use of permissive and participatory methods in management-employee relations. That is, a mutual exchange of information and explanation with the granting of individual freedom within certain restricted and defined limits. However, it is not our purpose to debate the merits of authoritarianism versus democracy. We recognize that within the small work group there is a need for freedom from constraint and an increase in participation in order to achieve organizational goals within the framework of the organizational environment.

Another aspect of climate is best expressed by this familiar, and true saying: actions speak louder than words. Of particular concern to us is this effect of management climate on the behavior of supervisors, particularly in employee-centered activities.

There have been reports of disappointment with efforts to make supervisors more employee-centered. Managers state that, since research has shown ways of improving human relations, supervisors should begin to practice these methods. Usually a training course in human relations is established, and supervisors are given this training. Managers then sit back and wait for the expected improvements, only to find that there are none.

If we wish to produce changes in the supervisor's behavior,the climate must be made appropriate and rewarding to the changed behavior. This means that top-level attitudes and behavior cannot deny or contradict the change we are attempting to effect. Basic changes in organizational behavior cannot be made with any permanence, unless we provide an environment that is receptive to the changes and rewards those persons who do change.

IMPROVING SUPERVISION

Anyone who has read this far might expect to find *A Dozen Rules for Dealing With Employees* or *29 Steps to Supervisory Success.* We will not provide such a list.

Simple rules suffer from their simplicity. They ignore the complexities of human behavior. Reliance upon rules may cause supervisors to concentrate on superficial aspects of their relations with employees. It may preclude genuine understanding.

The supervisor who relies on a list of rules tends to think of people in mechanistic terms. In a certain situation, he uses *Rule No. 3.* Employees are not treated as thinking and feeling persons, but rather as figures in a formula: Rule 3 applied to employee X = Production.

Employees usually recognize mechanical manipulation and become dissatisfied and resentful. They lose faith in, and respect for, their supervisor, and this may be reflected in lower morale and productivity.

We do not mean that supervisors must become social science experts if they wish to improve. Reports of current research indicate that there are two major parts of their job which can be strengthened through self-improvement: (1) Work planning, including technical skills. (2) Motivation of employees.

The most effective supervisors combine excellence in the administrative and technical aspects of their work with friendly and considerate personal relations with their employees.

CRITICAL PERSONAL RELATIONS

Later in this chaper we shall talk about administrative aspects of supervision, but first let us comment on *friendly and considerate personal relations.* We have discussed this subject throughout the preceding chapters, but we want to review some of the critical supervisory influences on personal relations.

Closeness of Supervision

The closeness of supervision has an important effect on productivity and morale. Mann and Dent found that supervisors of low-producing units supervise very closely, while high-producing supervisors exercise only general supervision. It was found that the low-producing supervisors:

- o   check on employees more frequently

- o   give more detailed and frequent instructions

- o   limit employee's freedom to do job in own way.

Workers who felt less closely supervised reported that they were better satisfied with their jobs and the company. We should note that the manner or attitude of the supervisor has an important bearing on whether employees perceive supervision as being close or general.

These findings are another way of saying that supervision does not mean standing over the employee and telling him what to do and when and how to do it. The more effective supervisor tells his employees what is required, giving general instructions.

COMMUNICATION

Supervisors of high-production units consider communication as one of the most important aspects of their job. Effective communication is used by these supervisors to achieve better interpersonal relations and improved employee motivation. Low-production supervisors do not rate communication as highly important.

High-producing supervisors find that an important aid to more effective communication is listening. They are ready to listen to both personal problems or interests and questions about the work. This does not mean that they are *nosey* or meddle in their employees' personal lives, but rather that they show a willingness to listen, and do listen, if their employees wish to discuss problems.

These supervisors inform employees about forthcoming changes in work; they discuss agency policy with employees; and they make sure that each employee knows how well he is doing. What these supervisors do is use two-way communication effectively. Unless the supervisor freely imparts information, he will not receive information in return.

Attitudes and perception are frequently affected by communication or the lack of it. Research surveys reveal that many supervisors are not aware of their employees' attitudes, nor do they know what personal reactions their supervision arouses. Through frank discussions with employees, they have been surprised to discover employee beliefs about which they were ignorant. Discussion sometimes reveals that the supervisor and his employees have totally different impressions about the same event. The supervisor should be constantly on the alert for misconceptions about his words and deeds. He must remember that, although his actions are perfectly clear to himself, they may be, and frequently are, viewed differently by employees.

Failure to communicate information results in misconceptions and false assumptions. What you say and how you say it will strongly affect your employees' attitudes and perceptions. By giving them available information you can prevent misconceptions; by discussion, you may be able to change attitudes; by questioning; you can discover what the perceptions and assumptions really are. And it need hardly be added that actions should conform very closely to words.

If we were to attempt to reduce the above discussion on communication to rules, we would have a long list which would be based on one cardinal principle: Don't make assumptions!

- o   Don't assume that your employees know; tell them.
- o   Don't assume that you know how they feel; find out.
- o   Don't assume that they understand; clarify.

———

20 SUPERVISORY HINTS

1. Avoid inconsistency.
2. Always give employees a chance to explain their actions before taking disciplinary action. Don't allow too much time for a "cooling off" period before disciplining an employee.
3. Be specific in your criticisms.
4. Delegate responsibility wisely.
5. Do not argue or lose your temper, and avoid being impatient.
6. Promote mutual respect and be fair, impartial and open-minded.
7. Keep in mind that asking for employees' advice and input can be helpful in decision making.
8. If you make promises, keep them.
9. Always keep the feelings, abilities, dignity and motives of your staff in mind.
10. Remain loyal to your employees' interests.
11. Never criticize employees in front of others, or treat employees like children.
12. Admit mistakes. Don't place blame on your employees, or make excuses.
13. Be reasonable in your expectations, give complete instructions, and establish well-planned goals.
14. Be knowledgeable about office details and procedures, but avoid becoming bogged down in details.
15. Avoid supervising too closely or too loosely. Employees should also view you as an approachable supervisor.
16. Remember that employees' personal problems may affect job performance, but become involved only when appropriate.
17. Work to develop workers, and to instill a feeling of cooperation while working toward mutual goals.
18. Do not overpraise or underpraise, be properly appreciative.
19. Never ask an employee to discipline someone for you.
20. A complaint, even if unjustified, should be taken seriously.

———

PHILOSOPHY, PRINCIPLES, PRACTICES AND TECHNICS
OF
SUPERVISION, ADMINISTRATION, MANAGEMENT AND ORGANIZATION

TABLE OF CONTENTS

PHILOSOPHY, PRINCIPLES, PRACTICES, AND TECHNICS
OF
SUPERVISION, ADMINISTRATION, MANAGEMENT AND ORGANIZATION

I. MEANING OF SUPERVISION

The extension of the democratic philosophy has been accompanied by an extension in the scope of supervision. Modern leaders and supervisors no longer think of supervision in the narrow sense of being confined chiefly to visiting employees, supplying materials, or rating the staff. They regard supervision as being intimately related to all the concerned agencies of society, they speak of the supervisor's function in terms of "growth", rather than the "improvement," of employees.

This modern concept of supervision may be defined as follows:

Supervision is leadership and the development of leadership within groups which are cooperatively engaged in inspection, research, training, guidance and evaluation.

II. THE OLD AND THE NEW SUPERVISION

TRADITIONAL
1. Inspection
2. Focused on the employee
3. Visitation
4. Random and haphazard
5. Imposed and authoritarian
6. One person usually

MODERN
1. Study and analysis
2. Focused on aims, materials, methods, supervisors, employees, environment
3. Demonstrations, intervisitation, workshops, directed reading, bulletins, etc.
4. Definitely organized and planned (scientific)
5. Cooperative and democratic
6. Many persons involved (creative)

III THE EIGHT (8) BASIC PRINCIPLES OF THE NEW SUPERVISION

1. *PRINCIPLE OF RESPONSIBILITY*
   Authority to act and responsibility for acting must be joined.
   a. If you give responsibility, give authority.
   b. Define employee duties clearly.
   c. Protect employees from criticism by others.
   d. Recognize the rights as well as obligations of employees.
   e. Achieve the aims of a democratic society insofar as it is possible within the area of your work.
   f. Establish a situation favorable to training and learning.
   g. Accept ultimate responsibility for everything done in your section, unit, office, division, department.
   h. Good administration and good supervision are inseparable.

2. PRINCIPLE OF AUTHORITY

The success of the supervisor is measured by the extent to which the power of authority is not used.

    a. Exercise simplicity and informality in supervision.
    b. Use the simplest machinery of supervision.
    c. If it is good for the organization as a whole, it is probably justified.
    d. Seldom be arbitrary or authoritative.
    e. Do not base your work on the power of position or of personality.
    f. Permit and encourage the free expression of opinions.

3. PRINCIPLE OF SELF-GROWTH

The success of the supervisor is measured by the extent to which, and the speed with which, he is no longer needed.

    a. Base criticism on principles, not on specifics.
    b. Point out higher activities to employees.
    c. Train for self-thinking by employees, to meet new situations.
    d. Stimulate initiative, self-reliance and individual responsibility.
    e. Concentrate on stimulating the growth of employees rather than on removing defects.

4. PRINCIPLE OF INDIVIDUAL WORTH

Respect for the individual is a paramount consideration in supervision.

    a. Be human and sympathetic in dealing with employees.
    b. Don't nag about things to be done.
    c. Recognize the individual differences among employees and seek opportunities to permit best expression of each personality.

5. PRINCIPLE OF CREATIVE LEADERSHIP

The best supervision is that which is not apparent to the employee.

    a. Stimulate, don't drive employees to creative action.
    b. Emphasize doing good things.
    c. Encourage employees to do what they do best.
    d. Do not be too greatly concerned with details of subject or method.
    e. Do not be concerned exclusively with immediate problems and activities.
    f. Reveal higher activities and make them both desired and maximally possible.
    g. Determine procedures in the light of each situation but see that these are derived from a sound basic philosophy.
    h. Aid, inspire and lead so as to liberate the creative spirit latent in all good employees.

6. PRINCIPLE OF SUCCESS AND FAILURE

There are no unsuccessful employees, only unsuccessful supervisors who have failed to give proper leadership.

    a. Adapt suggestions to the capacities, attitudes, and prejudices of employees.
    b. Be gradual, be progressive, be persistent.
    c. Help the employee find the general principle; have the employee apply his own problem to the general principle.
    d. Give adequate appreciation for good work and honest effort.
    e. Anticipate employee difficulties and help to prevent them.
    f. Encourage employees to do the desirable things they will do anyway.
    g. Judge your supervision by the results it secures.

7. *PRINCIPLE OF SCIENCE*

Successful supervision is scientific, objective, and experimental. It is based on facts, not on prejudices.

a. Be cumulative in results.
b. Never divorce your suggestions from the goals of training.
c. Don't be impatient of results.
d. Keep all matters on a professional, not a personal level.
e. Do not be concerned exclusively with immediate problems and activities.
f. Use objective means of determining achievement and rating where possible.

8. *PRINCIPLE OF COOPERATION*

Supervision is a cooperative enterprise between supervisor and employee.

a. Begin with conditions as they are.
b. Ask opinions of all involved when formulating policies.
c. Organization is as good as its weakest link.
d. Let employees help to determine policies and department programs.
e. Be approachable and accessible - physically and mentally.
f. Develop pleasant social relationships.

IV. WHAT IS ADMINISTRATION?

Administration is concerned with providing the environment, the material facilities, and the operational procedures that will promote the maximum growth and development of supervisors and employees. (Organization is an aspect, and a concomitant, of administration.)

There is no sharp line of demarcation between supervision and administration; these functions are intimately interrelated and, often, overlapping. They are complementary activities.

1. *PRACTICES COMMONLY CLASSED AS "SUPERVISORY"*

a. Conducting employees conferences
b. Visiting sections, units, offices, divisions, departments
c. Arranging for demonstrations
d. Examining plans
e. Suggesting professional reading
f. Interpreting bulletins
g. Recommending in-service training courses
h. Encouraging experimentation
i. Appraising employee morale
j. Providing for intervisitation

2. *PRACTICES COMMONLY CLASSIFIED AS "ADMINISTRATIVE"*

a. Management of the office
b. Arrangement of schedules for extra duties
c. Assignment of rooms or areas
d. Distribution of supplies
e. Keeping records and reports
f. Care of audio-visual materials
g. Keeping inventory records
h. Checking record cards and books
i. Programming special activities
j. Checking on the attendance and punctuality of employees

3. *PRACTICES COMMONLY CLASSIFIED AS BOTH "SUPERVISORY" AND "ADMINISTRATIVE"*
    a. Program construction
    b. Testing or evaluating outcomes
    c. Personnel accounting
    d. Ordering instructional materials

V. RESPONSIBILITIES OF THE SUPERVISOR

A person employed in a supervisory capacity must constantly be able to improve his own efficiency and ability. He represents the employer to the employees and only continuous self-examination can make him a capable supervisor.

Leadership and training are the supervisor's responsibility. An efficient working unit is one in which the employees work with the supervisor. It is his job to bring out the best in his employees. He must always be relaxed, courteous and calm in his association with his employees. Their feelings are important, and a harsh attitude does not develop the most efficient employees.

VI. COMPETENCIES OF THE SUPERVISOR

1. Complete knowledge of the duties and responsibilities of his position.
2. To be able to organize a job, plan ahead and carry through.
3. To have self-confidence and initiative.
4. To be able to handle the unexpected situation and make quick decisions.
5. To be able to properly train subordinates in the positions they are best suited for.
6. To be able to keep good human relations among his subordinates.
7. To be able to keep good human relations between his subordinates and himself and to earn their respect and trust.

VII. THE PROFESSIONAL SUPERVISOR-EMPLOYEE RELATIONSHIP

There are two kinds of efficiency: one kind is only apparent and is produced in organizations through the exercise of mere discipline; this is but a simulation of the second, or true, efficiency which springs from spontaneous cooperation. If you are a manager, no matter how great or small your responsibility, it is your job, in the final analysis, to create and develop this involuntary cooperation among the people whom you supervise. For, no matter how powerful a combination of money, machines, and materials a company may have, this is a dead and sterile thing without a team of willing, thinking and articulate people to guide it.

The following 21 points are presented as indicative of the exemplary basic relationship that should exist between supervisor and employee:

1. Each person wants to be liked and respected by his fellow employee and wants to be treated with consideration and respect by his superior.
2. The most competent employee will make an error. However, in a unit where good relations exist between the supervisor and his employees, tenseness and fear do not exist. Thus, errors are not hidden or covered up and the efficiency of a unit is not impaired.
3. Subordinates resent rules, regulations, or orders that are unreasonable or unexplained.
4. Subordinates are quick to resent unfairness, harshness, injustices and favoritism.
5. An employee will accept responsibility if he knows that he will be complimented for a job well done, and not too harshly chastised for failure; that his supervisor will check the cause of the failure, and, if it was the supervisor's fault, he will assume the blame therefore. If it was the employee's fault, his supervisor will explain the correct method or means of handling the responsibility.

6. An employee wants to receive credit for a suggestion he has made, that is used. If a suggestion cannot be used, the employee is entitled to an explanation. The supervisor should not say "no" and close the subject.
7. Fear and worry slow up a worker's ability. Poor working environment can impair his physical and mental health. A good supervisor avoids forceful methods, threats and arguments to get a job done.
8. A forceful supervisor is able to train his employees individually and as a team, and is able to motivate them in the proper channels.
9. A mature supervisor is able to properly evaluate his subordinates and to keep them happy and satisfied.
10. A sensitive supervisor will never patronize his subordinates.
11. A worthy supervisor will respect his employees' confidences.
12. Definite and clear-cut responsibilities should be assigned to each executive.
13. Responsibility should always be coupled with corresponding authority.
14. No change should be made in the scope or responsibilities of a position without a definite understanding to that effect on the part of all persons concerned.
15. No executive or employee, occupying a single position in the organization, should be subject to definite orders from more than one source.
16. Orders should never be given to subordinates over the head of a responsible executive. Rather than do this, the officer in question should be supplanted.
17. Criticisms of subordinates should, whoever possible, be made privately, and in no case should a subordinate be criticized in the presence of executives or employees of equal or lower rank.
18. No dispute or difference between executives or employees as to authority or responsibilities should be considered too trivial for prompt and careful adjudication.
19. Promotions, wage changes, and disciplinary action should always be approved by the executive immediately superior to the one directly responsible.
20. No executive or employee should ever be required, or expected, to be at the same time an assistant to, and critic of, another.
21. Any executive whose work is subject to regular inspection should, whever practicable, be given the assistance and facilities necessary to enable him to maintain an independent check of the quality of his work.

VIII. MINI-TEXT IN SUPERVISION, ADMINISTRATION, MANAGEMENT, AND ORGANIZATION

A. BRIEF HIGHLIGHTS

Listed concisely and sequentially are major headings and important data in the field for quick recall and review.

1. *LEVELS OF MANAGEMENT*

Any organization of some size has several levels of management. In terms of a ladder the levels are:

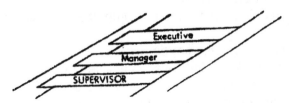

The first level is very important because it is the beginning point of management leadership.

2. WHAT THE SUPERVISOR MUST LEARN
A supervisor must learn to:
(1) Deal with people and their differences
(2) Get the job done through people
(3) Recognize the problems when they exist
(4) Overcome obstacles to good performance
(5) Evaluate the performance of people
(6) Check his own performance in terms of accomplishment

3. A DEFINITION OF SUPERVISOR
The term supervisor means any individual having authority, in the interests of the employer, to hire, transfer, suspend, lay-off, recall, promote, discharge, assign, reward, or discipline other employees or responsibility to direct them, or to adjust their grievances, or effectively to recommend such action, if, in connection with the foregoing, exercise of such authority is not of a merely routine or clerical nature but requires the use of independent judgment.

4. ELEMENTS OF THE TEAM CONCEPT
What is involved in teamwork? The component parts are:
(1) Members   (3) Goals   (5) Cooperation
(2) A leader   (4) Plans   (6) Spirit

5. PRINCIPLES OF ORGANIZATION
(1) A team member must know what his job is.
(2) Be sure that the nature and scope of a job are understood.
(3) Authority and responsibility should be carefully spelled out.
(4) A supervisor should be permitted to make the maximum number of decisions affecting his employees.
(5) Employees should report to only one supervisor.
(6) A supervisor should direct only as many employees as he can handle effectively.
(7) An organization plan should be flexible.
(8) Inspection and performance of work should be separate.
(9) Organizational problems should receive immediate attention.
(10) Assign work in line with ability and experience.

6. THE FOUR IMPORTANT PARTS OF EVERY JOB
(1) Inherent in every job is the *accountability* for results.
(2) A second set of factors in every job is *responsibilities.*
(3) Along with duties and responsibilities one must have the *authority* to act within certain limits without obtaining permission to proceed.
(4) No job exists in a vacuum. The supervisor is surrounded by key *relationships.*

7. PRINCIPLES OF DELEGATION
Where work is delegated for the first time, the supervisor should think in terms of these questions:
(1) Who is best qualified to do this?
(2) Can an employee improve his abilities by doing this?
(3) How long should an employee spend on this?
(4) Are there any special problems for which he will need guidance?
(5) How broad a delegation can I make?

8. PRINCIPLES OF EFFECTIVE COMMUNICATIONS
(1) Determine the media
(2) To whom directed?
(3) Identification and source authority
(4) Is communication understood?

9. PRINCIPLES OF WORK IMPROVEMENT
(1) Most people usually do only the work which is assigned to them
(2) Workers are likely to fit assigned work into the time available to perform it
(3) A good workload usually stimulates output
(4) People usually do their best work when they know that results will be reviewed or inspected
(5) Employees usually feel that someone else is responsible for conditions of work, workplace layout, job methods, type of tools/equipment, and other such factors
(6) Employees are usually defensive about their job security
(7) Employees have natural resistance to change
(8) Employees can support or destroy a supervisor
(9) A supervisor usually earns the respect of his people through his personal example of diligence and efficiency

10. AREAS OF JOB IMPROVEMENT
The areas of job improvement are quite numerous, but the most common ones which a supervisor can identify and utilize are:

(1) Departmental layout
(2) Flow of work
(3) Workplace layout
(4) Utilization of manpower
(5) Work methods
(6) Materials handling
(7) Utilization
(8) Motion economy

11. SEVEN KEY POINTS IN MAKING IMPROVEMENTS
(1) Select the job to be improved
(2) Study how it is being done now
(3) Question the present method
(4) Determine actions to be taken
(5) Chart proposed method
(6) Get approval and apply
(7) Solicit worker participation

12. CORRECTIVE TECHNIQUES OF JOB IMPROVEMENT

Specific Problems	General Improvement	Corrective Techniques
(1) Size of workload	(1) Departmental layout	(1) Study with scale model
(2) Inability to meet schedules	(2) Flow of work	(2) Flow chart study
(3) Strain and fatigue	(3) Work plan layout	(3) Motion analysis
(4) Improper use of men and skills	(4) Utilization of manpower	(4) Comparison of units produced to standard allowance
(5) Waste, poor quality, unsafe conditions	(5) Work methods	(5) Methods analysis
(6) Bottleneck conditions that hinder output	(6) Materials handling	(6) Flow chart & equipment study
(7) Poor utilization of equipment and machine	(7) Utilization of equipment	(7) Down time vs. running time
(8) Efficiency and productivity of labor	(8) Motion economy	(8) Motion analysis

13. A PLANNING CHECKLIST

(1) Objectives	(6) Resources	(11) Safety
(2) Controls	(7) Manpower	(12) Money
(3) Delegations	(8) Equipment	(13) Work
(4) Communications	(9) Supplies and materials	(14) Timing of improvements
(5) Resources	(10) Utilization of time	

14. FIVE CHARACTERISTICS OF GOOD DIRECTIONS

In order to get results, directions must be:

(1) Possible of accomplishment	(3) Related to mission	(5) Unmistakably clear
(2) Agreeable with worker interests	(4) Planned and complete	

15. TYPES OF DIRECTIONS

(1) Demands or direct orders	(3) Suggestion or implication
(2) Requests	(4) Volunteering

16. CONTROLS

A typical listing of the overall areas in which the supervisor should establish controls might be:

(1) Manpower	(3) Quality of work	(5) Time	(7) Money
(2) Materials	(4) Quantity of work	(6) Space	(8) Methods

17. ORIENTING THE NEW EMPLOYEE

(1) Prepare for him	(3) Orientation for the job
(2) Welcome the new employee	(4) Follow-up

18. CHECKLIST FOR ORIENTING NEW EMPLOYEES

                  Yes   No

(1) Do your appreciate the feelings of new employees when they first report for work?

(2) Are you aware of the fact that the new employee must make a big adjustment to his job?

(3) Have you given him good reasons for liking the job and the organization?

(4) Have you prepared for his first day on the job?

(5) Did you welcome him cordially and make him feel needed?

(6) Did you establish rapport with him so that he feels free to talk and discuss matters with you?

(7) Did you explain his job to him and his relationship to you?

(8) Does he know that his work will be evaluated periodically on a basis that is fair and objective?

(9) Did you introduce him to his fellow workers in such a way that they are likely to accept him?

(10) Does he know what employee benefits he will receive?

(11) Does he understand the importance of being on the job and what to do if he must leave his duty station?

(12) Has he been impressed with the importance of accident prevention and safe practice?

(13) Does he generally know his way around the department?

(14) Is he under the guidance of a sponsor who will teach the right ways of doing things?

(15) Do you plan to follow-up so that he will continue to adjust successfully to his job?

19. *PRINCIPLES OF LEARNING*
    (1) Motivation   (2) Demonstration or explanation   (3) Practice

20. *CAUSES OF POOR PERFORMANCE*
    (1) Improper training for job
    (2) Wrong tools
    (3) Inadequate directions
    (4) Lack of supervisory follow-up
    (5) Poor communications
    (6) Lack of standards of performance
    (7) Wrong work habits
    (8) Low morale
    (9) Other

21. *FOUR MAJOR STEPS IN ON-THE-JOB INSTRUCTION*
    (1) Prepare the worker
    (2) Present the operation
    (3) Tryout performance
    (4) Follow-up

22. *EMPLOYEES WANT FIVE THINGS*
    (1) Security (2) Opportunity (3) Recognition (4) Inclusion (5) Expression

23. *SOME DON'TS IN REGARD TO PRAISE*
    (1) Don't praise a person for something he hasn't done
    (2) Don't praise a person unless you can be sincere
    (3) Don't be sparing in praise just because your superior withholds it from you
    (4) Don't let too much time elapse between good performance and recognition of it

24. *HOW TO GAIN YOUR WORKERS' CONFIDENCE*
Methods of developing confidence include such things as:
    (1) Knowing the interests, habits, hobbies of employees
    (2) Admitting your own inadequacies
    (3) Sharing and telling of confidence in others
    (4) Supporting people when they are in trouble
    (5) Delegating matters that can be well handled
    (6) Being frank and straightforward about problems and working conditions
    (7) Encouraging others to bring their problems to you
    (8) Taking action on problems which impede worker progress

25. *SOURCES OF EMPLOYEE PROBLEMS*
On-the-job causes might be such things as:
    (1) A feeling that favoritism is exercised in assignments
    (2) Assignment of overtime
    (3) An undue amount of supervision
    (4) Changing methods or systems
    (5) Stealing of ideas or trade secrets
    (6) Lack of interest in job
    (7) Threat of reduction in force
    (8) Ignorance or lack of communications
    (9) Poor equipment
    (10) Lack of knowing how supervisor feels toward employee
    (11) Shift assignments

Off-the-job problems might have to do with:
    (1) Health   (2) Finances   (3) Housing   (4) Family

26. THE SUPERVISOR'S KEY TO DISCIPLINE

There are several key points about discipline which the supervisor should keep in mind:

(1) Job discipline is one of the disciplines of life and is directed by the supervisor.
(2) It is more important to correct an employee fault than to fix blame for it.
(3) Employee performance is affected by problems both on the job and off.
(4) Sudden or abrupt changes in behavior can be indications of important employee problems.
(5) Problems should be dealt with as soon as possible after they are identified.
(6) The attitude of the supervisor may have more to do with solving problems than the techniques of problem solving.
(7) Correction of employee behavior should be resorted to only after the supervisor is sure that training or counseling will not be helpful.
(8) Be sure to document your disciplinary actions.
(9) Make sure that you are disciplining on the basis of facts rather than personal feelings.
(10) Take each disciplinary step in order, being careful not to make snap judgments, or decisions based on impatience.

27. FIVE IMPORTANT PROCESSES OF MANAGEMENT

(1) Planning   (2) Organizing   (3) Scheduling
(4) Controlling   (5) Motivating

28. WHEN THE SUPERVISOR FAILS TO PLAN

(1) Supervisor creates impression of not knowing his job
(2) May lead to excessive overtime
(3) Job runs itself -- supervisor lacks control
(4) Deadlines and appointments missed
(5) Parts of the work go undone
(6) Work interrupted by emergencies
(7) Sets a bad example
(8) Uneven workload creates peaks and valleys
(9) Too much time on minor details at expense of more important tasks

29. FOURTEEN GENERAL PRINCIPLES OF MANAGEMENT

(1) Division of work
(2) Authority and responsibility
(3) Discipline
(4) Unity of command
(5) Unity of direction
(6) Subordination of individual interest to general interest
(7) Remuneration of personnel
(8) Centralization
(9) Scalar chain
(10) Order
(11) Equity
(12) Stability of tenure of personnel
(13) Initiative
(14) Esprit de corps

30. CHANGE

Bringing about change is perhaps attempted more often, and yet less well understood, than anything else the supervisor does. How do people generally react to change? (People tend to resist change that is imposed upon them by other individuals or circumstances.

Change is characteristic of every situation. It is a part of every real endeavor where the efforts of people are concerned.

A. Why do people resist change?

People may resist change because of:

    (1) Fear of the unknown

    (2) Implied criticism

    (3) Unpleasant experiences in the past

    (4) Fear of loss of status

    (5) Threat to the ego

    (6) Fear of loss of economic stability

B. How can we best overcome the resistance to change?

In initiating change, take these steps:

    (1) Get ready to sell

    (2) Identify sources of help

    (3) Anticipate objections

    (4) Sell benefits

    (5) Listen in depth

    (6) Follow up

B. BRIEF TOPICAL SUMMARIES

I. WHO/WHAT IS THE SUPERVISOR?

1. The supervisor is often called the "highest level employee and the lowest level manager."
2. A supervisor is a member of both management and the work group. He acts as a bridge between the two.
3. Most problems in supervision are in the area of human relations, or people problems.
4. Employees expect: Respect, opportunity to learn and to advance, and a sense of belonging, and so forth.
5. Supervisors are responsible for directing people and organizing work. Planning is of paramount importance.
6. A position description is a set of duties and responsibilities inherent to a given position.
7. It is important to keep the position description up-to-date and to provide each employee with his own copy.

II. THE SOCIOLOGY OF WORK

1. People are alike in many ways; however, each individual is unique.
2. The supervisor is challenged in getting to know employee differences. Acquiring skills in evaluating individuals is an asset.
3. Maintaining meaningful working relationships in the organization is of great importance.
4. The supervisor has an obligation to help individuals to develop to their fullest potential.
5. Job rotation on a planned basis helps to build versatility and to maintain interest and enthusiasm in work groups.
6. Cross training (job rotation) provides backup skills.
7. The supervisor can help reduce tension by maintaining a sense of humor, providing guidance to employees, and by making reasonable and timely decisions. Employees respond favorably to working under reasonably predictable circumstances.
8. Change is characteristic of all managerial behavior. The supervisor must adjust to changes in procedures, new methods, technological changes, and to a number of new and sometimes challenging situations.
9. To overcome the natural tendency for people to resist change, the supervisor should become more skillful in initiating change.

III. PRINCIPLES AND PRACTICES OF SUPERVISION

1. Employees should be required to answer to only one superior.
2. A supervisor can effectively direct only a limited number of employees, depending upon the complexity, variety, and proximity of the jobs involved.
3. The organizational chart presents the organization in graphic form. It reflects lines of authority and responsibility as well as interrelationships of units within the organization.
4. Distribution of work can be improved through an analysis using the "Work Distribution Chart."
5. The "Work Distribution Chart" reflects the division of work within a unit in understandable form.
6. When related tasks are given to an employee, he has a better chance of increasing his skills through training.
7. The individual who is given the responsibility for tasks must also be given the appropriate authority to insure adequate results.
8. The supervisor should delegate repetitive, routine work. Preparation of recurring reports, maintaining leave and attendance records are some examples.
9. Good discipline is essential to good task performance. Discipline is reflected in the actions of employees on the job in the absence of supervision.
10. Disciplinary action may have to be taken when the positive aspects of discipline have failed. Reprimand, warning, and suspension are examples of disciplinary action.
11. If a situation calls for a reprimand, be sure it is deserved and remember it is to be done in private.

IV. DYNAMIC LEADERSHIP

1. A style is a personal method or manner of exerting influence.
2. Authoritarian leaders often see themselves as the source of power and authority.
3. The democratic leader often perceives the group as the source of authority and power.
4. Supervisors tend to do better when using the pattern of leadership that is most natural for them.
5. Social scientists suggest that the effective supervisor use the leadership style that best fits the problem or circumstances involved.
6. All four styles -- telling, selling, consulting, joining -- have their place. Using one does not preclude using the other at another time.
7. The theory X point of view assumes that the average person dislikes work, will avoid it whenever possible, and must be coerced to achieve organizational objectives.
8. The theory Y point of view assumes that the average person considers work to be as natural as play, and, when the individual is committed, he requires little supervision or direction to accomplish desired objectives.
9. The leader's basic assumptions concerning human behavior and human nature affect his actions, decisions, and other managerial practices.
10. Dissatisfaction among employees is often present, but difficult to isolate. The supervisor should seek to weaken dissatisfaction by keeping promises, being sincere and considerate, keeping employees informed, and so forth.
11. Constructive suggestions should be encouraged during the natural progress of the work.

V. PROCESSES FOR SOLVING PROBLEMS

1. People find their daily tasks more meaningful and satisfying when they can improve them.
2. The causes of problems, or the key factors, are often hidden in the background. Ability to solve problems often involves the ability to isolate them from their backgrounds. There is some substance to the cliché that some persons "can't see the forest for the trees."
3. New procedures are often developed from old ones. Problems should be broken down into manageable parts. New ideas can be adapted from old ones.

4. People think differently in problem-solving situations. Using a logical, patterned approach is often useful. One approach found to be useful includes these steps:
    (a) Define the problem   (d) Weigh and decide
    (b) Establish objectives   (e) Take action
    (c) Get the facts   (f) Evaluate action

VI. TRAINING FOR RESULTS

1. Participants respond best when they feel training is important to them.
2. The supervisor has responsibility for the training and development of those who report to him.
3. When training is delegated to others, great care must be exercised to insure the trainer has knowledge, aptitude, and interest for his work as a trainer.
4. Training (learning) of some type goes on continually. The most successful supervisor makes certain the learning contributes in a productive manner to operational goals.
5. New employees are particularly susceptible to training. Older employees facing new job situations require specific training, as well as having need for development and growth opportunities.
6. Training needs require continuous monitoring.
7. The training officer of an agency is a professional with a responsibility to assist supervisors in solving training problems.
8. Many of the self-development steps important to the supervisor's own growth are equally important to the development of peers and subordinates. Knowledge of these is important when the supervisor consults with others on development and growth opportunities.

VII. HEALTH, SAFETY, AND ACCIDENT PREVENTION

1. Management-minded supervisors take appropriate measures to assist employees in maintaining health and in assuring safe practices in the work environment.
2. Effective safety training and practices help to avoid injury and accidents.
3. Safety should be a management goal. All infractions of safety which are observed should be corrected without exception.
4. Employees' safety attitude, training and instruction, provision of safe tools and equipment, supervision, and leadership are considered highly important factors which contribute to safety and which can be influenced directly by supervisors.
5. When accidents do occur they should be investigated promptly for very important reasons, including the fact that information which is gained can be used to prevent accidents in the future.

VIII. EQUAL EMPLOYMENT OPPORTUNITY

1. The supervisor should endeavor to treat all employees fairly, without regard to religion, race, sex, or national origin.
2. Groups tend to reflect the attitude of the leader. Prejudice can be detected even in very subtle form. Supervisors must strive to create a feeling of mutual respect and confidence in every employee.
3. Complete utilization of all human resources is a national goal. Equitable consideration should be accorded women in the work force, minority-group members, the physically and mentally handicapped, and the older employee. The important question is: "Who can do the job?"
4. Training opportunities, recognition for performance, overtime assignments, promotional opportunities, and all other personnel actions are to be handled on an equitable basis.

IX. IMPROVING COMMUNICATIONS

1. Communications is achieving understanding between the sender and the receiver of a message. It also means sharing information -- the creation of understanding.
2. Communication is basic to all human activity. Words are means of conveying meanings; however, real meanings are in people.
3. There are very practical differences in the effectiveness of one-way, impersonal, and two-way communications. Words spoken face-to-face are better understood. Telephone conversations are effective, but lack the rapport of person-to-person exchanges. The whole person communicates.
4. Cooperation and communication in an organization go hand in hand. When there is a mutual respect between people, spelling out rules and procedures for communicating is unnecessary.
5. There are several barriers to effective communications. These include failure to listen with respect and understanding, lack of skill in feedback, and misinterpreting the meanings of words used by the speaker. It is also common practice to listen to what we want to hear, and tune out things we do not want to hear.
6. Communication is management's chief problem. The supervisor should accept the challenge to communicate more effectively and to improve interagency and intra-agency communications.
7. The supervisor may often plan for and conduct meetings. The planning phase is critical and may determine the success or the failure of a meeting.
8. Speaking before groups usually requires extra effort. Stage fright may never disappear completely, but it can be controlled.

X. SELF-DEVELOPMENT

1. Every employee is responsible for his own self-development.
2. Toastmaster and toastmistress clubs offer opportunities to improve skills in oral communications.
3. Planning for one's own self-development is of vital importance. Supervisors know their own strengths and limitations better than anyone else.
4. Many opportunities are open to aid the supervisor in his developmental efforts, including job assignments; training opportunities, both governmental and non-governmental -- to include universities and professional conferences and seminars.
5. Programmed instruction offers a means of studying at one's own rate.
6. Where difficulties may arise from a supervisor's being away from his work for training, he may participate in televised home study or correspondence courses to meet his self-develop- ment needs.

XI. TEACHING AND TRAINING

A. The Teaching Process

Teaching is encouraging and guiding the learning activities of students toward established goals. In most cases this process consists in five steps: preparation, presentation, summarization, evaluation, and application.

1. Preparation

Preparation is twofold in nature; that of the supervisor and the employee.

Preparation by the supervisor is absolutely essential to success. He must know what, when, where, how, and whom he will teach. Some of the factors that should be considered are:

(1) The objectives	(5) Employee interest
(2) The materials needed	(6) Training aids
(3) The methods to be used	(7) Evaluation
(4) Employee participation	(8) Summarization

Employee preparation consists in preparing the employee to receive the material. Probably the most important single factor in the preparation of the employee is arousing and maintaining his interest. He must know the objectives of the training, why he is there, how the material can be used, and its importance to him.

2. Presentation
In presentation, have a carefully designed plan and follow it.
The plan should be accurate and complete, yet flexible enough to meet situations as they arise. The method of presentation will be determined by the particular situation and objectives.

3. Summary
A summary should be made at the end of every training unit and program. In addition, there may be internal summaries depending on the nature of the material being taught. The important thing is that the trainee must always be able to understand how each part of the new material relates to the whole.

4. Application
The supervisor must arrange work so the employee will be given a chance to apply new knowledge or skills while the material is still clear in his mind and interest is high. The trainee does not really know whether he has learned the material until he has been given a chance to apply it. If the material is not applied, it loses most of its value.

5. Evaluation

The purpose of all training is to promote learning. To determine whether the training has been a success or failure, the supervisor must evaluate this learning.

In the broadest sense evaluation includes all the devices, methods, skills, and techniques used by the supervisor to keep him self and the employees informed as to their progress toward the objectives they are pursuing. The extent to which the employee has mastered the knowledge, skills, and abilities, or changed his attitudes, as determined by the program objectives, is the extent to which instruction has succeeded or failed.

Evaluation should not be confined to the end of the lesson, day, or program but should be used continuously. We shall note later the way this relates to the rest of the teaching process.

B. Teaching Methods

A teaching method is a pattern of identifiable student and instructor activity used in presenting training material.
All supervisors are faced with the problem of deciding which method should be used at a given time.
As with all methods, there are certain advantages and disadvantages to each method.

1. Lecture
The lecture is direct oral presentation of material by the supervisor. The present trend is to place less emphasis on the trainer's activity and more on that of the trainee.

2. Discussion
Teaching by discussion or conference involves using questions and other techniques to arouse interest and focus attention upon certain areas, and by doing so creating a learning situation. This can be one of the most valuable methods because it gives the employees 'an opportunity to express their ideas and pool their knowledge.

3. Demonstration

The demonstration is used to teach how something works or how to do something. It can be used to show a principle or what the results of a series of actions will be. A well-staged demonstration is particularly effective because it shows proper methods of performance in a realistic manner.

4. Performance

Performance is one of the most fundamental of all learning techniques or teaching methods. The trainee may be able to tell how a specific operation should be performed but he cannot be sure he knows how to perform the operation until he has done so.

5. Which Method to Use

Moreover, there are other methods and techniques of teaching. It is difficult to use any method without other methods entering into it. In any learning situation a combination of methods is usually more effective than anyone method alone.

Finally, evaluation must be integrated into the other aspects of the teaching-learning process. It must be used in the motivation of the trainees; it must be used to assist in developing understanding during the training; and it must be related to employee application of the results of training.

This is distinctly the role of the supervisor.

———

PRINCIPLES AND PRACTICES OF ADMINISTRATION, SUPERVISION & MANAGEMENT

TABLE OF CONTENTS

PRINCIPLES AND PRACTICES OF ADMINISTRATION, SUPERVISION & MANAGEMENT

Most people are inclined to think of administration as something that only a few persons are responsible for in a large organization. Perhaps this is true if you are thinking of Administration with a capital *A*, but administration with a lower case a is a responsibility of supervisors at all levels each working day.

All of us feel we are pretty good supervisors and that we do a good job of administering the workings of our agency. By and large, this is true, but every so often it is good to check up on ourselves. Checklists appear from time to time in various publications which psychologists say, tell whether or not a person will make a good wife, husband, doctor, lawyer, or supervisor.

The following questions are an excellent checklist to test yourself as a supervisor and administrator.

Remember, Administration gives direction and points the way but administration carries the ideas to fruition. Each is dependent on the other for its success. Remember, too, that no unit is too small for these departmental functions to be carried out. These statements apply equally as well to the Chief Librarian as to the Department Head with but one or two persons to supervise.

GENERAL ADMINISTRATION - General Responsibilities of Supervisors

1. Have I prepared written statements of functions, activities, and duties for my organizational unit?

2. Have I prepared procedural guides for operating activities?

3. Have I established clearly in writing, lines of authority and responsibility for my organizational unit?

4. Do I make recommendations for improvements in organization, policies, administrative and operating routines and procedures, including simplification of work and elimination of non-essential operations?

5. Have I designated and trained an understudy to function in my absence?

6. Do I supervise and train personnel within the unit to effectively perform their assignments?

7. Do I assign personnel and distribute work on such a basis as to carry out the organizational unit's assignment or mission in the most effective and efficient manner?

8. Have I established administrative controls by:

   a. Fixing responsibility and accountability on all supervisors under my direction for the proper performance of their functions and duties.

b.   Preparing and submitting periodic work load and progress reports covering the operations of the unit to my immediate superior.

c.   Analysis and evaluation of such reports received from subordinate units.

d.   Submission of significant developments and problems arising within the organizational unit to my immediate superior.

e.   Conducting conferences, inspections, etc., as to the status and efficiency of unit operations.

9.   Do I maintain an adequate and competent working force?

10.   Have I fostered good employee-department relations, seeing that established rules, regulations, and instructions are being carried out properly?

11.   Do I collaborate and consult with other organizational units performing related functions to insure harmonious and efficient working relationships?

12.   Do I maintain liaison through prescribed channels with city departments and other governmental agencies concerned with the activities of the unit?

13.   Do I maintain contact with and keep abreast of the latest developments and techniques of administration (professional societies, groups, periodicals, etc.) as to their applicability to the activities of the unit?

14.   Do I communicate with superiors and subordinates through prescribed organizational channels?

15.   Do I notify superiors and subordinates in instances where bypassing is necessary as soon thereafter as practicable?

16.   Do I keep my superior informed of significant developments and problems?

SEVEN BASIC FUNCTIONS OF THE SUPERVISOR

1. PLANNING
This means working out goals and means to obtain goals. What needs to be done, who will do it, how, when, and where it is to be done.

SEVEN STEPS IN PLANNING

1. Define job or problem clearly.
2. Consider priority of job.
3. Consider time-limit - starting and completing.
4. Consider minimum distraction to, or interference with, other activities.
5. Consider and provide for contingencies - possible emergencies.
6. Break job down into components.
7. Consider the 5 W's and H:

WHY	...	is it necessary to do the job? (Is the purpose clearly defined?)
WHAT	...	needs to be done to accomplish the defined purpose?
	...	is needed to do the job? (money, materials, etc.)
WHO	...	is needed to do the job?
	...	will have responsibilities?
WHERE	...	is the work to be done?
WHEN	...	is the job to begin and end? (schedules, etc.)
HOW	...	is the job to be done? (methods, controls, records, etc.)

2. ORGANIZING
This means dividing up the work, establishing clear lines of responsibility and authority and coordinating efforts to get the job done.

3. STAFFING
The whole personnel function of bringing in and training staff, getting the right man and fitting him to the right job - the job to which he is best suited.
In the normal situation, the supervisor's responsibility regarding staffing normally includes providing accurate job descriptions, that is, duties of the jobs, requirements, education and experience, skills, physical, etc.; assigning the work for maximum use of skills; and proper utilization of the probationary period to weed out unsatisfactory employees.

4. DIRECTING
Providing the necessary leadership to the group supervised. Important work gets done to the supervisor's satisfaction.

5. COORDINATING
The all-important duty of inter-relating the various parts of the work.
The supervisor is also responsible for controlling the coordinated activities. This means measuring performance according to a time schedule and setting quotas to see that the goals previously set are being reached. Reports from workers should be analyzed, evaluated, and made part of all future plans.

6. REPORTING
This means proper and effective communication to your superiors, subordinates, and your peers (in definition of the job of the supervisor). Reports should be read and information contained therein should be used not be filed away and forgotten. Reports should be written in such a way that the desired action recommended by the report is forthcoming.

7. BUDGETING
This means controlling current costs and forecasting future costs. This forecast is based on past experience, future plans and programs, as well as current costs.

You will note that these seven functions can fall under three topics:

Planning	)	
Organizing	)	Make a Plan
Staffing	)	
Directing	)	Get things done
Controlling	)	

Reporting   )
Budgeting   )   Watch it work

PLANNING TO MEET MANAGEMENT GOALS

I. <u>WHAT IS PLANNING?</u>
   A. Thinking a job through before new work is done to determine the best way to do it
   B. A method of doing something
   C. Ways and means for achieving set goals
   D. A means of enabling a supervisor to deliver with a minimum of effort, all details involved in coordinating his work

II. <u>WHO SHOULD MAKE PLANS?</u>
   Everybody!
   All levels of supervision must plan work. (Top management, heads of divisions or bureaus, first line supervisors, and individual employees.) The higher the level, the more planning required.

III. <u>WHAT ARE THE RESULTS OF POOR PLANNING?</u>
   A. Failure to meet deadline
   B. Low employee morale
   C. Lack of job coordination
   D. Overtime is frequently necessary
   E. Excessive cost, waste of material and manhours

IV. <u>PRINCIPLES OF PLANNING</u>
   A. Getting a clear picture of your objectives. What exactly are you trying to accomplish?
   B. Plan the whole job, then the parts, in proper sequence.
   C. Delegate the planning of details to those responsible for executing them.
   D. Make your plan flexible.
   E. Coordinate your plan with the plans of others so that the work may be processed with a minimum of delay.
   F. Sell your plan before you execute it.
   G. Sell your plan to your superior, subordinate, in order to gain maximum participation and coordination.
   H. Your plan should take precedence. Use knowledge and skills that others have brought to a similar job.
   I. Your plan should take account of future contingencies; allow for future expansion.
   J. Plans should include minor details. Leave nothing to chance that can be anticipated.
   K. Your plan should be simple and provide standards and controls. Establish quality and quantity standards and set a standard method of doing the job. The controls will indicate whether the job is proceeding according to plan.
   L. Consider possible bottlenecks, breakdowns, or other difficulties that are likely to arise.

V. Q. WHAT ARE THE *YARDSTICKS* BY WHICH PLANNING SHOULD BE MEASURED?
   A. Any plan should:
      - Clearly state a definite course of action to be followed and goal to be achieved, with consideration for emergencies.
      - Be realistic and practical.

- State what's to be done, when it's to be done, where, how, and by whom.
- Establish the most efficient sequence of operating steps so that more is accomplished in less time, with the least effort, and with the best quality results.
- Assure meeting deliveries without delays.
- Establish the standard by which performance is to be judged.

Q. WHAT KINDS OF PLANS DOES EFFECTIVE SUPERVISION REQUIRE?
A. Plans should cover such factors as:
- Manpower - right number of properly trained employees on the job.
- Materials - adequate supply of the right materials and supplies.
- Machines - full utilization of machines and equipment, with proper maintenance.
- Methods - most efficient handling of operations.
- Deliveries - making deliveries on time.
- Tools - sufficient well-conditioned tools
- Layout - most effective use of space.
- Reports - maintaining proper records and reports.
- Supervision - planning work for employees and organizing supervisor's own time.

I. MANAGEMENT

Question: *What do we mean by management?*

Answer: *Getting work done through others.*

Management could also be defined as planning, directing, and controlling the operations of a bureau or division so that all factors will function properly and all persons cooperate efficiently for a common objective.

II. MANAGEMENT PRINCIPLES

1. There should be a hierarchy - wherein authority and responsibility run upward and downward through several levels - with a broad base at the bottom and a single head at the top.

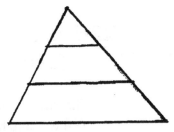

2. Each and every unit or person in the organization should be answerable ultimately to the manager at the apex. In other words, *The buck stops here!*

3. Every necessary function involved in the bureau's objectives is assigned to a unit in that bureau.

4. Responsibilities assigned to a unit are specifically clear-cut and understood.

5. Consistent methods of organizational structure should be applied at each level of the organization.

6. Each member of the bureau from top to bottom knows:
    to whom he reports
    who reports to him.

7. No member of one bureau reports to more than one supervisor.
    No dual functions

8. Responsibility for a function is matched by authority necessary to perform that function.
    Weight of authority

9. Individuals or units reporting to a supervisor do not exceed the number which can be feasibly and effectively coordinated and directed.
    Concept of *span of control*

10. Channels of command (management) are not violated by staff units, although there should be staff services to facilitate and coordinate management functions.

11. Authority and responsibility should be decentralized to units and individuals who are responsible for the actual performance of operations.
    Welfare - down to Welfare Centers
    Hospitals - down to local hospitals

12. Management should exercise control through attention to policy problems of exceptional importance, rather than through review of routine actions of subordinates.

13. Organizations should never be permitted to grow so elaborate as to hinder work accomplishments.
    Empire building

II. ORGANIZATION STRUCTURE
Types of Organizations.
The purest form is a leader and a few followers, such as:

```
                    ┌─────────────┐
                    │  Supervisor │
                    └─────────────┘
──────────────────────────────────────────────────
┌──────────┐   ┌──────────┐   ┌──────────┐   ┌──────────┐
│  Worker  │   │  Worker  │   │  Worker  │   │  Worker  │
└──────────┘   └──────────┘   └──────────┘   └──────────┘
```

(Refer to organization chart) from supervisor to workers.

The line of authority is direct,
The workers know exactly where they stand in relation to their boss, to whom they report for instructions and direction.

Unfortunately, in our present complex society, few organizations are similar to this example of a pure line organization. In this era of specialization, other people are often needed in the simplest of organizations. These specialists are known as staff. The sole purpose for their existence (staff) is to assist, advise, suggest, help or counsel line organizations. Staff has no authority to direct line people - nor do they give them direct instructions.

```
                        ┌─────────────┐
                        │ SUPERVISOR  │
                        └─────────────┘
                               │
 ┌─────────────────────────────┼─────────────────────────────┐
┌──────────┐      ┌────────────┐      ┌────────────┐      ┌────────┐
│Personnel │      │ Accounting │      │ Inspection │      │ Legal  │
└──────────┘      └────────────┘      └────────────┘      └────────┘
 ┌────────┐        ┌────────┐          ┌────────┐          ┌────────┐
 │ Worker │        │ Worker │          │ Worker │          │ Worker │
 └────────┘        └────────┘          └────────┘          └────────┘
```

Line Functions	Staff Functions
1. Directs	1. Advises
2. Orders	2. Persuades and sells
3. Responsibility for carrying out activities from beginning to end	3. Staff studies, reports, recommends but does not carry out
4. Follows chain of command	4. May advise across department lines
5. Is identified with what it does	5. May find its ideas identified with others
6. Decides when and how to use staff advice	6. Has to persuade line to want its advice
7. Line executes	7. Staff - Conducts studies and research. Provides advice and instructions in technical matters. Serves as technical specialist to render specific services

Types and Functions of Organization Charts.

An organization chart is a picture of the arrangement and inter-relationship of the subdivisions of an organization.

1. Types of Charts:
   a. Structural - basic relationships only
   b. Functional - includes functions or duties
   c. Personnel - positions, salaries, status, etc.
   d. Process Chart - work performed
   e. Gantt Chart - actual performance against planned
   f. Flow Chart - flow and distribution of work

2. Functions of Charts:
   a. Assist in management planning and control
   b. Indicate duplication of functions
   c. Indicate incorrect stressing of functions
   d. Indicate neglect of important functions
   e. Correct unclear authority
   f. Establish proper span of control

3. Limitations of Charts:
   a. Seldom maintained on current basis

b. Chart is oversimplified

c. Human factors cannot adequately be charted

4. Organization Charts should be:
   a. Simple
   b. Symmetrical
   c. Indicate authority
   d. Line and staff relationship differentiated
   e. Chart should be dated and bear signature of approving officer
   f. Chart should be displayed, not hidden

ORGANIZATION

There are four basic principles of organization:

1. Unity of command
2. Span of control
3. Uniformity of assignment
4. Assignment of responsibility and delegation of authority

Unity of Command

Unity of command means that each person in the organization should receive orders from one, and only one, supervisor. When a person has to take orders from two or more people, (a) the orders may be in conflict and the employee is upset because he does not know which he should obey, or, (b) different orders may reach him at the same time and he does not know which he should carry out first.

Equally as bad as having two bosses is the situation where the supervisor is by-passed. Let us suppose you are a supervisor whose boss by-passes you (deals directly with people reporting to you). To the worker, it is the same as having two bosses; but to you, the supervisor, it is equally serious. By-passing on the part of your boss will undermine your authority, and the people under you will begin looking to your boss for decisions and even for routine orders.

You can prevent by-passing by telling the people you supervise that if anyone tries to give them orders, they should direct that person to you.

Span of Control

Span of control on a given level involves:

a. The number of people being supervised

b. The distance

c. The time involved in supervising the people. (One supervisor cannot supervise too many workers effectively.)

Span of control means that a supervisor has the right number (not too many and not too few) of subordinates that he can supervise well.

Uniformity of Assignment

In assigning work, you as the supervisor should assign to each person jobs that are similar in nature. An employee who is assigned too many different types of jobs will waste time in going from one kind of work to another. It takes time for him to get to top production in one kind of task and, before he does so, he has to start on another.

When you assign work to people, remember that:

a. Job duties should be definite. Make it clear from the beginning <u>what</u> they are to do, <u>how</u> they are to do it, and <u>why</u> they are to do it. Let them know how much they are expected to do and how well they are expected to do it.

b. Check your assignments to be certain that there are no workers with too many unrelated duties, and that no two people have been given overlapping responsibilities. Your aim should be to have every task assigned to a specific person with the work fairly distributed and with each person doing his part.

<u>Assignment of Responsibility and Delegation of Authority</u>
A supervisor cannot delegate his final responsibility for the work of his department. The experienced supervisor knows that he gets his work done through people. He can't do it all himself. So he must assign the work and the responsibility for the work to his employees. Then they must be given the authority to carry out their responsibilities.

By assigning responsibility and delegating authority to carry out the responsibility, the supervisor builds in his workers initiative, resourcefulness, enthusiasm, and interest in their work. He is treating them as responsible adults. They can find satisfaction in their work, and they will respect the supervisor and be loyal to the supervisor.

PRINCIPLES OF ORGANIZATION

1. <u>Definition</u>
Organization is the method of dividing up the work to provide the best channels for coordinated effort to get the agency's mission accomplished.

2. <u>Purpose of Organization</u>
   a. To enable each employee within the organization to clearly know his responsibilities and relationships to his fellow employees and to organizational units.
   b. To avoid conflicts of authority and overlapping of jurisdiction.
   c. To ensure teamwork.

3. <u>Basic Considerations in Organizational Planning</u>
   a. The basic plans and objectives of the agency should be determined, and the organizational structure should be adapted to carry out effectively such plans and objectives.
   b. The organization should be built around the major functions of the agency and not individuals or groups of individuals.
   c. The organization should be sufficiently flexible to meet new and changing conditions which may be brought about from within or outside the department.
   d. The organizational structure should be as simple as possible and the number of organizational units kept at a minimum.
   e. The number of levels of authority should be kept at a minimum. Each additional management level lengthens the chain of authority and responsibility and increases the time for instructions to be distributed to operating levels and for decisions to be obtained from higher authority.

    f. The form of organization should permit each executive to exercise maximum initiative within the limits of delegated authority.

4. **Bases for Organization**
    a. Purpose (Examples: education, police, sanitation)
    b. Process (Examples: accounting, legal, purchasing)
    c. Clientele (Examples: welfare, parks, veteran)
    d. Geographic (Examples: borough offices, precincts, libraries)

5. **Assignments of Functions**
    a. Every function of the agency should be assigned to a specific organizational unit. Under normal circumstances, no single function should be assigned to more than one organizational unit.
    b. There should be no overlapping, duplication, or conflict between organizational elements.
    c. Line functions should be separated from staff functions, and proper emphasis should be placed on staff activities.
    d. Functions which are closely related or similar should normally be assigned to a single organizational unit.
    e. Functions should be properly distributed to promote balance, and to avoid overemphasis of less important functions and underemphasis of more essential functions.

6. **Delegation of Authority and Responsibility**
    a. Responsibilities assigned to a specific individual or organizational unit should carry corresponding authority, and all statements of authority or limitations thereof should be as specific as possible.
    b. Authority and responsibility for action should be decentralized to organizational units and individuals responsible for actual performance to the greatest extent possible, without relaxing necessary control over policy or the standardization of procedures. Delegation of authority will be consistent with decentralization of responsibility but such delegation will not divest an executive in higher authority of his overall responsibility.
    c. The heads of organizational units should concern themselves with important matters and should delegate to the maximum extent details and routines performed in the ordinary course of business.
    d. All responsibilities, authorities, and relationships should be stated in simple language to avoid misinterpretation.
    e. Each individual or organizational unit charged with a specific responsibility will be held responsible for results.

7. **Employee Relationships**
    a. The employees reporting to one executive should not exceed the number which can be effectively directed and coordinated. The number will depend largely upon the scope and extent of the responsibilities of the subordinates.
    b. No person should report to more than one supervisor. Every supervisor should know who reports to him, and every employee should know to whom he reports. Channels of authority and responsibility should not be violated by staff units.
    c. Relationships between organizational units within the agency and with outside organizations and associations should be clearly stated and thoroughly understood to avoid misunderstanding.

DELEGATING

1. <u>What is Delegating?</u>
Delegating is assigning a job to an employee, giving him the authority to get that job done, and giving him the responsibility for seeing to it that the job is done.

    a. <u>What to Delegate</u>
        (1) Routine details
        (2) Jobs which may be necessary and take a lot of time, but do not have to be done by the supervisor personally (preparing reports, attending meetings, etc.)
        (3) Routine decision-making (making decisions which do not require the supervisor's personal attention)

    b. <u>What Not to Delegate</u>
        (1) Job details which are *executive functions* (setting goals, organizing employees into a good team, analyzing results so as to plan for the future)
        (2) Disciplinary power (handling grievances, preparing service ratings, reprimands, etc.)
        (3) Decision-making which involves large numbers of employees or other bureaus and departments
        (4) Final and complete responsibility for the job done by the unit being supervised

    c. <u>Why Delegate?</u>
        (1) To strengthen the organization by developing a greater number of skilled employees
        (2) To improve the employee's performance by giving him the chance to learn more about the job, handle some responsibility, and become more interested in getting the job done
        (3) To improve a supervisor's performance by relieving him of routine jobs and giving him more time for *executive functions* (planning, organizing, controlling, etc.) which cannot be delegated

2. <u>To Whom to Delegate</u>
People with abilities not being used. Selection should be based on ability, not on favoritism.

REPORTS

<u>Definition</u>
    A report is an orderly presentation of factual information directed to a specific reader for a specific purpose.

<u>Purpose</u>
    The general purpose of a report is to bring to the reader useful and factual information about a condition or a problem. Some specific purposes of a report may be:

1. To enable the reader to appraise the efficiency or effectiveness of a person or an operation
2. To provide a basis for establishing standards
3. To reflect the results of expenditures of time, effort, and money
4. To provide a basis for developing or altering programs

<u>Types</u>
1. Information Report - Contains facts arranged in sequence
2. Summary (Examination) Report - Contains facts plus an analysis or discussion of the significance of the facts. Analysis may give advantages and disadvantages or give qualitative and quantitative comparisons
3. Recommendation Report - Contains facts, analysis, and conclusion logically drawn from the facts and analysis, plus a recommendation based upon the facts, analysis, and conclusions

<u>Factors to Consider Before Writing Report</u>

1. <u>Why</u> write the report - The purpose of the report should be clearly defined.
2. <u>Who</u> will read the report - What level of language should be used? Will the reader understand professional or technical language?
3. <u>What</u> should be said - What does the reader need or want to know about the subject?
4. <u>How</u> should it be said - Should the subject be presented tactfully? Convincingly? In a stimulating manner?

<u>Preparatory Steps</u>

1. Assemble the facts - Find out who, why, what, where, when, and how.
2. Organize the facts - Eliminate unnecessary information.
3. Prepare an outline - Check for orderliness, logical sequence.
4. Prepare a draft - Check for correctness, clearness, completeness, conciseness, and tone.
5. Prepare it in final form - Check for grammar, punctuation, appearance.

<u>Outline For a Recommendation Report</u>
Is the report:

1. Correct in information, grammar, and tone?
2. Clear?
3. Complete?
4. Concise?
5. Timely?
6. Worth its cost?

Will the report accomplish its purpose?

MANAGEMENT CONTROLS

1. <u>Control</u>
What is control? What is controlled? Who controls?

The essence of control is action which adjusts operations to predetermined standards, and its basis is information in the hands of managers. Control is checking to determine whether plans are being observed and suitable progress toward stated objectives is being made, and action is taken, if necessary, to correct deviations.

We have a ready-made model for this concept of control in the automatic systems which are widely used for process control in the chemical and petroleum industries. A process control system works this way. Suppose, for example, it is desired to maintain a constant rate of flow of oil through a pipe at a predetermined or set-point value. A signal, whose strength represents the rate of flow, can be produced in a measuring device and transmitted to a control mechanism. The control mechanism, when it detects any deviation of the actual from the set-point signal, will reposition the value regulating flow rate.

2. Basis For Control

A process control mechanism thus acts to adjust operations to predetermined standards and does so on the basis of information it receives. In a parallel way, information reaching a manager gives him the opportunity for corrective action and is his basis for control. He cannot exercise control without such information, and he cannot do a complete job of managing without controlling.

3. Policy
What is policy?

Policy is simply a statement of an organization's intention to act in certain ways when specified types of circumstances arise. It represents a general decision, predetermined and expressed as a principle or rule, establishing a normal pattern of conduct for dealing with given types of business events - usually recurrent. A statement is therefore useful in economizing the time of managers and in assisting them to discharge their responsibilities equitably and consistently.

Policy is not a means of control, but policy does generate the need for control.

Adherence to policies is not guaranteed nor can it be taken on faith. It has to be verified. Without verification, there is no basis for control. Policy and procedures, although closely related and interdependent to a certain extent, are not synonymous. A policy may be adopted, for example, to maintain a materials inventory not to exceed one million dollars. A procedure for inventory control would interpret that policy and convert it into methods for keeping within that limit, with consideration, too, of possible but foreseeable expedient deviation.

4. Procedure
What is procedure?

A procedure specifically prescribes:

    a. What work is to be performed by the various participants
    b. Who are the respective participants
    c. When and where the various steps in the different processes are to be performed
    d. The sequence of operations that will insure uniform handling of recurring transactions
    e. The *paper* that is involved, its origin, transition, and disposition

Necessary appurtenances to a procedure are:

    a. Detailed organizational chart

b. Flow charts

c. Exhibits of forms, all presented in close proximity to the text of the procedure

5. <u>Basis of Control - Information in the Hands of Managers</u>
If the basis of control is information in the hands of managers, then <u>reporting</u> is elevated to a level of very considerable importance.

Types of reporting may include:

a. Special reports and routine reports
b. Written, oral, and graphic reports
c. Staff meetings
d. Conferences
e. Television screens
f. Non-receipt of information, as where management is by exception
g. Any other means whereby information is transmitted to a manager as a basis for control action

FRAMEWORK OF MANAGEMENT

<u>Elements</u>
1. <u>Policy</u> - It has to be verified, controlled.

2. <u>Organization</u> - is part of the giving of an assignment. The organizational chart gives to each individual in his title, a first approximation of the nature of his assignment and orients him as being accountable to a certain individual. Organization is not in a true sense a means of control. Control is checking to ascertain whether the assignment is executed as intended and acting on the basis of that information.

3. <u>Budgets</u> - perform three functions:

a. They present the objectives, plans, and programs of the organization in financial terms.
b. They report the progress of actual performance against these predetermined objectives, plans, and programs.
c. Like organizational charts, delegations of authority, procedures and job descriptions, they define the assignments which have flowed from the Chief Executive. Budgets are a means of control in the respect that they report progress of actual performance against the program. They provide information which enables managers to take action directed toward bringing actual results into conformity with the program.

4. <u>Internal Check</u> - provides in practice for the principle that the same person should not have responsibility for all phases of a transaction. This makes it clearly an aspect of organization rather than of control. Internal Check is static, or built-in.

5. <u>Plans, Programs, Objectives</u>
People must know what they are trying to do. <u>Objectives</u> fulfill this need. Without them, people may work industriously and yet, working aimlessly, accomplish little.

Plans and Programs complement Objectives, since they propose how and according to what time schedule the objectives are to be reached.

6. <u>Delegations of Authority</u>

Among the ways we have for supplementing the titles and lines of authority of an organizational chart are delegations of authority. Delegations of authority clarify the extent of authority of individuals and in that way serve to define assignments. That they are not means of control is apparent from the very fact that wherever there has been a delegation of authority, the need for control increases. This could hardly be expected to happen if delegations of authority were themselves means of control.

Manager's Responsibility

Control becomes necessary whenever a manager delegates authority to a subordinate because he cannot delegate and then simply sit back and forget all about it. A manager's accountability to his own superior has not diminished one whit as a result of delegating part of his authority to a subordinate. The manager must exercise control over actions taken under the authority so delegated. That means checking serves as a basis for possible corrective action.

Objectives, plans, programs, organizational charts, and other elements of the managerial system are not fruitfully regarded as either <u>controls</u> or <u>means of control</u>. They are pre-established <u>standards</u> or <u>models of performance</u> to which operations are adjusted by the exercise of management control. These standards or models of performance are dynamic in character for they are constantly altered, modified, or revised. Policies, organizational set-up, procedures, delegations, etc. are constantly altered but, like objectives and plans, they remain in force until they are either abandoned or revised. All of the elements (or standards or models of performance), objectives, plans and prpgrams, policies, organization, etc. can be regarded as a *framework of management*.

Control Techniques

Examples of control techniques:
1. Compare against established standards
2. Compare with a similar operation
3. Compare with past operations
4. Compare with predictions of accomplishment

Where Forecasts Fit

Control is after-the-fact while forecasts are before. Forecasts and projections are important for setting objectives and formulating plans.

Information for aiming and planning does not have to before-the-fact. It may be an after-the-fact analysis proving that a certain policy has been impolitic in its effect on the relation of the company or department with customer, employee, taxpayer, or stockholder; or that a certain plan is no longer practical, or that a certain procedure is unworkable.

The prescription here certainly <u>would not be in control</u> (in these cases, control would simply bring operations into conformity with obsolete standards) but the establishment of new standards, a new policy, a new plan, and a new procedure to be controlled too.

Information is, of course, the basis for all communication in addition to furnishing evidence to management of the need for reconstructing the framework of management.

PROBLEM SOLVING

The accepted concept in modern management for problem solving is the utilization of the following steps:

1. Identify the problem
2. Gather data
3. List possible solutions
4. Test possible solutions
5. Select the best solution
6. Put the solution into actual practice

Occasions might arise where you would have to apply the second step of gathering data before completing the first step.

You might also find that it will be necessary to work on several steps at the same time.

1. Identify the Problem

Your first step is to define as precisely as possible the problem to be solved. While this may sound easy, it is often the most difficult part of the process.

It has been said of problem solving that you are halfway to the solution when you can write out a clear statement of the problem itself.

Our job now is to get below the surface manifestations of the trouble and pinpoint the problem. This is usually accomplished by a logical analysis, by going from the general to the particular; from the obvious to the not-so-obvious cause.
Let us say that production is behind schedule. WHY? Absenteeism is high. Now, is absenteeism the basic problem to be tackled, or is it merely a symptom of low morale among the workforce? Under these circumstances, you may decide that production is not the problem; the problem is *employee morale*.

In trying to define the problem, remember there is seldom one simple reason why production is lagging, or reports are late, etc.

Analysis usually leads to the discovery that an apparent problem is really made up of several subproblems which must be attacked separately.

Another way is to limit the problem, and thereby ease the task of finding a solution, and concentrate on the elements which are within the scope of your control.

When you have gone this far, write out a tentative statement of the problem to be solved.

2. Gather Data

In the second step, you must set out to collect all the information that might have a bearing on the problem. Do not settle for an assumption when reasonable fact and figures are available.

If you merely go through the motions of problem-solving, you will probably shortcut the information-gathering step. Therefore, do not stack the evidence by confining your research to your own preconceived ideas.

As you collect facts, organize them in some form that helps you make sense of them and spot possible relationships between them. For example: Plotting cost per unit figures on a graph can be more meaningful than a long column of figures.

Evaluate each item as you go along. Is the source material: absolutely reliable, probably reliable, or not to be trusted.

One of the best methods for gathering data is to go out and look the situation over carefully. Talk to the people on the job who are most affected by this problem.

Always keep in mind that a primary source is usually better than a secondary source of information.

3. List Possible Solutions

This is the creative thinking step of problem solving. This is a good time to bring into play whatever techniques of group dynamics the agency or bureau might have developed for a joint attack on problems.

Now the important thing for you to do is: Keep an open mind. Let your imagination roam freely over the facts you have collected. Jot down every possible solution that occurs to you. Resist the temptation to evaluate various proposals as you go along. List seemingly absurd ideas along with more plausible ones. The more possibilities you list during this step, the less risk you will run of settling for merely a workable, rather than the best, solution.

Keep studying the data as long as there seems to be any chance of deriving additional - ideas, solutions, explanations, or patterns from it.

4. Test Possible Solutions

Now you begin to evaluate the possible solutions. Take pains to be objective. Up to this point, you have suspended judgment but you might be tempted to select a solution you secretly favored all along and proclaim it as the best of the lot.

The secret of objectivity in this phase is to test the possible solutions separately, measuring each against a common yardstick. To make this yardstick try to enumerate as many specific criteria as you can think of. Criteria are best phrased as questions which you ask of each possible solution. They can be drawn from these general categories:

Suitability   -   Will this solution do the job?
                         Will it solve the problem completely or partially?

Is it a permanent or a stopgap solution?

Feasibility   -   Will this plan work in actual practice?
Can we afford this approach?
How much will it cost?

Acceptability -   Will the boss go along with the changes required in the plan?
Are we trying to drive a tack with a sledge hammer?

5.   Select the Best Solution

This is the area of executive decision.

Occasionally, one clearly superior solution will stand out at the conclusion of the testing process. But often it is not that simple. You may find that no one solution has come through all the tests with flying colors.

You may also find that a proposal, which flunked miserably on one of the essential tests, racked up a very high score on others.

The best solution frequently will turn out to be a combination.

Try to arrange a marriage that will bring together the strong points of one possible solution with the particular virtues of another. The more skill and imagination that you apply, the greater is the likelihood that you will come out with a solution that is not merely adequate and workable, but is the best possible under the circumstances.

6.   Put the Solution Into Actual Practice
As every executive knows, a plan which works perfectly on paper may develop all sorts of bugs when put into actual practice.

Problem-solving does not stop with selecting the solution which looks best in theory. The next step is to put the chosen solution into action and watch the results. The results may point towards modifications.

If the problem disappears when you put your solution into effect, you know you have the right solution.

If it does not disappear, even after you have adjusted your plan to cover unforeseen difficulties that turned up in practice, work your way back through the problem-solving solutions.

Would one of them have worked better?
Did you overlook some vital piece of data which would have given you a different slant on the whole situation? Did you apply all necessary criteria in testing solutions? If no light dawns after this much rechecking, it is a pretty good bet that you defined the problem incorrectly in the first place.

You came up with the wrong solution because you tackled the wrong problem.

Thus, step six may become step one of a new problem-solving cycle.

COMMUNICATION

1. <u>What is Communication?</u>
    We communicate through writing, speaking, action or inaction. In speaking to people face-to-face, there is opportunity to judge reactions and to adjust the message. This makes the supervisory chain one of the most, and in many instances the most, important channels of communication.

    In an organization, communication means keeping employees informed about the organization's objectives, policies, problems, and progress. Communication is the free interchange of information, ideas, and desirable attitudes between and among employees and between employees and management.

2. <u>Why is Communication Needed?</u>
    a. People have certain social needs
    b. Good communication is essential in meeting those social needs
    c. While people have similar basic needs, at the same time they differ from each other
    d. Communication must be adapted to these individual differences

    An employee cannot do his best work unless he knows why he is doing it. If he has the feeling that he is being kept in the dark about what is going on, his enthusiasm and productivity suffer.

    Effective communication is needed in an organization so that employees will understand what the organization is trying to accomplish; and how the work of one unit contributes to or affects the work of other units in the organization and other organizations.

3. <u>How is Communication Achieved?</u>
    Communication flows downward, upward, sideways.

    a. Communication may come from top management down to employees. This is <u>downward communication</u>.

        Some means of downward communication are:
        (1) Training (orientation, job instruction, supervision, public relations, etc.)
        (2) Conferences
        (3) Staff meetings
        (4) Policy statements
        (5) Bulletins
        (6) Newsletters
        (7) Memoranda
        (8) Circulation of important letters

        In downward communication, it is important that employees be informed in advance of changes that will affect them.

    b. Communications should also be developed so that the ideas, suggestions, and knowledge of employees will flow <u>upward</u> to top management.

Some means of upward communication are:

(1) Personal discussion conferences
(2) Committees
(3) Memoranda
(4) Employees suggestion program
(5) Questionnaires to be filled in giving comments and suggestions about proposed actions that will affect field operations

Upward communication requires that management be willing to listen, to accept, and to make changes when good ideas are present. Upward communication succeeds when there is no fear of punishment for speaking out or lack of interest at the top. Employees will share their knowledge and ideas with management when interest is shown and recognition is given.

c. The *advantages* of downward communication:

(1) It enables the passing down of orders, policies, and plans necessary to the continued operation of the station.
(2) By making information available, it diminishes the fears and suspicions which result from misinformation and misunderstanding.
(3) It fosters the pride people want to have in their work when they are told of good work.
(4) It improves the morale and stature of the individual to be *in the know.*
(5) It helps employees to understand, accept, and cooperate with changes when they know about them in advance.

d. The *advantages* of upward communication:

(1) It enables the passing upward of information, attitudes, and feelings.
(2) It makes it easier to find out how ready people are to receive downward communication.
(3) It reveals the degree to which the downward communication is understood and accepted.
(4) It helps to satisfy the basic *social* needs.
(5) It stimulates employees to participate in the operation of their organization.
(6) It encourages employees to contribute ideas for improving the efficiency and economy of operations.
(7) It helps to solve problem situations before they reach the explosion point.

4. Why Does Communication Fail?
   a. The technical difficulties of conveying information clearly
   b. The emotional content of communication which prevents complete transmission
   c. The fact that there is a difference between what management needs to say, what it wants to say, and what it does say
   d. The fact that there is a difference between what employees would like to say, what they think is profitable or safe to say, and what they do say

5. How to Improve Communication.
   As a supervisor, you are a key figure in communication. To improve as a communicator, you should:
   a. Know - Knowing your subordinates will help you to recognize and work with individual differences.

b. <u>Like</u> - If you like those who work for you and those for whom you work, this will foster the kind of friendly, warm, work atmosphere that will facilitate communication.

c. <u>Trust</u> - Showing a sincere desire to communicate will help to develop the mutual trust and confidence which are essential to the free flow of communication.

d. <u>Tell</u> - Tell your subordinates and superiors *what's doing*. Tell your subordinates *why* as well as *how*.

e. <u>Listen</u> - By listening, you help others to talk and you create good listeners. Don't forget that listening implies action.

f. <u>Stimulate</u> - Communication has to be stimulated and encouraged. Be receptive to ideas and suggestions and motivate your people so that each member of the team identifies himself with the job at hand.

g. <u>Consult</u> - The most effective way of consulting is to let your people participate, insofar as possible, in developing determinations which affect them or their work.

6. <u>How to Determine Whether You are Getting Across</u>.
   a. Check to see that communication is received and understood
   b. Judge this understanding by actions rather than words
   c. Adapt or vary communication, when necessary
   d. Remember that good communication cannot cure all problems

7. <u>The Key Attitude</u>.
   Try to see things from the other person's point of view. By doing this, you help to develop the permissive atmosphere and the shared confidence and understanding which are essential to effective two-way communication.

   Communication is a two-way process.
   a. The basic purpose of any communication is to get action.
   b. The only way to get action is through acceptance.
   c. In order to get acceptance, communication must be humanly satisfying as well as technically efficient.

HOW ORDERS AND INSTRUCTIONS SHOULD BE GIVEN

<u>Characteristics of Good Orders and Instructions</u>

1. <u>Clear</u>
   Orders should be definite as to
   - <u>What</u> is to be done
   - <u>Who</u> is to do it
   - <u>When</u> it is to be done
   - <u>Where</u> it is to be done
   - <u>How</u> it is to be done

2. <u>Concise</u>
   Avoid wordiness. Orders should be brief and to the point.

3. <u>Timely</u>
   Instructions and orders should be sent out at the proper time and not too long in advance of expected performance.

4. <u>Possibility of Performance</u>
   Orders should be feasible:
   a. Investigate before giving orders
   b. Consult those who are to carry out instructions before formulating and issuing them

5. <u>Properly Directed</u>
   Give the orders to the people concerned. Do not send orders to people who are not concerned. People who continually receive instructions that are not applicable to them get in the habit of neglecting instructions generally.

6. <u>Reviewed Before Issuance</u>
   Orders should be reviewed before issuance:
   a. Test them by putting yourself in the position of the recipient
   b. If they involve new procedures, have the persons who are to do the work review them for suggestions

7. <u>Reviewed After Issuance</u>
   Persons who receive orders should be allowed to raise questions and to point out unforeseen consequences of orders.

8. <u>Coordinated</u>
   Orders should be coordinated so that work runs smoothly.

9. <u>Courteous</u>
   Make a request rather than a demand. There is no need to continually call attention to the fact that you are the boss.

10. <u>Recognizable as an Order</u>
    Be sure that the order is recognizable as such.

11. <u>Complete</u>
    Be sure recipient has knowledge and experience sufficient to carry out order. Give illustrations and examples.

A DEPARTMENTAL PERSONNEL OFFICE IS RESPONSIBLE
<u>FOR THE FOLLOWING FUNCTIONS</u>

1. Policy
2. Personnel Programs
3. Recruitment and Placement
4. Position Classification
5. Salary and Wage Administration
6. Employee Performance Standards and Evaluation
7. Employee Relations
8. Disciplinary Actions and Separations
9. Health and Safety
10. Staff Training and Development
11. Personnel Records, Procedures, and Reports
12. Employee Services
13. Personnel Research

SUPERVISION

Leadership

All leadership is based essentially on authority. This comes from two sources: it is received from higher management or it is earned by the supervisor through his methods of supervision. Although effective leadership has always depended upon the leader's using his authority in such a way as to appeal successfully to the motives of the people supervised, the conditions for making this appeal are continually changing. The key to today's problem of leadership is flexibility and resourcefulness on the part of the leader in meeting changes in conditions as they occur.

Three basic approaches to leadership are generally recognized:

1. The Authoritarian Approach
   a. The methods and techniques used in this approach emphasize the *I* in leadership and depend primarily on the formal authority of the leader. This authority is sometimes exercised in a hardboiled manner and sometimes in a benevolent manner, but in either case the dominating role of the leader is reflected in the thinking, planning, and decisions of the group.
   b. Group results are to a large degree dependent on close supervision by the leader. Usually, the individuals in the group will not show a high degree of initiative or acceptance of responsibility and their capacity to grow and develop probably will not be fully utilized. The group may react with resentment or submission, depending upon the manner and skill of the leader in using his authority
   c. This approach develops as a natural outgrowth of the authority that goes with the leader's job and his feeling of sole responsibility for getting the job done. It is relatively easy to use and does not require much resourcefulness.
   d. The use of this approach is effective in times of emergencies, in meeting close deadlines as a final resort, in settling some issues, in disciplinary matters, and with dependent individuals and groups.

2. The Laissez-Faire or *Let 'em Alone* Approach
   a. This approach generally is characterized by an avoidance of leadership responsibility by the leader. The activities of the group depend largely on the choice of its members rather than the leader.
   b. Group results probably will be poor. Generally, there will be disagreements over petty things, bickering, and confusion. Except for a few aggressive people, individuals will not show much initiative and growth and development will be retarded. There may be a tendency for informal leaders to take over leadership of the group.
   c. This approach frequently results from the leader's dislike of responsibility, from his lack of confidence, from failure of other methods to work, from disappointment or criticism. It is usually the easiest of the three to use and requires both understanding and resourcefulness on the part of the leader.
   d. This approach is occasionally useful and effective, particularly in forcing dependent individuals or groups to rely on themselves, to give someone a chance to save face by clearing his own difficulties, or when action should be delayed temporarily for good cause.

3. <u>The Democratic Approach</u>
   a. The methods and techniques used in this approach emphasize the *we* in leadership and build up the responsibility of the group to attain its objectives. Reliance is placed largely on the earned authority of the leader.
   b. Group results are likely to be good because most of the job motives of the people will be satisfied. Cooperation and teamwork, initiative, acceptance of responsibility, and the individual's capacity for growth probably will show a high degree of development.
   c. This approach grows out of a desire or necessity of the leader to find ways to appeal effectively to the motivation of his group. It is the best approach to build up inside the person a strong desire to cooperate and apply himself to the job.
      It is the most difficult to develop, and requires both understanding and resourcefulness on the part of the leader.
   d. The value of this approach increases over a long period where sustained efficiency and development of people are important. It may not be fully effective in all situations, however, particularly when there is not sufficient time to use it properly or where quick decisions must be made.

All three approaches are used by most leaders and have a place in supervising people. The extent of their use varies with individual leaders, with some using one approach predominantly. The leader who uses these three approaches, and varies their use with time and circumstance, is probably the most effective. Leadership which is used predominantly with a democratic approach requires more resourcefulness on the part of the leader but offers the greatest possibilities in terms of teamwork and cooperation.

The one best way of developing democratic leadership is to provide a real sense of participation on the part of the group, since this satisfies most of the chief job motives. Although there are many ways of providing participation, consulting as frequently as possible with individuals and groups on things that affect them seems to offer the most in building cooperation and responsibility. Consultation takes different forms, but it is most constructive when people feel they are actually helping in finding the answers to the problems on the job.

There are some requirements of leaders in respect to human relations which should be considered in their selection and development. Generally, the leader should be interested in working with other people, emotionally stable, self-confident, and sensitive to the reactions of others. In addition, his viewpoint should be one of getting the job done through people who work cooperatively in response to his leadership. He should have a knowledge of individual and group behavior, but, most important of all, he should work to combine all of these requirements into a definite, practical skill in leadership.

<u>Nine Points of Contrast Between *Boss* and *Leader*</u>

1. The boss drives his men; the leader coaches them.
2. The boss depends on authority; the leader on good will.
3. The boss inspires fear; the leader inspires enthusiasm.
4. The boss says J; the leader says *We.*
5. The boss says *Get here on time;* the leader gets there ahead of time.
6. The boss fixes the blame for the breakdown; the leader fixes the breakdown.
7. The boss knows how it is done; the leader shows how.
8. The boss makes work a drudgery; the leader makes work a game.
9. The boss says *Go*; the leader says *Let's go.*

EMPLOYEE MORALE

Employee morale is the way employees feel about each other, the organization or unit in which they work, and the work they perform.

<u>Some Ways to Develop and Maintain Good Employee Morale</u>

1. Give adequate credit and praise when due.
2. Recognize importance of all jobs and equalize load with proper assignments, always giving consideration to personality differences and abilities.
3. Welcome suggestions and do not have an *all-wise* attitude. Request employees' assistance in solving problems and use assistants when conducting group meetings on certain subjects.
4. Properly assign responsibilities and give adequate authority for fulfillment of such assignments.
5. Keep employees informed about matters that affect them.
6. Criticize and reprimand employees privately.
7. Be accessible and willing to listen.
8. Be fair.
9. Be alert to detect training possibilities so that you will not miss an opportunity to help each employee do a better job, and if possible with less effort on his part.
10. Set a good example.
11. Apply the golden rule.

<u>Some Indicators of Good Morale</u>

1. Good quality of work
2. Good quantity
3. Good attitude of employees
4. Good discipline
5. Teamwork
6. Good attendance
7. Employee participation

MOTIVATION

<u>Drives</u>

A *drive,* stated simply, is a desire or force which causes a person to do or say certain things. These are some of the most usual drives and some of their identifying characteristics recognizable in people motivated by such drives:

1. <u>Security</u> (desire to provide for the future)
    Always on time for work
    Works for the same employer for many years
    Never takes unnecessary chances Seldom resists doing what he is told

2. <u>Recognition</u> (desire to be rewarded for accomplishment)
    Likes to be asked for his opinion
    Becomes very disturbed when he makes a mistake
    Does things to attract attention

Likes to see his name in print

3. <u>Position</u> (desire to hold certain status in relation to others)
   Boasts about important people he knows
   Wants to be known as a key man
   Likes titles
   Demands respect
   Belongs to clubs, for prestige

4. <u>Accomplishment</u> (desire to get things done)
   Complains when things are held up
   Likes to do things that have tangible results
   Never lies down on the job
   Is proud of turning out good work

5. <u>Companionship</u> (desire to associate with other people)
   Likes to work with others
   Tells stories and jokes
   Indulges in horseplay
   Finds excuses to talk to others on the job

6. <u>Possession</u> (desire to collect and hoard objects)
   Likes to collect things
   Puts his name on things belonging to him
   Insists on the same work location

Supervisors may find that identifying the drives of employees is a helpful step toward motivating them to self-improvement and better job performance. For example: An employee's job performance is below average. His supervisor, having previously determined that the employee is motivated by a drive for security, suggests that taking training courses will help the employee to improve, advance, and earn more money. Since earning more money can be a step toward greater security, the employee's drive for security would motivate him to take the training suggested by the supervisor. In essence, this is the process of charting an employee's future course by using his motivating drives to positive advantage.

EMPLOYEE PARTICIPATION

<u>What is Participation?</u>

Employee participation is the employee's giving freely of his time, skill and knowledge to an extent which cannot be obtained by demand.

<u>Why is it Important?</u>

The supervisor's responsibility is to get the job done through people. A good supervisor gets the job done through people who work willingly and well. The participation of employees is important because:
1. Employees develop a greater sense of responsibility when they share in working out operating plans and goals.
2. Participation provides greater opportunity and stimulation for employees to learn, and to develop their ability.

3. Participation sometimes provides better solutions to problems because such solutions may combine the experience and knowledge of interested employees who want the solutions to work.
4. An employee or group may offer a solution which the supervisor might hesitate to make for fear of demanding too much.
5. Since the group wants to make the solution work, they exert *pressure* in a constructive way on each other.
6. Participation usually results in reducing the need for close supervision.

How May Supervisors Obtain It?

Participation is encouraged when employees feel that they share some responsibility for the work and that their ideas are sincerely wanted and valued. Some ways of obtaining employee participation are:

1. Conduct orientation programs for new employees to inform them about the organization and their rights and responsibilities as employees.
2. Explain the aims and objectives of the agency. On a continuing basis, be sure that the employees know what these aims and objectives are.
3. Share job successes and responsibilities and give credit for success.
4. Consult with employees, both as individuals and in groups, about things that affect them.
5. Encourage suggestions for job improvements. Help employees to develop good suggestions. The suggestions can bring them recognition. The city's suggestion program offers additional encouragement through cash awards.

The supervisor who encourages employee participation is not surrendering his authority. He must still make decisions and initiate action, and he must continue to be ultimately responsible for the work of those he supervises. But, through employee participation, he is helping his group to develop greater ability and a sense of responsibility while getting the job done faster and better.

STEPS IN HANDLING A GRIEVANCE

1. Get the facts
   a. Listen sympathetically.
   b. Let him talk himself out.
   c. Get his story straight.
   d. Get his point of view.
   e. Don't argue with him.
   f. Give him plenty of time.
   g. Conduct the interview privately.
   h. Don't try to shift the blame or pass the buck.

2. Consider the facts
   a. Consider the employee's viewpoint.
   b. How will the decision affect similar cases.
   c. Consider each decision as a possible precedent.
   d. Avoid snap judgments - don't jump to conclusions.

3. Make or get a decision
   a. Frame an effective counter-proposal.
   b. Make sure it is fair to all.
   c. Have confidence in your judgment.
   d. Be sure you can substantiate your decision.

4. Notify the employee of your decision
   Be sure he is told; try to convince him that the decision is fair and just.

5. Take action when needed and if within your authority
   Otherwise, tell employee that the matter will be called to the attention of the proper person or that nothing can be done, and why it cannot.

6. Follow through to see that the desired result is achieved.

7. Record key facts concerning the complaint and the action taken.

8. Leave the way open to him to appeal your decision to a higher authority.

9. Report all grievances to your superior, whether they are appealed or not.

DISCIPLINE

Discipline is training that develops self-control, orderly conduct, and efficiency.

To discipline does not necessarily mean to punish.

To discipline does mean to train, to regulate, and to govern conduct.

The Disciplinary Interview

Most employees sincerely want to do what is expected of them. In other words, they are self-disciplined. Some employees, however, fail to observe established rules and standards, and disciplinary action by the supervisor is required.

The primary purpose of disciplinary action is to improve conduct without creating dissatisfaction, bitterness, or resentment in the process.

Constructive disciplinary action is more concerned with causes and explanations of breaches of conduct than with punishment. The disciplinary interview is held to get at the causes of apparent misbehavior and to motivate better performance in the future.

It is important that the interview be kept on as impersonal a basis as possible. If the supervisor lets the interview descend to the plane of an argument, it loses its effectiveness.

Planning the Interview

Get all pertinent facts concerning the situation so that you can talk in specific terms to the employee.

Review the employee's record, appraisal ratings, etc.

Consider what you know about the temperament of the employee. Consider your attitude toward the employee. Remember that the primary requisite of disciplinary action is fairness.

Don't enter upon the interview when angry.

Schedule the interview for a place which is private and out of hearing of others.

<u>Conducting the Interview</u>

1. Make an effort to establish accord.

2. Question the employee about the apparent breach of discipline. Be sure that the question is not so worded as to be itself an accusation.

3. Give the employee a chance to tell his side of the story. Give him ample opportunity to talk.

4. Use understanding-listening except where it is necessary to ask a question or to point out some details of which the employee may not be aware. If the employee misrepresents facts, make a plain, accurate statement of the facts, but don't argue and don't engage in personal controversy.

5. Listen and try to understand the reasons for the employee's (mis)conduct. First of all, don't assume that there has been a breach of discipline. Evaluate the employee's reasons for his conduct in the light of his opinions and feelings concerning the consistency and reasonableness of the standards which he was expected to follow. Has the supervisor done his part in explaining the reasons for the rules? Was the employee's behavior unintentional or deliberate? Does he think he had real reasons for his actions? What new facts is he telling? Do the facts justify his actions? What causes, other than those mentioned, could have stimulated the behavior?

6. After listening to the employee's version of the situation, and if censure of his actions is warranted, the supervisor should proceed with whatever criticism is justified. Emphasis should be placed on future improvement rather than exclusively on the employee's failure to measure up to expected standards of job conduct.

7. Fit the criticism to the individual. With one employee, a word of correction may be all that is required.

8. Attempt to distinguish between unintentional error and deliberate misbehavior. An error due to ignorance requires training and not censure.

9. Administer criticism in a controlled, even tone of voice, never in anger. Make it clear that you are acting as an agent of the department. In general, criticism should refer to the job or the employee's actions and not to the person. Criticism of the employee's work is not an attack on the individual.

10. Be sure the interview does not destroy the employee's self-confidence. Mention his good qualities and assure him that you feel confident that he can improve his performance.

11. Wherever possible, before the employee leaves the interview, satisfy him that the incident is closed, that nothing more will be said on the subject unless the offense is repeated.

———————

CPSIA information can be obtained
at www.ICGtesting.com
Printed in the USA
LVHW021912171219
640814LV00021B/248

9 781731 838155